Colección T.

SERIE A: MONOGRAFÍAS, 282

A COMPANION TO
PORTUGUESE LITERATURE

Tamesis

Founding Editors
† J. E. Varey
† Alan Deyermond

General Editor
Stephen M. Hart

Series Editor of
Fuentes para la historia del teatro en España
Charles Davis

Advisory Board
Rolena Adorno
John Beverley
Efraín Kristal
Jo Labanyi
Alison Sinclair
Isabel Torres
Julian Weiss

A COMPANION TO
PORTUGUESE LITERATURE

Edited by

Stephen Parkinson
Cláudia Pazos Alonso
T. F. Earle

TAMESIS

© Contributors 2009

All Rights Reserved. Except as permitted under current legislation
no part of this work may be photocopied, stored in a retrieval system,
published, performed in public, adapted, broadcast,
transmitted, recorded or reproduced in any form or by any means,
without the prior permission of the copyright owner

First published 2009 by Tamesis, Woodbridge
Paperback edition 2013

ISBN 978 1 85566 194 3 hardback
ISBN 978 1 85566 267 4 paperback

Transferred to digital printing

Tamesis is an imprint of Boydell & Brewer Ltd
PO Box 9, Woodbridge, Suffolk IP12 3DF, UK
and of Boydell & Brewer Inc,
668 Mt Hope Avenue, Rochester, NY 14620–2731, USA
website: www.boydellandbrewer.com

The publisher has no responsibility for the continued existence or accuracy of
URLs for external or third-party internet websites referred to in this book,
and does not guarantee that any content on such websites is,
or will remain, accurate or appropriate

A CIP catalogue record for this book is available
from the British Library

This publication is printed on acid-free paper

CONTENTS

ACKNOWLEDGEMENTS

The editors gratefully acknowledge the financial support of the Faculty of Medieval and Modern Languages of the University of Oxford. We thank all contributors for their diligent and cooperative work towards this trailblazing volume. Finally, we must give due thanks to our commissioning editor Ellie Ferguson, without whose patience and persistence this project would never have come to fruition.

NOTES ON THE CONTRIBUTORS

Vanda Anastácio is an Associate Professor at the Faculdade de Letras of the University of Lisbon, where she teaches Portuguese Culture and Literature and Brazilian Literature of the Colonial Period. She directs the team preparing the critical edition of the works and letters of the Marquesa of Alorna with the support of the *Fundação das Casas de Fronteira e de Alorna*. She has published a number of scholarly editions of Portuguese authors of the sixteenth and eighteenth centuries, including the *Sonnets* of the Marquesa of Alorna.

Helena Carvalhão Buescu is Professor of Comparative Literature at the University of Lisbon. Her main research areas are Comparative Literature and the construction of modernity. She has published ten books, most recently *Emendar a Morte* (2008), and co-edited *A Revisionary History of Portuguese Literature* (1999). She directs the Centre for Comparative Studies and is a member of the Academia Europaea.

Mariana Gray de Castro is currently completing her Ph.D. thesis on Pessoa and Shakespeare at King's College, London. Her main research interest lies in comparative modernist literature, and she has lectured on Fernando Pessoa and modernism at the University of Oxford. She has published articles in Portugal, Brazil, and the UK, and is editing a book of essays on Pessoa from a comparative perspective.

Teresa Pinto Coelho is Professor of Anglo-Portuguese Studies at the Universidade Nova, Lisbon. She has published extensively on Eça de Queirós, on whom she wrote her Oxford D.Phil. thesis (*Apocalipse e Regeneração*, 1986). A parallel interest is Anglo-Portuguese rivalry for the possession of southern Africa at the turn of the nineteenth century, one of the the themes of her study *A Agulha de Cleópatra* (2000). She is preparing a book on Eça and the English press.

Rip Cohen is Visiting Scholar in the Department of German and Romance Languages and Literatures at the Johns Hopkins University. He has published a critical edition of the 500 *Cantigas d'Amigo* (2003) and has written and lectured widely on medieval Galician-Portuguese philology and poetry.

Tom Earle is King John II Professor of Portuguese at the University of Oxford and a Fellow of St Peter's College. Most of his publications are about the literature of the Renaissance in Portugal. He has a book in press, *Portuguese Writers and English Readers: Books by Portuguese Writers Printed before 1640 in the Libraries of Oxford and Cambridge*, and is working, with Prof. José Camões of the University of Lisbon, on an edition of the comedies of Francisco de Sá de Miranda.

David Frier is Senior Lecturer in Portuguese at the University of Leeds. He has published widely on the novels of José Saramago and Camilo Castelo Branco, and he is currently working on the late novels of Eça de Queirós and preparing a volume of edited essays on Fernando Pessoa.

Luís Gomes teaches Portuguese Language at the University of Glasgow. He has worked on the poet Vasco Mousinho de Quevedo and on literature in the Dual Monarchy. He is currently editing a selection of works on Portuguese emblems (from the sixteenth to the eighteenth century) for *Glasgow Emblem Studies*.

Helder Macedo is Emeritus Professor of Portuguese at King's College, London. He was the founding editor of the journal *Portuguese Studies*, and has published ten scholarly books, six collections of poetry and five novels. He was awarded prizes by the Academy of Sciences of Lisbon, the Portuguese PEN Club and the International Association of Literary Critics for his work on Portuguese Renaissance Literature.

Patricia Odber de Baubeta is Head of Department of Hispanic Studies and Director of the *Cátedra Gil Vicente* in the University of Birmingham, where she has lectured since 1981. She began her academic career as a medievalist, has carried out research on the language of advertising, fairy tale motifs in contemporary literature, and translation issues, and is now working on Portuguese literature in English translation, and the anthology in Portugal.

Hilary Owen is Professor of Portuguese and Luso-African Studies at the University of Manchester. She has worked extensively on feminism, women's writing and postcolonial theory in Portugal and Mozambique. She is the author of *Mother Africa, Father Marx: Women's Writing of Mozambique, 1942–2002* (2007).

Stephen Parkinson is Lecturer in Portuguese Language and Linguistics at the University of Oxford, and is a Fellow of Linacre College. He has published widely on the text and manuscripts of the *Cantigas de Santa Maria*, for which he has created an online database of ancillary information <http://csm.mml.ox.ac.uk>, and is currently preparing a new critical edition of the text. He has been General Editor of the bibliographical journal *The Year's Work in Modern Language Studies* since 1997.

Cláudia Pazos Alonso is University Lecturer in Portuguese and Brazilian Studies at the University of Oxford, and a Fellow of Wadham College. She has published widely on twentieth-century women writers and representations of gender. She is currently co-authoring with Hilary Owen a book entitled *Antigone's Daughters? Gender, Genius and the Politics of Authorship in 20th-Century Portuguese Women's Writing.*

Juliet Perkins is Senior Lecturer in Portuguese and Brazilian Studies at King's College, London. Her principal publications are on twentieth-century Portuguese poetry and fiction, eighteenth-century musical theatre, and the Inês de Castro story. Her current projects include a survey of Portuguese travel literature in English translation, and a group of essays on the work of José Cardoso Pires.

Phillip Rothwell is Professor of Portuguese at Rutgers, the State University of New Jersey. He is author of *A Canon of Empty Fathers: Paternity in Portuguese Narrative* and *A Postmodern Nationalist: Truth, Orality and Gender in the Work of Mia Couto.* He is executive editor of *ellipsis: The Journal of the American Portuguese Studies Association.*

Mark Sabine is Lecturer in Lusophone Studies at the University of Nottingham. He has published extensively on the work of José Saramago and Fernando Pessoa, and has also authored studies of representations of empire and nationality, and of gender, sexuality and desire, in nineteenth- and twentieth-century Portuguese and Lusophone African literature and film.

Claire Williams is Lecturer in Brazilian Literature and Culture at the University of Oxford, and is a Fellow of St Peter's College. She has published widely on Lusophone women's writing, particularly the authors Clarice Lispector (Brazil), Maria Gabriela Llansol (Portugal) and Lília Momplé (Mozambique).

Clive Willis is Emeritus Professor of Portuguese Studies at Manchester University. He has published widely on the language, literature and history of the Portuguese-speaking countries. Recent publications include *Luso-Asian Voices* (with David Brookshaw, 2000) and *China and Macau* (2002). *Early Brazil* (with Stuart Schwartz) is to be published in 2010. *Camões, Prince of Poets* is currently in preparation.

INTRODUCTION

This *Companion to Portuguese Literature* is the first in English. It is intended as a companion in a literal sense – a guide, friendly and accessible, but we hope authoritative, for readers to take with them on one of the most interesting but least known literary adventures that Western Europe can offer. The book has been written for readers who, for whatever reason, are new to Portuguese literature, who would like to have some idea of the terrain in advance, but who do not expect an answer to every question. So each chapter provides an outline of the work of a writer or group of writers, and establishes the main issues in view, in a way that encourages further exploration. At the same time it gives a clear overview of areas which undergraduate and graduate students may be about to study in greater depth.

This is a Companion, not a history or dictionary of literature. There have been histories of Portuguese literature by English writers – for example, Aubrey Bell's now quite outmoded *Portuguese Literature* of 1932. There are other, and much more distinguished histories in Portuguese. The best-known modern one is A. J. Saraiva and Óscar Lopes's brilliantly polemic *História da Literatura Portuguesa* of the 1950s. These writers' left-wing political convictions led them to shed light on many neglected matters, but they were extremely partial. The more recent *Revisionist History of Portuguese Literature*, in English but written mostly by a group of Portuguese scholars, also seeks to challenge conventional wisdom. In a Companion, however, unlike a history, there is no single point of view, apart from the wish to guide readers on their way. In any case, in a book with eighteen authors editorial single-mindedness is impossible.

In recent years Portuguese scholars have produced a number of excellent dictionaries of literature and of the work of individual writers. A list of some of them is given at the end of this Introduction. Compilers of dictionaries normally try to give a complete coverage of their subject, but that is not the ambition of this book. After all, no one on a journey would tolerate a companion who insisted on explaining everything, without distinguishing the wood from the trees. The individual chapters of this volume, prepared and coordinated by specialists working in or in close association with the main centres of British Lusophone Studies, focus on the major schools and authors of the medieval, Renaissance and modern periods. Most of the authors selected for comment are, therefore, canonical, but we have also included some less well known women and contemporary writers.

The Companion presents Portuguese literature as a landscape of writers and their books, arranged from a chronological perspective. There is some grouping by genre – the familiar genres of verse, prose and drama – but the emphasis throughout is on individual achievement. We have, then, followed a traditional, humanistic agenda, but one which is flexible enough to accommodate many different styles of criticism. We have avoided a thematic approach, partly because of our wish not to be dogmatic editors, partly because thematic divisions are subject to fashion and can very soon go out of date. Nor does the chronological perspective imply any particular view of the development of Portuguese history or culture. Rather our intention has been to allow the reader to see the work of individual writers in the context of their times.

We begin with Helder Macedo's survey of the whole field, eight centuries of Portuguese history and literature. The survey provides, amongst many other things, an outline of the history of Portugal as it impinges on literature, and for that reason the reader of subsequent chapters will need to refer back to it. It is also a personal view of the whole of Portuguese literature, its dominant themes, personalities and fault-lines, from the perspective of a noted scholar and critic who is himself a creative writer, in verse and prose. Because it is a personal view, it is tempered, in different ways, by the chapters that follow.

In the medieval period, our account centres on the Galician-Portuguese lyric (including the *Cantigas de Santa Maria*) and the chronicles of Fernão Lopes; in the Renaissance, the epic and lyric works of Luís de Camões, the plays of Gil Vicente, and the poetry and drama of Francisco de Sá de Miranda and António Ferreira. A section is included on the travel literature produced by voyagers to Africa, India and the Far East. Briefer surveys are provided for the relatively quiet periods of the seventeenth and eighteenth centuries. For Romantic and post-Romantic literature the spotlight falls on the works of Almeida Garrett, and the novels of Camilo Castelo Branco and José Maria Eça de Queirós. In the early twentieth century we focus on the modernist poetry of Fernando Pessoa; the later twentieth century and its continuation into the new millennium have no single dominant figure in prose, poetry or drama, and are accordingly represented by overlapping surveys of women writers and the main genres in the periods before and after the 1974 'Carnation Revolution'. A final chapter on Portuguese literature in translation directs the English-speaking reader to the largely undiscovered literary riches of Portuguese. We have made no attempt to cover Brazilian Literature or the Literature of Portuguese-speaking Africa, whose inclusion would necessarily have led to tokenism and subalternisation. Both of these bodies of literature, as well as film and cultural studies in the Portuguese-speaking world, merit independent volumes.

All quotations from Portuguese have been translated, in many cases by the authors of the chapters concerned, with the original reproduced where appropriate. Literary works are referred to by their Portuguese title, supplemented on first mention by a translation and where appropriate the titles of published English translations; second and subsequent references will use only the Portuguese title, in full or abbreviated. References to critical literature, particularly in Portuguese, have been kept to a minimum. Each chapter ends with a list of editions of the main authors cited, and of available English translations of their work, and a selection of further reading, primarily in English. The index contains an exhaustive listing of authors, anonymous works, and historical figures.

A few explanatory notes are required to explain some basic Portuguese cultural and historical conventions and their rendering in English. Portuguese monarchs (and other members of the royalty or the nobility) are traditionally referred to in Portuguese as 'Dom' (abbreviated 'D.') and 'Dona' instead of or in addition to the title of King, Queen or Prince. In this volume we will use the English labels 'King', 'Queen' and 'Prince', in conjunction with modernised but un-Anglicised forms of Portuguese first names. Thus the monarch known as 'D. José' and often translated as 'King Joseph' will appear as King José; the medieval poet-King 'D. Denis' or 'D. Diniz' will be King Dinis; 'el-Rei D. Afonso Quinto' will be (King) Afonso V; and 'D(ona) Maria II' will be (Queen) Maria II. Similarly, no attempt will be made to anglicise names such as Sancho, Pedro, Fernando, Filipe, Miguel, Manuel, Sebastião, and Carlos. Exceptionally the 'Infante D. Henrique' of the fifteenth century will be 'Prince Henry the Navigator', as he is known to British historians, and the Marquesa de Alorna will be 'Marquise de Alorna'. Aristocratic titles such as Marquês and Duque, when associated with particular domains, will normally be translated, as in the 'Marquis of Pombal'. The title 'D(om)' will be used for nobles without specific titles. Names of historical and political institutions (e.g. *Estado Novo*, *Cortes*) are given in Portuguese and translated on first occurrence where appropriate.

Portuguese authors will generally be referred to by whichever distinctive combination of given names and surnames is current in literary discourse. This may not correspond to the form under which they will be listed in alphabetically organised bibliographies, which will place authors under their final surname.[1] Thus José Maria Eça de Queirós is more commonly referred

---

[1]   Portuguese follows English rather than Spanish naming conventions, in that the final surname is invariably the paternal or marital surname. This is often preceded by two or more parental and grandparental surnames. Many Portuguese writers have created double-barrelled surnames, in the English manner, so as to officialise multiple surnames.

to as 'Eça' or 'Eça de Queirós' than 'Queirós', António Lobo Antunes is known as 'Lobo Antunes' and José Cardoso Pires is 'Cardoso Pires'. At the same time, we only occasionally defer to the Portuguese predilection for using the given name of a few cherished authors, when this name is distinctive enough to identify them: well-known examples include Camilo (Castelo Branco), Cesário (Verde), Antero (de Quental), Florbela (Espanca), Agustina (Bessa Luís), Sophia (de Mello Breyner Andresen). Medieval authors, and particularly the poets of the early *cancioneiros*, are usually identified by a given name and a nickname or patronymic, as the modern use of surnames was not yet established.

Portuguese literary terminology will be used sparingly and with English equivalents or translations. Poetic examples will not require any understanding of Portuguese metrical terminology or conventions.[2]

Though the availability of good translations of modern Portuguese poetry and fiction is gradually increasing, Portuguese literature is still remarkably poorly known. We hope that this work will contribute to a greater understanding and appreciation of the literary culture of Britain's oldest ally.

Stephen Parkinson, Cláudia Pazos Alonso, T. F. Earle

Further reading

In English

General

Moss, Joyce (ed.), *Spanish and Portuguese Literatures and Their Times (The Iberian Peninsula)*, World Literature and its Times vol. 5 (Detroit, MI: Gale, 2002)

Rector, Monica and Fred M. Clark (eds), *Portuguese Writers*, Dictionary of Literary Biography vol. 287 (Detroit, MI: Thomson Gale, 2004)

Tamen, Miguel and Helena Carvalhão Buescu (eds), *A Revisionary History of Portuguese Literature* (New York, Garland, 1999)

Historical background

Birmingham, David, *A Concise History of Portugal* (Cambridge: Cambridge University Press, 1993)

---

[2] Portuguese poetic metre is conventionally analysed using the same counting system as French poetry, in which syllables are counted up to but not beyond the final stressed syllable, as opposed to Spanish counting which adds a final unstressed syllable (real or potential) after the final stressed syllable. Thus a Portuguese decasyllabic line is equivalent to a Spanish hendecasyllable, and the seven-syllable Portuguese *redondilha* corresponds to the Spanish eight-syllable *redondilla*. Unlike their Italian, French and Spanish counterparts, Portuguese lines of verse rarely have any prescribed rhythmic regularities, such as stress on the fourth or sixth line of the decasyllable.

Saraiva, José Hermano, *Portugal: A Companion History* (Manchester: Carcanet, 1997)

Wheeler, Douglas L., *Historical Dictionary of Portugal* (Lanham, MD: Scarecrow Press, 1993)

In Portuguese
General
Coelho, Jacinto do Prado (ed.), *Dicionário de Literatura: Literatura Portuguesa, Literatura Brasileira, Literatura Galega, estilística literária*, 5 vols (Oporto: Figueirinhas, 1969)

Reis, Carlos (ed.), *História Crítica da Literatura Portuguesa*, 9 vols (Lisbon: Verbo, 1993–2005) [vols IV and VIII are still to be published]

Saraiva, António José, and Óscar Lopes, *História da Literatura Portuguesa*, 17th edn (Oporto: Porto Editora, 2008 [1st edn 1955])

Historical background
Marques, A. H. de Oliveira and Joel Serrão (General editors), *Nova História de Portugal*, 12 vols (Lisbon: Presença, 1986–92)

Mattoso, José (General editor), *História de Portugal*, 15 vols (Lisbon: Círculo de Leitores, 1992–)

On specific periods and authors
Buescu, Helena Carvalhão (ed.), *Dicionário do Romantismo Literário Português* (Lisbon: Caminho, 1997)

Cabral, Alexandre (ed.), *Dicionário de Camilo Castelo Branco* (Lisbon: Caminho, 1988)

Lanciani, Giulia and Giuseppe Tavani (eds), *Dicionário de Literatura Medieval Galega e Portuguesa* (Lisbon: Caminho, 1993)

Martins, Fernando Cabral (ed.), *Dicionário de Fernando Pessoa e do Modernismo Português* (Lisbon: Caminho, 2008)

Matos, A. Campos (ed.), *Dicionário de Eça de Queirós* (Lisbon: Caminho, 1988; revised and expanded 2000)

Seixo, Maria Alzira, *Dicionário da Obra de António Lobo Antunes*, 2 vols (Lisbon: Imprensa Nacional–Casa da Moeda, 2008)

Eight Centuries of Portuguese Literature:
An Overview

HELDER MACEDO

Portugal was a by-product of the Christian Reconquest of the Iberian Peninsula. In the 11th century, Henry, a younger son of the Duke of Burgundy,
joined the campaign of King Alfonso VI of León and Castile in the fight
against the Moors. As a reward, he was married to the king's illegitimate
daughter, Teresa, and was given as a dowry a territory then integrated into
Galicia, becoming Count of Portugal in 1093. Henry's son Afonso Henriques
(1109–85) conducted a series of brilliant campaigns both against the royal
power of León-Castile and against the Moors. In 1139 he was proclaimed king
of Portugal. León-Castile recognised the new kingdom in 1143 and a papal
bull of 1179 acknowledged Afonso Henriques as the first king of Portugal.
His successors consolidated the kingdom's independence, expanding its
territory to what are virtually Portugal's present frontiers, in a process that
culminated with the conquest of the Algarve in 1249–50. A new dynasty, the
Dynasty of Aviz, which came to power in the course of a civil war of resistance to Portugal's annexation by Castile in 1383–85, initiated the European
imperial expansion that shaped the modern world.

The language of this small country has become the official language of
more than two hundred million people in four continents. It has a literary
tradition going back some eight centuries that began in a language not yet
distinguishable from its Galician roots and gave rise to a remarkable poetic
flowering which lasted from the early thirteenth century to the middle of
the fourteenth century. Practitioners in other areas of the Iberian Peninsula
included King Alfonso X of Castile (1221–84), later known as 'the Learned'
(*el Sabio*), who commissioned the famous *Cantigas de Santa Maria*. The
secular *cantigas*, collected in three *Cancioneiros*, are divided into three main
categories: *cantigas de amigo* (literally 'songs of the lover'), *cantigas de
amor* ('songs of love'), which are often compared with the Provençal love
lyric, and *cantigas de escarnho e maldizer* ('songs of mockery and slander'),
which are frequently slanderous, bawdy and misogynistic.

The most original features of Galician-Portuguese lyricism are found in the *cantigas de amigo*, poems in the female voice written by male authors, in which an underlying oral and musical tradition is incorporated into a literary genre that is highly sophisticated psychologically and strictly prescribed in poetic terms. In a distinctive subgroup of these miniature masterpieces, patterns based on parallel verses, refrain and word-repetition are modulated to define metaphorical correspondences with natural surroundings and human feelings. A factual sea and the plausible ships sailing on it become metaphors for lovers' meetings; hair and fountains are emblems of female sexuality; the phallic flowers of 'the green pine' announce the arrival of the woman's beloved; the wind blows into the water the intimate garments of a nubile and amorous maiden or, in an equivalent sexual metaphor, a mountain deer stirs the waters of a fountain. The dramatic personification inherent in these poems of latent animistic significance can be understood as a narcissistic male usurpation of the female or as a male projection into the female. In either case, they transpose the subjectivity of love into an objective expression of feeling. Practitioners are drawn from all social classes, ranging from King Dinis (1261–1325), grandson of Alfonso the Learned and founder of the first Portuguese university in 1288, to enigmatic minstrels like Martin Codax. Many poets move from one genre to another, each distinguished by its different and even opposed attitudes to women (deification in the *cantigas de amor*, degradation in the *cantigas de escarnho*, and identification in the *cantigas de amigo*). Some even make poems combining the attitudes of all three genres, as when João Garcia de Guilhade uses the female voice of the *cantiga de amigo* with the tone of a *cantiga de escarnho*, to make fun of the stereotyped male attitudes of the *cantigas de amor*.

Portugal shared the European medieval tradition of chivalric literature and religious edification through adaptations and fragmentary translations. The development of Portuguese prose is largely attributable to the contribution of Dom Pedro, Count of Barcelos, the illegitimate son of King Dinis who was responsible for a genealogical work, the *Livro de Linhagens* (*The Book of Lineages*), and a Portuguese version of a chronicle of Spain, the *Crónica Geral de Espanha*. In these formative works, historical record blends with the magical and symbolic, as in the complex narrative of events leading to the fall of the last Visigothic king and the invasion of the Peninsula by the Moors of North Africa, adapted from an Arabic chronicle by Mohammed Ar-Razi (887–935?).

Historical record and literary construction were to converge in the chronicles of Fernão Lopes, a commoner who was born circa 1380 and died circa 1459. To use the term 'chronicles' to designate a vast tetralogy in which this prodigious narrator depicts the transformation of a medieval kingdom into a new nation forged by the collective will of its people is not wrong, but it is as reductive as it would be to consider Shakespeare's history plays as dramatised chronicles rather than as dramatic representations of history. Situated in the context of the Hundred Years War and giving considerable attention to the English intervention in the Iberian Peninsula, the historical period covered by Fernão Lopes encompasses the reigns of Pedro I (1320–67) and Fernando (1348–83); the dynastic crisis of 1383–85; and the reign of the founder of a new dynasty, João I (1357–1433). Conceptually, the work centres on the dynastic crisis, which, in accordance with prevailing rules on succession, would have led to the annexation of Portugal by Castile since the heiress-apparent was married to the Castilian king. A majority of the Portuguese aristocracy sided with Castile while a large group of the population, drawn initially mainly from urban areas but later including some of the less favoured minor nobility and people from rural areas, took up arms against this technically legitimate succession. The least likely of the potential claimants to the Portuguese throne, Dom João, Master of Avis (the illegitimate son of King Pedro I and a commoner), emerged from the resulting civil war and Castilian invasion as the king legitimised by popular will, marking the beginning of what Fernão Lopes characterised as a new age.

Fernão Lopes wrote his chronicles at the behest of the future king Duarte (1391–1438), son of João I and of Philippa of Lancaster, daughter of John of Gaunt. The implicit purpose of this commission was to legitimise the anomaly of the people's election of a king who had acquired his right to govern through rebellion and the force of arms. With supreme literary mastery, Fernão Lopes transforms the factual sequence of Portugal's history up to his own time into a demonstration of its historical legitimacy: the historical outcome is legitimised in an innovative concept of justice as equity, with equity seen as the service of the collectivity, and the benefit of the collectivity as the justification of royal power. In this way Fernão Lopes gives a new dimension to the concept of royal charisma, seeing the imponderable quality that makes a man a king among men as an actuating quality whose absence deprives a king of his royalty. This was the same problem that Shakespeare confronted more than a century and a half later in *Richard II*, a tragedy on the legitimacy of power and royal charisma centred on a dynastic crisis that was contemporaneous with the crisis in Portugal and led to the accession to the English throne of the first cousin of the Avis princes, Henry Bolingbroke. The chronicles of Fernão Lopes are a foundational work: in signifying the transformation of the old feudal order into a new national order they can be seen as a pioneering example of the Renaissance epic that was to culminate in Tasso and Camões. They also have something of the quality of a *Bildungsroman*, the process of apprenticeship unfolding not so much in the development of a single hero as in that of the collectivity, represented from generation to generation by paradigmatic characters and social groups who determine the course of history. Extraordinary individual portraits are placed alongside marvellous descriptions of mass movements, with a capacity for psychological analysis and visualisation of action possibly equalled only in nineteenth-century fiction.

King Duarte, whose remarkable brothers included Prince Henry the Navigator and Prince Pedro, the cosmopolitan traveller whose treatise on the virtues of benefaction, *A Virtuosa Benfeitoria*, was a forerunner of a civic humanism inspired by Cicero, left a collection of essays, *O Leal Conselheiro* (*The Loyal Counsellor*), which contains perceptive analyses of feelings and behaviour, and includes a remarkable description of the 'melancholy humour' from which he suffered and of how he cured it. He tackles moral issues raised by the concept of the 'just war' and the limits of religious freedom, and analyses a wide range of beliefs and superstitions in what can only be described as a spirit of rationalist humanism, with an emphasis on the value of experience as the basis of knowledge.

With the generation of the Princes of Avis, Portugal began its overseas expansion, at first in North Africa, in pursuit of what was essentially a policy of conquest of neighbouring territories suitable for occupation. Subsequent exploration of the African coast in search of a sea route to India initiated a policy of armed trade and development of the slave trade, particularly after the beginning of the colonisation of Brazil in 1500. The two policies were seen as complementary but if the policy of occupying lands in North Africa had been successful it could have contributed to the economic welfare of the common people whereas expansion of overseas trade led to the creation of a financial hierarchy in a domestically impoverished rural country. The negative consequences of empire building became evident only gradually, however, and in its golden age Portugal was in the vanguard of naval technology, mathematics, and geographical knowledge in Renaissance Europe.

The chronicles of Fernão Lopes mark the beginning of an outstanding tradition of historical literature, which includes accounts by some astute observers with personal experience of the Empire, like Gaspar Correia (1495–1564), Fernão Lopes de Castanheda (1510–59) and Diogo do Couto (1542–1616). The foremost chronicler of the period was João de Barros (c.1496–1570), who used the methods of a modern researcher, consulting documentary sources. Most famous for his monumental *Décadas da Ásia* (*Asia: The Four Decades*), he was the author of many other works, including a celebrated allegorical chivalrous romance (*Clarimundo*), a daring philosophical debate on religion (*Ropica Pnefma* (*Spiritual Merchandise*)), and a Grammar of Portuguese. A reader of Erasmus, whose *Praise of Folly* he admiringly mentions, and of Thomas More, whose *Utopia* he characterises as a 'modern fable designed to teach the English how to govern themselves', this historian of empire seems to anticipate the end of empires when he comments, as a justification for his Grammar, that the arms and stone pillars that Portugal had scattered throughout the world were material things that time could destroy, but the Portuguese language would not so easily be destroyed by time.

The works of the Portuguese chroniclers not only provide an inestimably valuable historical record of Europe's first encounters with other peoples in other continents and fill significant gaps in the historiography of these peoples – it would be difficult, for instance, to write the history of the Ottoman Empire without referring to Portuguese Renaissance historiographers – but also reflect the increasing political, cultural, religious and ethnic complexity of Portuguese society during the period of discovery and expansion. Under João II (1455–95), who consolidated royal power, the discovery of a sea route to India became a tangible reality when Portuguese caravels rounded the Cape of Good Hope in 1488; it was also during his reign that, with supreme arrogance, the world still unknown to Europeans was divided between Portugal and Spain by the Treaty of Tordesillas (1494). In the Peninsular context, the period encompassed such momentous events as the unification of the kingdoms of Castile and Aragon and the establishment of the Spanish Inquisition in 1478; and, in 1492, the fall of Granada, marking the end of the long process of *Reconquista*, the discovery of the Americas by Columbus, and the expulsion of the Moors and Jews from Spain. In the rest of Europe, this period was characterised by major controversies and religious wars in Christendom consequent upon the dissident Protestant movements within the Roman Church, reformation attempts at the heart of what came to be known as 'Catholicism' in opposition to 'Protestantism', and the strict orthodoxy of the Counter-Reformation.

King João II allowed Jews expelled from Spain to enter Portugal, encouraging settlement by the wealthier among them and those with professions considered useful, while prescribing that all the others would be reduced to servitude if they did not leave the country after a short period of transit. His successor, King Manuel I (1469–1521), carried out a policy of fostering mixed marriages designed to achieve the peaceful integration of Jews into all levels of Portuguese society, but he also resorted to forced conversion and 'confiscation' of the children of those who refused to convert. The percentage of 'New Christians' increased substantially, although many continued to practise their Jewish faith in secret and, as later Portuguese Inquisition records were to show, many women of Jewish origin educated their children in their secret faith and led their Christian husbands to 'Judaise'.

The expulsion from Spain led to the intensification of the old Jewish millenarian tradition, which found fertile soil in Portugal in a Christian millenarianism of Joachimite origin in which the advent of the Age of the Holy Spirit could be understood as corresponding to the advent of the Messiah. Medieval Spanish Cabbalism, with its controversial female personification of the divine, was virtually neutralised by Jewish orthodoxy but found renewed favour among the communities expelled from Spain. In a parallel development within Spanish and Portuguese Christianity, the *Alumbrados* ('Enlightened') practised a heterodox form of worship of the female personification of the divine, which found followers in all social classes. Equally symptomatic of parallel developments and possible convergences between Jewish and Christian beliefs is the fact that while some aspects of Spanish Cabbalism had been integrated into Christian thinking by Pico della Mirandola, the *Dialoghi d'Amore* by the Portuguese Jew León Hebreo, or Yehudah Abravanel (born in Lisbon, around 1465), son of Isaac Abravanel, who had served in the Portuguese court, became a canonical work of Christian Neoplatonism in the tradition of Marsilio Ficino.

Sixteenth-century Portugal was rife with conflicting tensions. Lisbon, as the main European port for trade with the Orient, was a market for exotic products, new ideas, sex and drugs. Violence proliferated. More than ten percent of the Lisbon population was black; Jews and Moors conducted their trade alongside Christians coming from all parts of Europe; questions of faith were openly debated. Sailors related their improbable encounters with peoples and worlds until then unknown to other Europeans. It is not surprising that Thomas More's *Utopia* was set in an island supposedly brought to his attention by a Portuguese sailor whose emblematic name Hythlodaeus characterises him as a teller of tall tales. The first encounters of the Portuguese with the cultures of other continents took place under the sign of improbability, with desire or expectation often superimposed upon the reality observed. Álvaro Velho, presumed author of the account of Vasco da Gama's first voyage to India, identified the Hindus encountered by the Portuguese as the Christians they wanted them to be and a statue of the bloodthirsty goddess Durga as an image of the loving Virgin Mary. Pêro Vaz de Caminha, in his letter to King Manuel I describing the discovery of the land that became Brazil, *Carta sobre o Achamento das Terras de Vera Cruz* (*Letter on the Discovery of the Lands of the True Cross*), saw the nakedness of the Amerindians he encountered as proof of the existence of an innocent race, living in a sin-free state like Adam and Eve before the Fall. But the harsh realities of the voyages were also to be recorded in the anonymous narratives of shipwreck collected under the title *História Trágico-Marítima* (translated as *The Tragic History of the Sea*).

The ambiguous integration of the Jews into Portuguese society and contacts with ideas in other European countries created in Portugal what could have become a Catholic culture with crypto-Jewish reformist elements. The Portuguese Inquisition was established in 1536 by King Manuel's successor, João III, fifty-eight years after its establishment in Spain, and the first *auto da fé* in Portugal was held in Lisbon in 1540. Erasmus had dedicated his *Chrysostomi Lucubrationes* to King João III whose brother, Cardinal Henrique (the Portuguese Grand Inquisitor), had been a disciple of the Flemish humanist Clenardus. He had also corresponded with Damião de Góis (1502–74), a Portuguese humanist friend and student of Erasmus whose portrait was drawn by Dürer and whose contacts with Luther and Melanchthon led to his investigation by the Inquisition. Portuguese professors teaching at universities abroad were attracted back to Portugal by the creation, in 1547, of one of Europe's most progressive colleges, the *Colégio das Artes* (College of Arts) in Coimbra. Michel de Montaigne characterised the College's founding rector, André de Gouveia, formerly the prestigious principal of the colleges of Sainte-Barbe in Paris and Guienne in Bordeaux, as 'the greatest principal in France'. But the Coimbra *Colégio das Artes* was closed down, and its professors investigated by the Inquisition on suspicion of Protestantism. This would not have been wholly unfounded considering that the teaching staff included the subsequently self-confessed Calvinist, George Buchanan, and that André de Gouveia himself had been accused of heterodoxy by his uncle and earlier mentor in Paris, Diogo de Gouveia. The College was entrusted to the Company of Jesus, the name originally given to the religious order founded by Ignatius of Loyola, Diogo de Gouveia's protégé in Paris.

Portugal's literature had flourished during the 'Age of Discovery', from the publication of Garcia de Resende's anthology, the *Cancioneiro Geral* (*General Songbook*), in 1516 to the publication of *Os Lusíadas* (translated as *The Lusiads*) by Luís de Camões in 1572. The *Cancioneiro Geral* is a vast compilation of Portuguese court poetry, which includes compositions by 286 authors dating back to the reign of Afonso V. Most of its contents, are, however, representative of cultural life at the courts of João II and Manuel I, where performances of theatrical intermezzos or *momos* (mummers' plays) were combined with dancing, music, and the reciting of poems often organised in residually dramatic debates or long sequences based on set themes. Garcia de Resende followed the model of contemporaneous Spanish *cancioneros* and the influence of Castilian poetry is evident in some of the poetic forms and in the bilingualism of some of the Portuguese poets in the *Cancioneiro Geral*. There are Petrarchan echoes in some poems and allusions to Dante in the compositions known as *infernos de namorados* ('lovers' infernos'), of which the best example is Garcia de Resende's own poem written in the voice of Inês de Castro, the mistress of Pedro I killed for reasons of State, with consequences recorded by Fernão Lopes. With more or less macabre additions, the story provided the subject of many poems and plays in various languages. The *Cancioneiro Geral* also includes satirical poems, largely scatological and obscene, as well as poems of social criticism and chivalresque celebration, integrated into 'cousas de folgar e gentilezas' (entertainments and courtesies). These account for a large part of the *Cancioneiro*'s material, as the compiler, in his voice as chronicler, gently deplores in the Prologue, in which he foresees a need for poetry to be devoted in future to themes that perpetuate the memory of Portuguese deeds. But 'entertainments' can also reflect deeper concerns. The sequence of poems that opens the *Cancioneiro*, a lengthy debate on the theme of *Cuidar e Sospirar* ('To muse or to sigh') – whether love should be interiorised or expressed – can be seen as corresponding, albeit on a frivolous and unconscious level, to the great contemporary debate on whether religious faith should be expressed in the spirituality of inner devotion or in the material form of good works. Among many fine compositions, the *Cancioneiro* includes the first printed poems of three major figures in Portuguese literature: Gil Vicente, Sá de Miranda and Bernardim Ribeiro.

Gil Vicente (c.1465–c.1536) is considered Portugal's foremost dramatist, with at least forty-four theatrical works in Portuguese and Castilian, including moralities, farces, comedies, tragicomedies and devotional plays, which combine the allegorical and the realistic, celebration of war and pastoral nostalgia, moral edification and social criticism, the purest lyricism and the liveliest colloquialism. His innovative *autos* brought into court entertainment virtually all aspects of Portuguese life through typical characters placed in paradigmatic situations: disappointed returnees from India, adulterous wives, wise women, bawds, corrupt clergy, merrymaking friars, overweening nobles, cowardly braggarts, ridiculous versifiers, charlatan doctors, venal judges, grasping functionaries, dishonest tradesmen, thieving usurers, gullible peasants, wise fools, astrologers, witches, Jews, Moors, gypsies, blacks – in short, virtually the whole of Portuguese society. His satirising of paid indulgences, the idolatrous cult of saints, rote prayers and superstitious beliefs indicates that a reforming attitude within Catholic orthodoxy was still acceptable in the courts to which he was attached. Gil Vicente's work had some popular followers in Portugal but it was in Spain, with Lope de Vega and Calderón de la Barca, that his legacy had worthy continuity.

Francisco de Sá de Miranda (1487–1558), who, like Gil Vicente, wrote several works in Castilian, travelled in Italy and Spain from 1521 to 1526 and introduced Renaissance poetic forms associated with the *dolce stil nuovo* into Portugal. A few years after his return, he turned his back on the court, where he had been close to King João III, and settled in the rural north of the country. Here, as his anonymous first biographer records, towards the end of his life 'tears would flow down his cheeks [...] in pity for what his spirit revealed to him of his country's misfortunes'. The continuous thread running through his vast and complex work is the imperative of reason in a world subject to deception, whether arising from an apparent love that usurps individual identity, or exercised by a political or religious power incompatible with collective liberty. In the eclogue *Basto* he attributes strong feelings of social injustice to the shepherd representing his own position, who says: 'I find you have harsh masters, here. They want us to worship them', and adds: 'they will not let us have minds of our own.' The eclogue concludes with the vision of a society collectively gone mad, in which madness has become normality. Sá de Miranda's verse letters, including one addressed to João III, offer a radical condemnation of Portuguese imperial policy, which he sees as a cause of the country's economic decadence, moral corruption and materialism. His disciplined and austere lyric poetry, inspired by Horace, confronts the essential paradox of finite humanity and the cyclic renewal of Nature in a troubled search for a meaning that would make life more than simply 'being born and dying'.

Bernardim Ribeiro, who was probably born towards the end of the 1480s and whose date of death is unknown, is the author of one of the most beautiful and enigmatic works in literature, the novel *História da Menina e Moça ou Saudades* (translated as *The Young Girl's Story, or The Book of Longings*). In a poem published in the *Cancioneiro Geral*, Bernardim Ribeiro crystallises his existential situation as that of a self divided by an inner conflict that makes him his own enemy. His eclogues have autobiographical suggestions of an unfulfilled love that might be at the heart of this self-conflict. In one of his elegies, the spectral apparition of the beloved woman leads to a vision of darkness as the image of life. A nihilistic sestina expresses a longing for the destruction of the spiritual will (*vontade*) buried in matter. These themes are taken up in the novel, which is an extended soliloquy in a female voice that brings other voices and different times into the same ambiguous space from which it emerges, a place of exile between 'mountains that never change and the sea's waters that are never still', emblematic of woman's constancy in contrast to the inconstancy of men in a world in which 'change possesses all'. In this long *cantiga de amigo*, which is also a romance of chivalry told from a female perspective, there is no discernible distinction between the observed and the imagined, the objective and subjective, cause and effect, dream and reality, life and death, present, past and future. The novel is addressed to an *amigo* about whom the narrator now knows nothing except that 'alive or dead, the earth possesses him without any joy'. The inconclusive fate of this 'friend' seems to coincide with that of one of the male characters whose emblematic stories provide the main body of the narrative, a knight-poet disguised as a herdsman whose assumed name, an anagram of his own true name, is Binmarder, which is also an anagram of the author's name, Bernardim. The book, which the narrator says she is writing while she awaits her 'last hour', not knowing whether she will be able to finish it, remains unfinished, coming to an abrupt end, in mid-sentence.

The first edition of *Menina e Moça* was published in Ferrara in 1554 by the exiled Portuguese Jew, Abraham Usque. This was thirty-eight years after the publication of Bernardim Ribeiro's poems in the *Cancioneiro Geral*. Nothing is known of what happened to Bernardim Ribeiro between 1516 and 1554, apart from what can be gathered from references made by Sá de Miranda in two of his eclogues written at the end of the 1520s in which he indicates that his friend 'the poet Ribeiro' had fallen into disgrace at Court and had gone to 'better parts'. Usque published works of a religious or philosophical character destined for a Jewish audience, including the *Consolação das tribulações de Israel* (*Consolation for the Tribulations of Israel*) by his relative Samuel Usque, which is a book of spiritual resistance addressed to the Jewish communities persecuted in the Iberian Peninsula. The favourable reception of Bernardim Ribeiro's book by the exiled Jewish community makes it plausible, in the Portuguese context of the time, that he himself was a Jew who had converted to Christianity because of the material benefits this would bring him and then reconverted to Judaism for the sake of a love that not only divided him from himself but laid him open to the charge of heresy, punishable by death even before the establishment of the Inquisition in Portugal. This idea is not, however, accepted by traditionalist criticism.

The influence of Sá de Miranda and Bernardim Ribeiro was considerable. The Spanish poet Alonso Núñez de Reynoso paraphrased verses by both poets in his eclogue *Baltea*. In Portugal, the celebrated eclogue *Crisfal*, attributed to Cristóvão Falcão (1515?–57?), is so clearly akin to the work of Bernardim Ribeiro that it was included in the Ferrara edition of his works. Sá de Miranda's main successor was António Ferreira (1528–69), a notable poet in the same classical and Italianate tradition. He was the author of the tragedy *Castro*, which is generally considered the greatest work in Portuguese theatre after Gil Vicente. In this tragedy, the dramatic focus is transferred from the love affair of Inês de Castro and Pedro to the dilemma facing Afonso IV, who must choose between his compassion as a father and his duty as king.

The major trends of Portuguese Renaissance literature converge in the work of Portugal's greatest poet, Luís de Camões (c.1524–80). Having served as an imperial soldier for more than seventeen years, first in Ceuta and then in the East, Camões was the first European poet to have extensive knowledge of the cultures of other continents. Both in his unruly youth and in his life in the service of the Empire he fell foul of the law on a number of occasions and was imprisoned in Portugal and India. In social and literary terms he was an outsider, who, by virtue of his genius, has remained the central figure in Portuguese culture up to our own time. An anti-Petrarchan giving a new dimension to an ostensibly Petrarchan poetic diction, he is a disturbingly modern poet, a poet of uncertainty in a world in transition who used the Humanist and Christian Neoplatonic tradition to which he belonged in a quest for meaning that counterposes doubt and belief, rupture and continuity, immanence and transcendence, sexuality and spirituality, experience and faith. At the end of his life – 'a life scattered around the world in fragments' – he seems to have found only fragmentation instead of the totality he had been seeking. In a body of work built upon antinomies, the existential peregrination it depicts postulates something as innovatory as the right to happiness on earth. Love, the love of 'a man of flesh and blood', is not for him a simulacrum of the divine but the supreme expression of human knowledge. This concept of love, which permeates his lyric poetry, is central to the concept of *Os Lusíadas* and makes the celebration of the imperial feats of the Portuguese in the East the supreme epic of the European Renaissance. Like his lyric poetry his epic is compounded of antinomies. The most significant of these is the correlation it establishes between pastoral critique and epic celebration. From the pastoral perspective, associated with the myth of the Golden Age, the very subject matter of epic – voyages and quests, wars and conquests, wealth and power – reflects the decadence that led humans to fall into the Iron Age. Epic celebrates the deeds that pastoral condemns. *Os Lusíadas* is an epic poem that makes a pastoral critique of the very deeds it celebrates. The climax of the poem is, then, not Vasco da Gama's successful arrival in India after the voyage that provides its historical framework, but the discovery, on the voyage home, of an Island of Love, metaphor for a new Golden Age where all opposites could be reconciled in historical time.

A contemporary of Camões in the East, who travelled mainly in China and Japan, was Fernão Mendes Pinto (1510?–83), whose memoir *Peregrinação* (translated as *Peregrination*, or *Travels of Mendes Pinto*) can be seen as in many respects complementary to *Os Lusíadas*. The work is an extraordinary combination of fact and fiction in which the narrator, a picaresque 'poor me', whose travels are based on those of Fernão Mendes Pinto himself, includes in his narration exploits attributed to a bellicose and arrogant trader, António de Faria, which also correspond to episodes in the author's own life. In the same way, what the book admiringly describes of China and Japan is part fact, part fiction, using these nations and cultures as a critical mirror of Portuguese society and European culture in his own time. In its creative mixture of truth and fiction and of the factually autobiographical and the autobiographically transposed, *Peregrinação* is a strikingly original literary work, which could be said to anticipate fantastic realism and the post-modern novel.

Criticism of the abuses of Empire reached a peak in the *Diálogo do Soldado Prático* (*Dialogue of the Practical Soldier*) by the chronicler Diogo do Couto, the continuator of João de Barros's *Ásia* and a companion of Camões in India. This criticism coincided with an intensified Christian militancy in the home country. Following the establishment of the Inquisition, the old Humanist spirit of the Portuguese Crown had given way to religious fanaticism as the perceived decadence of the country continued. Imported wealth benefited the new mercantile oligarchy rather than the common people. The project to conquer 'infidel' lands in North Africa, 'the Algarves abroad', never entirely abandoned since it was first proposed under the Aviz princes, began to be seen as desirable both for future agricultural colonisation and for the service of Christ in a 'just war'. Camões himself gives voice to this unholy alliance of faith and profit in *Os Lusíadas*. In 1578, Sebastião, the fanatical young king to whom the poem is dedicated, invaded North Africa at the head of an army that included all the military forces available in the kingdom and the flower of the Portuguese aristocracy. Sebastião's opportune birth in 1554, two weeks after the death of his father, heir to the throne as the only surviving son of King João III, seemed to guarantee that the crown would not pass to his uncle, Philip II of Spain. But he died childless in the disastrous Battle of Alcácer-Quibir, and Portugal was annexed by Spain two years later in 1580.

The traumatised nation refused to accept the untimely death of King Sebastião, awaiting his imminent return to deliver Portugal from Spanish rule. (Many false Sebastians were to appear over coming decades.) The latent millenarianism resulting from the convergence between Jewish and Christian prophetic traditions was magnified into a persistent affirmation of subjugated national identity, in what came to be known as Sebastianism, with the dead king transformed into a nebulous Hidden King, a bizarre hybrid of King Arthur, Emperor Frederic Barbarossa and a militantly Catholic Messiah. In the aftermath of the union with Spain, epic exaltation gave way to pastoral melancholy, as in the revealingly entitled work *Corte na Aldeia* (*Village Court*) written in Portugal by the New-Christian Francisco Rodrigues Lobo (1573–1621), which gives a paradoxical pastoral dimension to Castiglione's *Il Cortegiano* by using tales told during metaphorical 'winter nights' to nostalgically glorify the 'golden age' when the Portuguese did not yet live exiled in their own country.

Between 1580 and the restoration of independence in 1640, Portugal found itself involved in Spain's European wars and its empire was under threat, mainly from the Dutch, in the East, in Africa and in Brazil. While Portuguese power in the East waned, it grew stronger in the Americas. Angola remained Portuguese thanks to the intervention of slave traders in Brazil, which had become the basis of the Portuguese economy. Large numbers of the Portuguese mercantile class, including a considerable proportion of New Christians, moved to Spain, accentuating the growing economic and cultural provincialisation of Portugal.

The contradictions inherent in a culture simultaneously provincialised and imperial, repressed and repressive, permeate the work of the two outstanding figures of Portuguese seventeenth-century literature, the aristocrat Dom Francisco Manuel de Melo (1608–66) and the Jesuit, Father António Vieira (1608–97), who were both concerned with social issues. António Vieira lived in Brazil from the age of six to the age of thirty, when he went back to Portugal. He exercised diplomatic functions in Europe, was investigated and imprisoned by the Inquisition and returned to Brazil at the age of seventy. Francisco Manuel de Melo alternated between Portugal and Spain as a diplomat and courtier, frequenting the brilliant court in Madrid. He supported the future King João IV during the movement to cast off Spanish rule but after the restoration of Portuguese independence he was imprisoned in Lisbon for eleven years, for reasons never entirely clarified. In 1655, his sentence was commuted to exile in Brazil, where he recouped his fortunes by participating in the slavocratic sugar trade. In the Iberian context, he was active in defending the rights of his aristocratic class and his oppressed nation. He is the author of a large and important body of work on historical, pedagogical and literary subjects, written in both Spanish and Portuguese, that includes a classic history of the Catalan war, as well as innovative Portuguese poems in blank verse and free verse, and a sarcastic farce on the aristocratic pretensions of aspiring commoners, *O Fidalgo Aprendiz* (*The Apprentice Nobleman*), which anticipates Molière's *Bourgeois Gentilhomme*. His study of Cabbalism, *Tratado da Ciência Cabala*, published posthumously, is revealing of how much prophetism, which he condemns in all its forms, continued to be active in the Portugal of his time. He makes an interesting distinction between what he designates as the 'unjust Cabbala' practised by the Jews and a 'just Cabbala' that could be used legitimately by Christians because it corresponded to traditional rhetoric, and suggests in the prologue that his book could be useful for Inquisitorial investigations of New Christians.

António Vieira, whose admirable sermons and letters have justly earned him fame as the supreme master of Portuguese prose, fought for the rights denied to the people oppressed by his country, both at home and abroad, protected the Amerindians, roundly condemned slavery ('a contract made by the Devil') and protested against the persecution of New Christians by the Inquisition. He acted and wrote in the context of a universal humanitarianism, and it was from that perspective that he desired the restoration of Portugal's independence. His most disturbing work is a brilliant intellectual construction of prophetic nationalism that Francisco Manuel de Melo would certainly have condemned, *A História do Futuro* (*The History of the Future*). Vieira takes up and recasts the Sebastianic tradition, not to announce the literal return of the Hidden King but to foresee the coming of an age in which the Sebastianic essence could be embodied in other Portuguese monarchs. This age would usher in a spiritual Fifth Empire when universal peace would reconcile all peoples and nations until the end of time. What distinguishes this work from other prophetic visions is the exercise of an exegetical logic that literalises prophecy as a product of reason rather than faith. His vision is not expressed in a metaphorical representation of a desired future but in what he calls 'the picture of the copy before the original'. It is as though prophetic mysticism was being merged with science fiction about future worlds.

The restoration of the Portuguese royal house did not create the Portugal that, from their different perspectives, Francisco Manuel de Melo or António Vieira would have wished. In order to guarantee an alliance that would strengthen his position in the country, King João IV included Bombay in the dowry for Catharine of Braganza's marriage to Charles II, in this way helping England to gain the sovereignty over India that Portugal never had. Brazil was already the priority in Portugal's imperial policy and would continue to be so until its independence in 1822. Wealth from Brazil permitted the upkeep of a sumptuous court in a country that produced little wealth of its own. Religious repression in Portugal increased, if anything, after the Restoration, with disastrous consequences for culture. Sacred music and baroque architecture flourished but the theatre, discouraged by the country's provincialisation during its union with Spain, would find only brief but remarkable original expression in the first third of the seventeenth century with the works of António José da Silva (1705–39) popularly known as 'O Judeu' ('the Jew'). He was born in Rio de Janeiro, where his New-Christian family had taken refuge from the Inquisition, but returned to Portugal in 1712 where he delighted Lisbon audiences with his musical comedies, ingeniously performed by marionettes. Notwithstanding his popularity, he was condemned to death by the Inquisition and was burned in an *auto da fé*.

The Portuguese baroque literature of which Francisco Manuel de Melo was one of the first representatives drifted into a cultism that was occasionally brilliant formally (and in some aspects a forerunner of modern visual poetry) but symptomatic of a repressed society that revealed itself in a monkish waggishness, necrophiliac morbidity and caricatural depictions of women. But these social circumstances also led to the tentative emergence of a woman's convent literature that would later find representation in *Lettres Portugaises*, a work attributed by its anonymous French author to an emblematic Portuguese nun. In Brazil, the poet Gregório de Matos (1633–96), known as 'Boca de Inferno' (Hell's Mouth) because of his libertine ways and obscene poetic expression, personified the colonial antithesis of Portuguese conventual hypocrisy. This satirical vein had a counterpart in the rarefied atmosphere of eighteenth-century Arcadian literature in Portugal, however, in the more obscene, and perhaps also more original, compositions of the bohemian and adventurous pre-Romantic poet Manuel Maria Barbosa du Bocage (1765–1805). Somewhat surprisingly, Bocage benefited from the patronage of the Marquise de Alorna (1750–1839), the cultured hostess of a celebrated literary salon who was also a cosmopolitan polygraph.

In the second half of the eighteenth century, the retrograde and pious country was forcibly modernised by the Marquis of Pombal (1699–1782), the despotic but enlightened prime minister of José I (1714–77). Having consolidated his power by undertaking the rebuilding of Lisbon after it was razed by the earthquake of 1755, Pombal encouraged the creation of a Portuguese middle class to promote the development of agriculture and industry in combination with a policy of investment in Brazil and nationalisation of colonial trade. These measures served to mitigate some of the effects of the Methuen Treaty of 1703 governing trading relations between England and Portugal, under the provisions of which Portugal had renounced further development of manufacturing. In addition, Pombal expelled the Jesuits, whose activities in Portugal and Brazil he considered to be detrimental to the proper exercise of royal power, and abolished the legal distinction between 'Old Christians' and 'New Christians' in 1773, a measure taken in Spain only in 1865. Pombal's industrial, commercial and social reforms laid the foundations for many developments in the nineteenth century, but he was rowing against the tide and his modernising project had little immediate continuity.

In 1807–08 Napoleon's armies invaded Spain and Portugal; England intervened and the Portuguese court moved to Brazil, where it remained throughout the ensuing Peninsular War, making Rio de Janeiro the first non-European capital of a pluri-continental empire. In 1821, following the outbreak of a radical liberal revolution in Portugal in the previous year, the royal family returned to Portugal leaving behind the prince royal, Pedro (1798–1834), who allied himself with the Brazilian independence movement and was proclaimed Emperor of Brazil in 1822. His brother Miguel (1802–66), who had acted as regent when Pedro abdicated, assumed the throne as monarch and restored the old absolutist regime. Portugal was torn apart in a destructive civil war. Pedro gave up his imperial Brazilian crown and returned to Portugal, leading a troop of exiled liberals, whose number included some notable intellectuals, against Miguel's absolutists. Having reassumed the Portuguese crown as Pedro IV, he established a constitutional regime that was more moderate than the revolutionaries would have wanted but more radical than the absolutists wished. The country was exhausted, divided and virtually ruined; the common people, dominated by the clergy, had deposited in 'Miguelism' renewed Sebastianic hopes, and the new governing class proved unequal to the task of meeting the country's needs.

Even so, Portugal entered a new culturally creative era, marked, from a broad historical perspective, by two defining events: the independence of Brazil in 1822 and the independence of the African colonies in 1975 when, finally free of the doubtful benefits of empire, the country returned to its medieval frontiers. This century and a half of history encompasses periods of political agitation and social stagnation; a regicide consequent upon a British ultimatum; the transformation of the liberal monarchy into a Republican regime that hardly differed from it; participation in the First World War; a dictatorship lasting forty-eight years; non-participation in the Second World War; thirteen years of colonial war; and, finally, the establishment of the post-colonial democracy in which the country now lives.

As in the case of other European countries, nineteenth-century liberalism in Portugal coincided with literary Romanticism. The two leading Portuguese exponents of the movement were Alexandre Herculano (1810–77) and Almeida Garrett (1799–1854), both of whom had chosen to live in exile during the Miguelist repression and had fought in the Liberal armies. Herculano was instrumental in helping the Portuguese to recover an idea of a national identity that preceded the imperial expansion. He explored this both in his monumental and carefully researched works on regional municipalities and the Middle Ages and in his historical novels and the legends and tales recorded in his *Lendas e Narrativas* (*Legends and Tales*). Almeida Garrett was a man who in his time played many parts. He took up arms

for a cause, he was an active liberal politician, he directed cultural institutions, and he was a courageous political commentator and lucid aesthetic
theorist. Entrusted with reviving the moribund Portuguese theatre, he himself
wrote the plays that were lacking. He compiled an anthology of traditional
folk ballads, integrating the oral tradition of popular culture into the written
culture. In his plays, poems and novels he recovered the national themes of a
culture that had forgotten its own traditions. He wrote a long narrative poem
on Camões, who is characterised as 'a Romantic before his time', and a play
whose title refers back to Gil Vicente (*Um Auto de Gil Vicente; A Play by Gil
Vicente*) and whose main character is Bernardim Ribeiro. His play *Frei Luís
de Sousa* (translated as *Brother Luís de Sousa*) is a masterpiece of European
Romantic theatre and his experimental novel, *Viagens na Minha Terra* (translated as *Travels in My Homeland*), with its innovative structural integration
of a novella into the factual account of his travels, is the first truly modern
work of Portuguese fiction. Both play and novel envisage the creation of a
new national consciousness, the play centred on the old Sebastianic ghosts
and the novel on the recent nightmares of the civil war. With its explicit references to Camões and Bernardim Ribeiro, the novel is an account of a journey
up the Tagus ('Tejo arriba'), which, being symbolically the opposite of the
maritime voyage celebrated in *Os Lusíadas*, becomes an equivalent quest for
the essence of the nation before it was corrupted by materialism. Garrett's
early poetry, shaped by neoclassical taste, does not have the colloquial liveli-
ness of his prose and plays. In his later years, however, he found a voice for
his Byronic sensuality, expressing the conflicts of loveless sexuality or shared
passion that leads to the satiated mutual recognition of the undoing of love,
without desire or regret.

The initial vigour of Portuguese Romanticism gave way to a new literary
academicism, which was followed by a morbid and socially disengaged senti-
mentalism. This was not the case in the work of Camilo Castelo Branco
(1825–90). Although this prolific novelist, author of over a hundred books,
is usually characterised as Romantic, his work can be better understood as
the product of a realist attitude not attributable to a literary school. This
was expressed in his treatment of novelistic situations as exemplary of
their society, of characters as emblematic of their circumstances, and their
circumstances as representative of the society in which they live. Camilo
was the first Portuguese writer to support himself entirely from his writing,
and he understood his public well. He was a master of literary manipulation
of sentimentality without being sentimental himself, sometimes even taking
the risk of distancing his readers by ironically warning them before one of
his characteristic 'heart-breaking' scenes that they were about to have their
hearts broken and then coldly, even cruelly perhaps, proceeding to break
them. His novels are set mostly in the rural north of Portugal, still feudal
in outlook and dominated by an impoverished old aristocracy. A favourite

theme is the conflict between the obligations of honour and the reasons of the heart. Women are sacrificial and men are domineering. A superb stylist and consummate storyteller, Camilo's best novels have the inexorable drive of classic tragedy, transcending the time and place in which they are set. They are magnificent literary constructions that have survived the society to which they bear witness.

In his 'Travels' Garrett had written: 'the ordinary people, the people [who are really] people' (*o povo, o povo povo*) are fine, it is we who are corrupt, who think we know it all and know nothing'. Camilo knew the ordinary people better than Garrett but idealised them less than another writer in transition to realism, Júlio Dinis (1839–71), whose country Edens sometimes offer glimpses of real snakes in imaginary gardens. The realist writers of the so-called *Geração de '70* (Generation of 1870) took up literary arms against 'the lack of good sense and good taste' of the ultra-Romantics, diagnosed in a famous pamphlet by Antero de Quental (1842–91). They returned to the aesthetic and ideological concerns of the earlier Romantic generation of Garrett and Herculano, reformulating them in their own terms, in the light of Auguste Comte's positivism, Proudhon's socialism, and Herbert Spencer's social evolutionism, and a literary realism inspired by French models. Antero, who was to reveal himself as a notable poet of metaphysical bent, was the Generation's political and philosophical thinker. Eça de Queirós (1845–1900) was not only the Generation's leading novelist but is one of the major figures of nineteenth-century European fiction. It was, however, Oliveira Martins (1846–94), a historian whose work was simultaneously meticulous and apocalyptic, who produced the haunting vision of Portugal that is still relevant for the Portuguese in their understanding of themselves. At the heart of this understanding is the idea of a process of national decadence, which each of these writers depicted in their work, from different perspectives but with the shared purpose of recording it as a way of helping to reverse the process.

In a book entitled *Portugal na Balança da Europa* (*Portugal in the Balance of Power of Europe*) Garrett had analysed the causes of the failure of the liberal revolution, attributing this to the marginalisation of the common people. In *Causas da Decadência dos Povos Peninsulares* (*Causes of the Decadence of the Peninsular Peoples*) Antero saw the decadence of the Peninsular peoples as a result of the convergence between Counter-Reformation Catholicism, absolutist monarchy and, unusually for his time, the overseas expansion, which had exhausted the country's energies while creating habits of idleness disguised by apparent imperial grandeur. Eça de Queirós, in his masterpiece *Os Maias* (translated as *The Maias*), depicts a nation incestuously turned in upon itself and complacent in its alienation. Oliveira Martins in his *History of Portugal* uses the organicist metaphor of 'the survival of the fittest' (the phrase coined by Herbert Spencer to describe his social Darwinism) to depict a country that had always been non-viable and, indeed, had long since died, living on only as a phantom. The portrait is striking as literature but implausible as history. The truth is that Portugal's decadence was, and continues to be, very much exaggerated.

In 1808, Brazilian ports had been opened to all nations and the subsequent commercial treaty with England, signed two years later, seriously undermined the foundations of the Portuguese economy. The proclamation of Brazil's independence in 1822 further aggravated the precarious situation of the national revenues. It became necessary to create new sources of wealth, which would no longer be dependent on the colonies but would come from within the country itself. Some of the economic policies introduced by the Marquês de Pombal were recovered and continued through a number of new initiatives. Some saw the solution in terms of an agricultural revival and, for the first time in many centuries, Portugal managed to export wheat. For others, the priority was industrial development, producing positive results in the case of the textile industry, but also leading to the development of other industries. The two approaches converged and were served by the development of transport and communications, with the construction of an extensive railroad network reaching the remotest areas of the country. Liberal policy was the economic expression of that 'inward gaze' to which Almeida Garrett, one of Liberalism's main defenders and, for that reason, also one of its severest critics, had given literary expression.

Antero de Quental was the only member of the Generation of 1870 who, like Sá de Miranda at the dawn of the overseas expansion, saw the Empire as a factor in the decadence of Portugal; the others, including Oliveira Martins, continued to view Portuguese decadence in terms of its past imperial glories. With the loss of Brazil and only a nominal presence in India, Africa was rediscovered. During World War I the Republican government, established in 1910, agreed that Portugal would enter the war on the side of Britain in order to save its African colonies from partition between Britain and Germany in accordance with two secret treaties signed between the two powers in the years before the war. Some fifteen years earlier, however, the needless national humiliation of the British Ultimatum of 1890 on ownership of the nominally Portuguese territories between Angola and Mozambique had caused an outbreak of nationalist fervour that led to the assassination of King Carlos in 1908 and the proclamation of the Republic in 1910. The Republican poet Guerra Junqueiro (1850–1923) was quick to transpose the view of the nation's decadence crystallised by Oliveira Martins in his history of Portugal into the thunderous verses of his dramatic poem *Pátria* (*Fatherland*), with Sebastianic yearnings focused in a vision of the Republic as national salvation.

Political ideologies and aesthetic theories have always influenced literature, but the best literature and, above all, poetry overcome such constraints. This was the case of two remarkable poets who wrote at the end of the nineteenth century, Cesário Verde (1855–86) and António Nobre (1867–1900). Cesário came from a middle-class background but identified with revolutionary socialism, Nobre from a wealthy rural family identified with traditionalist Catholicism; both were masters of an original and innovatory poetic diction, even in what they shared with fin-de-siècle European aesthetic movements. Cesário uses a 'compass and square' to construct meticulous poems in 'polyhedrons' that have affinities both with subsequent Cubist aesthetics and with cinematic techniques of cut and montage. Nobre uses the free melodic flow of his verse to create a space between strident protest and a masochistic acceptance of the evils of the world, while Cesário gave objective expression to these evils. Their contrasting poetic dictions converged, however, in a type of imagery that not only can be characterised as symbolist but came to be characterised as 'surrealistic', foreshadowing that of the Portuguese Modernist movement.

Thematically, Nobre's poetry had points of contact with a neo-pastoralism evident in the contemplative lyricism of João de Deus (1830–96), who was considered the greatest poet of his generation. This neo-pastoralism, with its emphasis on a return to rural values and national cultural roots, was given a political bias by so-called 'neo-Garrettism', whose proto-Fascist tendencies were as remote from Garrett as they were from João de Deus. Neo-Garrettism was reconfigured in the literary and philosophical movement known as *Saudosismo*, led by Teixeira de Pascoais (1877–1962). The movement envisaged a recovery of the spiritual and historical essence of Portugal through a nationalistic concept of *saudade* (nostalgia or longing), seen as the key to the transformation of Sebastianic yearnings into a new Portuguese universality. Implicitly accepting the funereal historical vision of Oliveira Martins, *Saudosismo* was a poetic recycling of the logical prophetism of Vieira's *História do Futuro*.

The ideas underlying *Saudosismo* were taken up by Fernando Pessoa (1888–1935) in the only book he published during his lifetime, *Mensagem* (*Message*). Pessoa, now recognised as one of the greatest European poets of the twentieth century, was the dominant figure of the Portuguese Modernist movement whose work was associated with the short-lived publication *Orpheu* (*Orpheus*). Pessoa created several heteronyms, alternative poetic selves who wrote very differently from one another. He was the artificer, the *fingidor*, who imitates God so that, by dividing his soul 'into fragments and different people', he can become both an artefact of eternity and a map of human finitude.

Portuguese Modernism was initially associated with a Futurism of Italian inspiration; among its most notable practitioners were the poet and novelist Mário de Sá-Carneiro (1890–1916) and the painter, poet and prose writer José de Almada Negreiros (1893–1970). The work of these seminal iconoclasts, like that of the symbolist poet Camilo Pessanha (1857–1926), who was

adopted by them as part of their poetic family, began to be widely published
and recognised only in the 1940s. The '*Orpheu* lunatics', as the group was
referred to, may have caused a brief scandal, but literary life continued
without the various 'isms' with which its members were associated. Their
belated fame has led to the retrospective marginalisation of other writers
of the time. To ignore these writers is to reduce Portuguese literature in the
early twentieth century to a kind of monoculture of underdevelopment, with
'Pessoa & Co.' as its only significant manifestation. The crepuscular sensuality of Pessanha's symbolism has little to do with the somewhat mechanical
symbolism practised by the leading literary personality of the time, Eugénio
de Castro (1869–1944), but it can be better understood when thematically
linked to the fiction and dramatic works of Raul Brandão (1867–1930) and
António Patrício (1878–1930), whose morbid sensuality has affinities with
the suicidal narcissism of Sá-Carneiro and even with the voluptuously feminine sado-masochistic poetry of Florbela Espanca (1894–1930). The libertine
eroticism that reduces women to mere physicality, depicted in simultaneously
critical and complicit terms in the stories of Teixeira Gomes (1860–1941),
finds corresponding expression in the hedonistic homosexual physicality
celebrated in the poetry of António Botto (1897–1959). Both have elements
in common with Sá-Carneiro's psychological ghost story *A Confissão de
Lúcio* (translated as *Lucio's Confession*), in which the suppressed homosexuality of two close male friends is physically expressed through the phantom
body of a woman.

In 1926 a military *coup d'état* put an end to the democratic regime in
which, despite a number of crises (including the end of the Monarchy and
the proclamation of the Republic in 1910), Portugal had lived for a century.
António de Oliveira Salazar (1899–1970) established the so-called *Estado
Novo* (*New State*), becoming the country's *de facto* dictator until 1968.
Democracy would only be restored in 1974, following another military coup.
From a cultural perspective, the most obvious impact of the dictatorial regime
was the establishment of State censorship. Many Portuguese intellectuals
felt that they were living exiled in their own country, as in the time of the
sixteenth-century 'Village Court' and, as then, waiting for liberation.

In the year following the 1926 military coup, a group of Coimbra students
founded the literary magazine *Presença* (*Presence*), later associated with
what came to be called 'Second Modernism'. The group's leading personalities were the poet, novelist and playwright José Régio (1901–69), the poet and
short-story writer Miguel Torga (1907–95), and the novelist and literary critic
João Gaspar Simões (1903–87). *Presença* certainly contributed considerably to the wider recognition of the *Orpheu* poets, particularly through the
critical writings of Gaspar Simões. His monumental study of the life and
work of Fernando Pessoa, published in 1950, was instrumental in promoting
the poet's work, despite what are currently considered the limitations of his

psychological approach. Régio preferred Sá-Carneiro to Pessoa and in his 1950 anthology *Líricas Portuguesas* (*Portuguese Lyrics*) suggested that, in the case of the latter, it was 'too soon to make one of those judgements that only time could confirm'. Whether 'second modernists' or not, the *Presença* poets owed more to an earlier literary tradition than to Modernism.

This is also true of the politically committed left-wing writers opposed to the dictatorial regime, who were identified as 'neo-realists'. These writers condemned what they considered to be a kind of political absenteeism on the part of the *Presença* writers. The accusation was, in fact, exaggerated and, in many cases, unfair. None of the *Presencistas* supported the dictatorship and some of them actively opposed it but they were not Marxists, which the neo-realists considered themselves to be. Besides sharing a common literary tradition, both *Presencistas* and neo-realists were generally more interested in provincial lives than in those lived in the capital where political power was exercised.

Despite the appearance of notable works of fiction and drama, both subject to special vigilance on the part of the censors, the genre that best survived the dictatorship was poetry, since metaphors always manage to say what those in power wish to silence: 'poppies growing in the wheat fields' signified the red of revolution in an agrarian country; 'News from the Blockade' was the title of a love poem sending messages of an impossible love in a blockaded nation.

During the 1939–45 war, Portugal's capital became a point of convergence in the tragedy unfolding in the rest of Europe, with Allies and Nazis coexisting under the paternalistic gaze of the political police, while members of the Gestapo and Jewish refugees passed each other in the streets and frequented the same cafés. These were extraordinary times, hardly reflected in the Portuguese literature of the period. The fact is that the country remained on the periphery of the war and that the broad ideological issues at stake (dictatorship versus democracy) were seen in the narrower context of their impact on the national situation. The liberation that Portuguese intellectuals had hoped the end of the war would bring did not come. Instead, the Cold War enabled the dictatorial regime to consolidate itself with the support of the anti-Communist democracies. Economically, Portugal remained 'underdeveloped'. Salazar did not believe in economic development, he believed in financial, social and political stability; development would threaten the status quo, permitting greater social mobility and creating the risk of democratisation. Frustrated expectations can be expressed in resignation or resistance and both attitudes existed side by side.

Post-war literature reflected a consolidation of the modernist inheritance of the early years of the century, as the work of Fernando Pessoa's generation became more widely known. Jorge de Sena (1919–78), poet, critic and essayist, was the leading writer of the post-war period. Other notable writers of the period include Sophia de Mello Breyner Andresen (1919–2004), who is considered one of Portugal's finest contemporary poets, David Mourão-Ferreira (1927–96), a poet and novelist of subtly celebratory sensuality, and Carlos de Oliveira (1921–81) and Egito Gonçalves (1922–2000), both of whom combine literary innovation with political commitment. The post-war years were also characterised by Surrealist experimentation, not merely as a belated aesthetic movement but as an expression of political, moral and social defiance. Mário Cesariny de Vasconcelos (1923–2006) and Alexandre O'Neill (1924–86) were the leading Portuguese surrealist poets linked to this trend. In the late 1950s, Herberto Helder (b. 1930), the most powerful poetic talent to emerge in the second half of the twentieth century, began to write poems of extraordinary bardic fluency, strictly organised in a combinatory art of perspectives, voices and quotations, in which the frontiers between the literal and the metaphorical, subjectivity and objectivity, are obliterated. Other poets who emerged in the late 1950s followed a 'baroque' line, using strict formal structures within which they practised a deliberate disjunction or syntactic disorientation that allows words to explode within their confining cocoon. 'Baroque' disguise was also practised in the Concretist poetry that flourished in the 1960s. In fiction it was perhaps José Cardoso Pires (1925–98) who best managed to depict Portugal's social and political situation in narratives that are both specific and have broad and timeless resonance. In his painstaking attitude to writing, he pioneered what was to become the new Portuguese fiction after the 1974 revolution.

During the 1960s the country was faced with insurgency in its African colonies. The Salazar regime prided itself that Portugal, having been the first of modern Europe's colonial empires, was also the only one to have survived the general decolonisation brought about by the 'wind of change'. To keep things unchanged, it launched a colonial war that changed everything. The wealth of the African colonies had never been as intensively exploited as those of Brazil and in the first half of the twentieth century most Portuguese intellectuals had given little attention to Africa. In 1965, however, for political as much as for literary reasons, the Portuguese Writers' Association awarded its fiction prize to the collection of short stories *Luuanda*, whose author Luandino Vieira (b. 1935) had been arrested in Angola in 1961 for 'conspiratorial activities' and had spent eleven years in the prison camp of Tarrafal in Cape Verde. The Writers' Association was abolished and its directors were imprisoned. The colonial wars had become a literary subject; but the explosion of literature directly connected with these wars only began in earnest after they ended, with the overthrow of the regime in 1974.

The most significant indication of a change in the rigid social and political structure was the increasing presence of women at the centre of Portuguese literature. This was not so much a result of the emergence of feminist writing, although there were instances of this, as of the more significant fact that women were assuming themselves as writers who also happened to be women. In poetry, the first explicit reference to the colonial war probably occurs in a 'cantiga de amigo' by Fiama Hasse Pais Brandão (1938–2007), in which the boats of the absent lovers in the medieval tradition become the troopships carrying lovers away to war. The female voice assumed by men in the medieval *cantigas* had become the real female voice of a woman poet. A book published in 1972, *Novas Cartas Portuguesas* (translated as *New Portuguese Letters* – a title that makes ironic reference to the seventeenth-century *Lettres Portugaises*), written by the so-called 'Three Marias', namely Maria Teresa Horta (b. 1937), Maria Velho da Costa (b. 1938) and Maria Isabel Barreno (b. 1939), was internationally adopted as an emblematic work of the feminist cause. The Portuguese political police persecuted the three authors not only for 'outrage to public morals' but for their condemnation of the colonial war and economic emigration. Their depiction of the marginalisation of women became a metaphor for the marginalised condition of all Portuguese, both men and women. Maria Teresa Horta's poetry uninhibitedly celebrates the sexual pleasure shared with a male body that she also celebrates, while the world of Maria Velho da Costa's novels is thematically as wide-ranging as it is female in outlook. One of the first and best novels on the colonial war, *A Costa dos Murmúrios* (translated as *The Murmuring Coast*) by Lídia Jorge (b. 1946), is written from a female perspective that is more insightful and far-reaching than other 'masculine' works on the same subject. Other notable women writers who do not confine themselves to feminist issues are Agustina Bessa Luís (b. 1922) and Maria Gabriela Llansol (1931–2008). The novels of Bessa Luís have kept alive a mainstream narrative tradition that goes back to Camilo Castelo Branco, while creating characters that have an almost mythic quality. The hermetic sensuality of Maria Gabriela Llansol creates a deliberate blurring of the narrative subject that transcends gender distinctions, with planes of reality flowing together in a distinctive poetic style.

On 25 April 1974 the Portuguese army gave up fighting wars it had not yet lost but could not win and overthrew the colonial regime it had served, adopting the independence of the colonies as a common cause for both colonisers and colonised. The armed forces became the unlikely implementers of a new Portuguese democracy. Portugal has become a nation no less efficient and no more corrupt than other European democracies. It is a reasonably successful member of the European Union, has built roads that have opened up the interior of the country, produces more and is more efficient in marketing what it produces, has powerful banking institutions and fosters investment in Brazil and its former African colonies. For the first time in its history, it is now a country of immigration as well as of emigration, with immigrants from eastern Europe, the former African colonies and, increasingly, from Brazil. The country's overall situation has visibly improved. But for this it was necessary not only for the former colonies to become independent but for Portugal to have become independent of its colonies.

As Portugal settles into a post-colonial and post-Sebastianic present, exciting new literary trends are emerging. The closer we are in time to a literary period, however, the more we are subject to the twin errors of over-inclusion or omission. Names not mentioned here may come to be regarded as the most significant writers of the late twentieth and early twenty-first centuries. Mention should be made, however, of two widely-acclaimed contemporary novelists who are considered to have an assured place in the history of Portuguese literature: José Saramago (b. 1922), winner of the 1998 Nobel Prize for Literature, and António Lobo Antunes (b. 1942) who is regarded by many as being worthy of that prize.

Lobo Antunes writes about inner worlds even when he externalises these in factual narratives. He served in the colonial war in Angola, and his nightmarish war experiences have become an integral part of his way of seeing the world and understanding his country's history. For Lobo Antunes, as for Fernando Pessoa, the country is once more the Portugal of Oliveira Martins, the living corpse that has survived its own death. His work is a brilliant literary construct, whose reality is in the truth of the writing. José Saramago has never written about Africa or the colonial wars. Like Garrett, he sought to rediscover Portugal in his early novels. When he retrieves Fernando Pessoa for literary purposes, it is to write about another war, the Spanish Civil War, imaginatively experienced in a rain-drenched Lisbon by one of Pessoa's heteronyms, Ricardo Reis, who, after his creator's death, has returned to the city 'where the sea ends and the land begins', as if making a Garrettean journey in the opposite direction to that celebrated in *Os Lusíadas*. Even when he writes historical novels objectively structured down to the last detail, Saramago writes fables. He never speaks of himself, he speaks from himself to the world. Many of his novels could begin not with the words 'once upon a time' of traditional tales but with the 'what if' of tales about possible worlds. In other words, he is more Camonian than Pessoan. But Portuguese literature can accommodate both Camões and Pessoa.

2

The Medieval Galician-Portuguese Lyric

RIP COHEN and STEPHEN PARKINSON

The secular genres (Rip Cohen)

The medieval Galician-Portuguese lyric (not counting the *Cantigas de Santa Maria*) is a corpus of around 1,680 texts, composed by some one hundred and sixty poets, and traditionally divided into three genres, *cantigas de amigo* (female-voiced lyric), *cantigas de amor* (male-voiced lyric) and *cantigas de escarnho e de mal dizer* (poetry of mockery and insult), hereinafter *Amigo*, *Amor*, and *CEM*.[1] This division, which could have been induced from the poetry itself, is based on evidence from the manuscript tradition, from the fragmentary and untitled *Arte de Trovar* (as it is often called by modern scholars), and from references in the texts themselves.[2] There is no good reason to challenge it, even if there are some hybrid cases, and a substantial number of texts which are grouped with the *CEM* while having nothing to do with insult or mockery.[3]

---

[1]   The forms *cantiga d'amigo*, *cantiga d'amor*, and *cantiga d'escarnho* are preferred by many writers. *Amigo* and *CEM* are identified by their numeration in the editions of Cohen and Lapa, respectively. For *Amor*, references are to the editions by Michaëlis (= *CA*) or Nunes (see 'Texts and Translations', p. 43, for details of these editions). In the literature poems are also identified by their number in the two main manuscripts, B and V, or by their number in Giuseppe Tavani, *Repertorio metrico della lirica galego-portoghese* (Rome: Ateneo, 1967).

[2]   Giuseppe Tavani, *Arte de Trovar do Cancioneiro da Biblioteca Nacional de Lisboa* (Lisbon: Colibri, 1999). On the importance of genre in the structure of the manuscript tradition, see António Resende de Oliveira, *Depois do Espectáculo Trovadoresco: a estrutura dos cancioneiros peninsulares e as recolhas dos séculos XIII e XIV* (Lisbon: Colibri, 1994).

[3]   There is no space here to cover the so-called 'minor genres'. There are numerous *tenções* (poetic contests or debates) which do not qualify as *CEM* and form a genre apart. The *pastorela* is an imported product, not a *cantiga de amigo*, as is clear from the form (no *cantiga de amigo* has the form of any of the *pastorelas*). The *lais* found at the beginning of MS B are based on Arthurian material. There are a few *encomia* and *threnoi*, important mainly for the dates they provide. And there is also a parody of French epic, and a few other odds and ends.

The three main genres can be distinguished for present purposes using the concept of 'matrix'. The matrix of a genre is a complex of form, pragmatics, and rhetoric. By 'form' I mean strophic form, verse length, rhyme-schemes, and virtuosic techniques such as *coblas unissonans* ('unison verses', using the same rhyme-sounds in each strophe) *coblas doblas* ('double verses', alternating two sets of rhyme-sounds), or *dobre* (using the same word twice in the same position in each strophe). Pragmatics includes the identity, social condition, and relationship of speaker and addressee, the background situation, the speech-action (i.e. the action(s) being performed by speech within the text), and emotion(s). By rhetoric is meant lexicon, phraseology, the interrelation of syntax and strophic form, and the many techniques, including figures of speech and thought, which are used to communicate a message (in Roman Jakobson's sense) and perform a social act.

The *cantigas de amigo* are female-voiced love lyric, and this is what marks them off not only from the other two genres, but from nearly all of medieval Romance love lyric. In them we find, in relation to the other two genres, simpler strophic forms, such as aaB and aaBB, simpler rhyme-systems, and far fewer virtuosic techniques, though individual *cantigas de amigo* may be more complex than individual poems in the other two genres. A subset of *cantigas de amigo*, sometimes seen as representing the traditional form of this lyric, make systematic use of the techniques of parallelistic repetition and *leixa-pren*.[4] Another striking feature has to do with the pragmatics: relative to *Amor*, there are more speaking personae – the girl (G), her mother (M), the girl's female friend (F), and the boy (B) – and the combinations of speaker and addressee give a far more rounded view of ongoing situations and actions. The Girl can address any of the other three, and any of them can address her. The range of situations, though limited, is still considerably greater than in the *cantigas de amor*. And the range of speech-actions, or 'moves' is even larger. Here is a partial list:

> The **girl** says goodbye to her boy, or waits for him, or greets him on his return. She gets sad or angry, or even renounces him if he has left without her permission, failed to show up for a tryst, or talked with another girl.[5] She asks him to come back after a fight. At other times the girl asks her mother for permission to go to see the boy, or says she is going to see him or has seen him. Often she narrates, anticipates, or performs an action, whether speaking to her mother or to her girlfriend(s) or to nobody in particular.

---

4   Stephen Reckert and Helder Macedo, *Do Cancioneiro de Amigo*, 3rd edn (Lisbon: Assírio & Alvim, 1996).

5   On the 'other girl', see Rip Cohen and Federico Corriente, '*Lelia doura* Revisited', *La Corónica* 31.1 (2002), 19–40.

The (girl's girl-)**friend** tries to persuade the girl to be receptive to the boy, or to take him back after a quarrel, and a few times counsels her to renounce him. Once she seems deliberately to provoke the girl's jealousy by reporting that another girl is after the boy.[6]

The **mother** lets the girl go and see the boy, or offers to go with her, or refuses permission, or else advises her how to make peace after a quarrel, or says 'I told you so' when things have gone wrong.

The **boy** (always in dialogue) bids the girl farewell, or greets her on his return, asks for her favours, or begs for forgiveness.

All told, there are a few dozen of these kinds of action.

The rhetoric, on the other hand, though generally simpler than that used in the other two genres, is more complex than has often been allowed, slowly articulating a present action (or emotion) by repetition with variation, and usually withholding essential information until the end of the song. There are some insults, but they are very mild compared with what we find in *CEM*. Any kind of obscenity or open reference to sexuality is taboo.

There is a simmering issue regarding this genre. For more than a century some scholars have thought that some sets by the same author constitute organised sequences meant for performance.[7] Favourite candidates have been the sets of Pero Meogo, unified among other things by the recurrent stags and fountains, and Martin Codax, where in addition to fairly obvious formal and thematic factors (parallelism and *leixa-pren*, references to Vigo), there is exceptional documentary evidence in the *Pergaminho Vindel*, the only surviving manuscript source of the complete works of a single poet.[8] If they exist, these would be the earliest organised sequences of love songs in any medieval Romance language, but scholars have not yet reached a consensus on the issue.

The *cantigas de amor* are male-voiced love lyric. They make use of more complex forms, including many never found in *Amigo* and some very complex ones that are drawn directly from Occitan or Old French lyric.[9] On the other hand, we find an extreme paucity of personae (almost always the man speaks to or about a woman) and of situations. Usually the man is wooing the woman

---

6   Dinis 42.

7   Julian Weiss, 'Lyric Sequences in the *Cantigas d'amigo*', *Bulletin of Hispanic Studies* 65 (1988), 21–37; Rip Cohen, *Thirty-two 'Cantigas d'amigo' of Dom Dinis: Typology of a Portuguese Renunciation* (Madison, WI: Hispanic Seminary of Medieval Studies, 1987), and 'Dança jurídica', *Coloquio/Letras* 142 (1996), 5–49.

8   Manuel Pedro Ferreira, *The Sound of Martin Codax / O som de Martin Codax* (Lisbon: Unisys, 1986).

9   Paolo Canettieri and Carlo Pulsoni. 'Per uno studio storico-geografico e tipologico dell'imitazione metrica nella lirica galego-portoghese', in Dominique Billy et al., *La lirica galego-portoghese: saggi di metrica e musica comparata* (Rome: Carocci, 2002), pp. 113–65.

(often by means of a complaint that she is being cruel, despite his loyalty and love-service), though on occasion he is leaving or coming back, sometimes he is away from her, and, rarely, so frustrated, angry or jealous that he renounces and even insults her. The rhetoric is more complex, and the relationship between metrical and syntactic units is far more varied, with a much higher frequency of enjambment.[10] Here again obscenity and explicit references to sexuality are not permitted.

The *cantigas de escarnho e de mal dizer* are poetry of insult and mockery, always with comic intent. They are often referred to as satire, incorrectly, as they normally insult named individuals, rather than poking fun at classes of people. Here we find more complex forms, a great variety of personae, and a rhetoric midway in complexity between *Amor* and *Amigo*. Insult or mockery constitutes the essence of this rhetoric, though techniques vary greatly, including praising in order to blame, defending in order to accuse, and thanking in order to insult. Obscenity is normal in *cantigas de mal dizer* (as mentioned in the *Arte de Trovar*), while in those *de escarnho* mockery is indirect. The physical and social world of the time, almost entirely absent in the other two genres, is present in force, making this genre, together with the *Cantigas de Santa Maria* (*CSM*), a mine for the study of social and cultural history. And the lexicon is far larger than in either of the other two genres, rivalled only by that of the *CSM*. The poetics of the insult reflected here bears comparison with the greatest masters of antiquity.[11] We find sexual themes, mockery of other singers and their song, social conflicts, legal and political questions, religion, and parodies of the other two genres.[12] There are also parodies of organised sequences, probably modelled on those in *Amigo*.

In *CEM* the speaker can be anyone but is rarely female. The addressee (who can be anyone) may be the object of insult, or a rhetorical 'you' serving as a kind of resonating chamber for the discourse, or a party to the action described or enacted. The rhetorical intent, however, is always to insult or belittle. The object of the insult is normally an individual, although in some texts a class of people (e.g. *infanções*, 'minor nobility') is mocked, resulting in songs which could legitimately be called satire. The rhetorical techniques by which the insult is articulated are extremely diverse, and this allows a brilliance of *elocutio* hardly possible elsewhere.

Now let us look at some examples of each genre. Limitations of space allow for only a few specimens.[13]

---

10 On the rhetoric of the *cantiga de amor*, see Vicenç Beltrán, *A cantiga de amor* (Vigo: Edicións Xerais, 1995).

11 Archilochus, Hipponax and Catullus; Aristotle, *Poetics* 1448b, calls such poems *psogoi*.

12 Alfonso X mocks the Pope, Pero Garcia Burgalês writes humorous blasphemies against Jesus and Mary (*CA* 221, 223).

13 All translations from Galician-Portuguese are my own.

Cantigas de amigo
Bernal de Bonaval[14]

> Filha fremosa, vedes que vos digo:
> que non faledes ao voss' amigo
> sen mi, ai filha fremosa.
>
> E se vós, filha, meu amor queredes,
> rogo vos eu que nunca lhi faledes
> sen mi, ai filha fremosa.
>
> E al á i de que vos non guardades:
> perdedes i de quanto lhi falades
> sen mi, ai filha fremosa.

> Lovely daughter, look what I'm telling you:
> Don't talk with your boyfriend
> Without me, oh lovely daughter.
>
> And, daughter, if you want my love,
> I ask you that you never talk with him
> Without me, oh lovely daughter.
>
> And there's something else you're not aware of:
> You lose every word you talk with him
> Without me, oh lovely daughter.

In the poem preceding this one the girl has asked her mother for permission to go and see the boy. This speech-action is represented in a score of *cantigas* and seems one of the most fundamental 'scripts' (in the sense explained below). In this poem the mother warns her daughter not to speak with the boy without her. As guardian of her daughter's sexuality, which is in effect family property, the mother must be involved in any negotiations if they are to be legitimised. The genre is loaded with code-words like *falar* ('talk'), *fazer ben* ('give favours'), etc. which can connote sexual favours, apparently an integral part of the wooing process.

Another mode of encryption is through symbols, as in this song:[15]

---

[14] Bonaval 8.

[15] On symbols, see Reckert and Macedo (note 4 above), Alan Deyermond, 'Pero Meogo's Stags and Fountains: Symbol and Anecdote in the Traditional Lyric', *Romance Philology* 33 (1979–80), 265–83, and Maria do Rosário Ferreira, *Águas doces, águas salgadas: da funcionalidade dos motivos aquáticos nas cantigas de amigo* (Oporto: Granito, 1999 [2000]) on water imagery.

Pero Meogo[16]

Enas verdes ervas
vi anda-las cervas,
meu amigo

Enos verdes prados
vi os cervos bravos,
meu amigo

E con sabor delas
lavei mhas garcetas,
meu amigo

E con sabor delos
lavei meus cabelos,
meu amigo

Des que los lavei,
d' ouro los liei,
meu amigo

Des que las lavara,
d' ouro las liara,
meu amigo

D' ouro los liei
e vos asperei,
meu amigo

D' ouro las liara
e vos asperava,
meu amigo

In the green grasses
I saw the deer running,
My friend.

In the green meadows
I saw the wild stags,
My friend.

And with pleasure
I washed my hair,
My friend.

And with pleasure
I washed my tresses,
My friend.

---

[16] Meogo 6.

After I washed it
I bound it with gold,
My friend.

After I'd washed them
I'd bound them with gold,
My friend.

I bound it with gold
And waited for you,
My friend.

I'd bound them with gold
And was waiting for you,
My friend.

This is a song of waiting, but note that the girl has washed her hair (a prenuptial rite also found in Sephardic songs) and bound it (an old Germanic custom denoting betrothal or marriage). The stags and fountains of Meogo have nearly come to symbolise the genre for many readers whose familiarity is restricted to anthologies, but in fact the stags occur only in Meogo and the fountains rarely outside his work. Nature symbolism, however important and influential it has been in the study of the genre, is found in less than 10% of the texts.

The genre is not without humour, as we can see in this song by João Garcia de Guilhade, where a girl specifies under what conditions she will believe her boyfriend:[17]

Cada que ven o meu amig' aqui
diz m', ai amigas, que perdeu o sen
por mi, e diz que morre por meu ben,
mais eu ben cuido que non ést' assi,
ca nunca lh' eu vejo morte prender
nen o ar vejo nunca ensandecer.

El chora muito e filha s' a jurar
que é sandeu e quer me fazer fis
que por mi morr', e, pois morrer non quis,
mui ben sei eu que á ele vagar,
ca nunca lh' eu vejo morte prender
nen o ar vejo nunca ensandecer.

Ora vejamos o que nos dirá,
pois veer viv' e pois sandeu non for;
ar direi lh' eu: 'Non morrestes d' amor?'
mais ben se quite de meu preito ja,

---

[17] Guilhade 15.

ca nunca lh' eu vejo morte prender
nen o ar vejo nunca ensandecer.

E ja mais nunca mi fará creer
que por mi morre, ergo se morrer.

Every time that my boy comes here
He tells me, oh friends, that he's gone crazy
For me, and says he's dying for my favours,
But I don't really think that this is so,
Because I never see him die
And I don't ever see him lose his mind.

He cries a lot and begins to swear
He's lost his mind, and he'd have me believe
That he's dying for me, and since he's not dead
I just think he's taking his sweet time,
Because I never see him die
And I don't ever see him lose his mind.

Now let's see what he'll say to us
When he shows up alive and hasn't lost his mind,
And I'll say to him, 'Haven't you died of love?'
But he can forget about anything with me,
Because I never see him die
And I don't ever see him lose his mind.

And he will never make me believe
That he's dying for me, unless he dies.

Her boyfriend claims he is dying and losing his mind, but he never completes either task. If he were truthful he would go mad and drop dead. When he appears, she will say, 'What, aren't you dead yet?' His very existence proves he is false, so she wants nothing more to do with him (v. 16). In this song Guilhade parodies the courtly themes of 'dying of love' and losing one's mind, mocking poetic practice.

Cantigas de amor

Some very early *cantigas de amor* hardly differ from early *cantigas de amigo* except in the gender of the speaking voice. Here is an example by Bernal de Bonaval:[18]

A dona que eu am' e tenho por senhor
amostrade-mh-a, Deus, se vos én prazer for;
se non, dade-mh-a morte.

---

[18] Nunes, *Amor*, 423.

A que tenh' eu por lume d' estes olhos meus
e por que choran sempr', amostrade-mh-a Deus;
se non, dade-mh-a morte.

Essa que vós fezestes melhor parecer
de quantas sei, ai Deus, fazede-mh-a veer;
se non, dade-mh-a morte.

Ai Deus, que mh-a fezestes mais ca min amar,
mostrade-mh-a u possa con ela falar;
se non, dade-mh a morte.

The lady I love and call my Lady –
Show her to me, God, if you please,
and if not, just give me death.

The one who's the light of these eyes of mine,
for whom they're always weeping, show her to me, God,
and if not, just give me death.

That one that you made the most beautiful
of all, oh God, please just let me see her,
and if not, just give me death.

Oh God, who made me love her more than me,
show her to me, where I can talk with her,
and if not, just give me death.

In this song, which uses an aaB strophic form (rare in *Amor*, common in *Amigo*), the speaker praises the lady, declares his love, loyalty and mortal suffering, and asks God either to grant him what he wants or to let him die. Curiously, what he wants is to see her and talk with her – just as in the *cantigas de amigo*.

Compare the formal and rhetorical complexity of a roughly contemporary *cantiga de amor* by Osoir' Eanes, *Sazon é ja de me partir*, which begins:[19]

Sazon é ja de me partir
de mha senhor, ca ja temp' ei
que a servi, ca perdud' ei
o seu amor, e quero m' ir;
mais pero direi lh' ant' assi:
'Senhor, e que vos mereci?
ca non foi eu depois peor
des quando ganhei voss' amor?'

E averedes a sentir
camanha mingua vos farei,

---

[19] *CA* 321 (B 38), lightly modified.

e veeredes, eu o sei
como poss' eu sen vós guarir,
e diredes depois por min:
'Mesela, por que o perdi?
e que farei quando s' el for
alhur servir outra senhor?'
[...]

It's time for me to go away
from my Lady, for it's been a while
that I've served her, and I've lost
her love, and so I'll go.
But first I'll say this to her:
'Lady, did I deserve this?
For wasn't I even worse off
after I gained your love?'

And you'll be forced to feel
how much you'll miss me,
and you'll see, I know,
that I can live without you,
and you'll say of me:
'Poor girl! why did I lose him?
And what will I do when he goes
elsewhere to serve another Lady?'

The man is leaving, but before he does he will complain about the woman's unfairness; and then the poet introduces the woman's voice within a male-voiced frame. After he leaves (he tells her) she will say, 'Oh no, why did I lose him? now another girl will get him and I'll be sorry. ...' This intermingling of male and female voices in an early (1220s) poem might be taken as evidence that *Amigo* comes from *Amor*. What it suggests is rather that *Amigo*-like songs existed before the earliest known *Amor*, and that the female-voiced tradition could be incorporated into the male-voiced genre. Particularly interesting is the reference to the other girl, who is moreover a *vezinha* ('neighbour') – a word not found in *Amigo*. The dramatic complexity of the situation, which outstrips that of nearly any other *cantiga de amor*, could be attributed either to an early experimental stage in the development of the genre in the thirteenth century, or to a long-standing tradition which was subsequently abandoned in favour of simpler scenarios.

As the thirteenth century progresses the genre tends to become less flexible. What poets aim at is elegance of form and subtlety of argument and expression in handling a few fixed kinds of situation. Rare is the poem which stands out for the situation it represents. But there are exceptions, including parodies. For instance, a common motif is the need to keep the love affair secret; so some poets blurt out the lady's name. Then this transgression is itself parodied.[20] What we might call 'original' motifs are rare. One occurs in a song of João Garcia de Guilhade in which the speaker has gone back to the place where he used to see his Lady and now wants nothing more than to gaze at those houses and remember.[21] Where does this motif come from? How did it get into a *cantiga de amor*, where references to the physical world are so rare? Despite the apparent lack of Classical influence in Galician-Portuguese lyric, it is just possible that there is a reference here to Ovid's *Remedies of Love*, in which the master advises the lover who would renounce *not* to return to the places where he had been with the beloved; yet that is precisely what Guilhade says he has done, is doing, and wants to continue to do.[22]

Cantigas de escarnho e de mal dizer

Although nearly anybody can be an object of insult in *CEM*, and nearly any technique can be used to insult, I have chosen examples of sexual insults – partly because they are among the most accessible (and entertaining) for modern readers, and partly because the very different image of woman and sexuality provides a point of comparison with *Amigo* and *Amor*.

Roí Páez de Ribela (*CEM* 412)

> A donzela de Biscaia
> Ainda mi a preito saia
> De noit' ou lũar!
>
> Pois m'agora assi desdenha,
> Ainda mi a preito venha
> De noit' ou lũar!
>
> Pois dela sõo maltreito,
> Ainda mi venha a preito
> De noit' ou lũar!

The insinuations in this song may be brought out better in a blues version, where the meaning of 'vĩir a preito' (not merely meaning 'come to the tryst') can be clarified.

----

[20] Pero Garcia Burgalês (*CA* 104–6).

[21] *CA* 236.

[22] *Remedia Amoris*, 725–34. There may be a couple of other cases, particularly in songs by Osoir' Eanes and Roi Fernandiz, where either Ovid or Propertius could be the source. If Osoir' Eanes studied in Paris, there is a possible explanation (there are almost no manuscripts of Classical poetry in Portugal).

That little girl from Bequick –
Let her still come do me the trick
In the night, in the moonlight.

Though she now shows me her frown
Let her still come and take me down
In the night, in the moonlight.

Though she treats me really bad
Let her still come and make me glad
In the night, in the moonlight.

Why cannot this be a *cantiga de amor*? How can we tell this is an insult
and not an amorous invitation? There are several ways. First, though her
name is not given, the woman is identified (line 1), violating the conventions
of a *cantiga de amor*. Second, the speaker asks her to come out once more
to a rendezvous at night, under the moonlight, a scandalous suggestion in the
social context of the thirteenth century. And finally, this invitation, framed as
if it were a romantic plea for reconciliation, clearly presupposes prior sexual
activities. On all three counts the speaker insults the lady and her father (the
guardian of the family's honour).

Less subtle is the following *cantiga de mal dizer*, one of a pair by João
Garcia de Guilhade:[23]

Martin jograr, que gran cousa:
ja sempre convosco pousa
vossa molher.

Veedes m' andar morrendo,
e vós jazedes fodendo
vossa molher.

Do meu mal non vos doedes,
e moir' eu, e vós fodedes
vossa molher.

Martin the strummer, what a bummer,
She's always lying with you –
Your woman.

You see *me* here dying,
and *you* lie there fucking
Your woman.

You don't care about *my* pain,
and I die, and *you* just fuck
Your woman.

---

23 *CEM* 207–8.

In the typical 'courtly love' poem, the singer woos a woman of a higher social class, typically the wife of a great lord, praising her virtues and lamenting her inaccessibility. Here Guilhade sings of the sexual desirability of the wife (or woman) of a man below him, a *jograr* or minstrel (Guilhade was a *cavaleiro*, or 'knight'), pretending to maintain the pose of a wronged lover for whom his lady has no mercy. The careful placing of obscenities (all located in the verse just before the refrain, and only used in the last two strophes) is typical of the genre: part of the art of the insult is setting it up, and delivering it in climactic position.

The origins: scripts in the matrix

In the body of song that preceded the thirteenth century there must have been songs that were formally, rhetorically, and pragmatically like those we find in the extant corpus of Galician-Portuguese lyric.[24] There must, in other words, have been a matrix, with form, rhetoric and pragmatics (and here I use 'matrix' to refer to this hypothetical tradition). The aaB(B) forms of the *cantigas d' amigo* can safely be seen as preceding the earliest extant texts. And certain rhetorical procedures, nearly ubiquitous in the corpus, such as repetition with variation, must also have been a common part of this tradition.[25] In addition, we can attempt a kind of prehistory of the pragmatics, and in particular of what I will call the *scripts* of each of the three genres.

A script is an underlying pragmatic structure that includes speaker, addressee, background information – including action(s) and utterance(s) – and often also new information (just received by the speaker), and a present act and/or emotion. If we call the speaker P^1 and the addressee P^2, designate the utterance within brackets $\{\ \}$, and within those brackets refer to background information with the letters x and y, new information with the letter z, the resulting action and/or emotion (preceded by an arrow) with a capital A, then the general form of a script is

$$P^1 - P^2 \{x, y + z \rightarrow A\}$$

The only thing that is essential to the script is a present action or emotion, but usually we find at least $\{x \rightarrow A\}$ or $\{z \rightarrow A\}$, that is, either background

---

[24] I purposely omit mention of the Romandalusi (Moçarabe) *kharajat*, on which see Federico Corriente, *Poesía dialectal árabe y romance en Alandalús / cejeles y xarajat de muwassahat* (Madrid: Gredos, 1997). The early trend (after the Hebrew series was deciphered in 1948) towards seeing a genetic link between *kharajat* and *cantigas de amigo* seems now to have been over-hasty.

[25] This was argued by H. R. Lang, *Der Liederbuch des Königs Denis* (Halle, 1894).

or new information, plus an action and/or emotion. If those possibilities mark
the limit at one end (that of reduction) of the script, it is rare to find a script
in *Amigo* that exceeds the general form given above, and those are texts
where both strophic form and script overstep the boundaries of the matrix.
In *Amor* the elements of the script rarely vary much, while in *CEM* they can
be almost anything.

To see how a script is enacted (performed) in a text, let us take this *cantiga
de amigo* of Pero Garcia Burgalês.[26]

> Non vos nembra, meu amigo, o torto que mi fezestes?
> posestes de falar migo, fui eu e vós non veestes;
> e queredes falar migo, e non querrei eu, amigo.
>
> Jurastes que toda via verriades de bon grado
> ante que saiss' o dia; mentistes mi, ai perjurado,
> e queredes falar migo, e non querrei eu, amigo.
>
> E ainda me rogaredes que fal' eu algur con vosco?
> e, por quanto mi fazedes, direi que vos non conhosco;
> e queredes falar migo, e non querrei ·eu, amigo.

> Don't you remember, my friend, the wrong you did to me?
> You promised to talk with me, I went, and you didn't come.
> And you want to talk with me? Well I don't want to, friend.
>
> You swore that no matter what, you would come willingly
> Before the day had ended; you broke your word, you liar!
> And you want to talk with me? Well I don't want to, friend.
>
> And you're still asking me to talk with you somewhere?
> Because of what you did to me I'll say I don't even know you.
> And you want to talk with me? Well I don't want to, friend.

The background information (x, y) is: (1) 'you swore to come'; (2) 'you
didn't come'; the new information (z) is: (3) 'and now you want to talk with
me'; the present action is a rejection of the boy ('I don't want to talk with
you; I'll say I don't even know you'). Thus we can represent the script as:

$$G - B \text{ \{oath, no-show + wants to talk } \rightarrow \text{ rejection\}}$$

In *Amigo*, with very few exceptions, each poem in the corpus enacts
(performs) one of a few dozen basic scripts. There are constraints on the
possible combinations of speaker and addressee, which can be represented
as in Figure 1.

---

26 Pero Garcia Burgalês 2. The strophic form given here, aaB (with internal rhyme in all
verses), seems preferable to the ababCC version given in Cohen's edition.

Figure 1

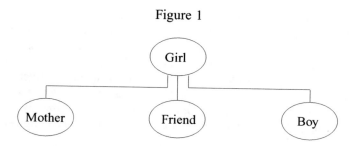

The Girl can address or be addressed by any of the other three, but they do not speak to one another 'on-stage'. These combinatory possibilities, their flexibility and constraints, point to a pre-existing tradition; and together with the rhetoric and form of the *cantigas de amigo*, suggest that tradition was old. It has the hallmarks of an oral genre of folksong that must have been at least centuries old when the first surviving texts were written down, roughly in the 1220s.

The early forms of *Amigo* (aaB, aaBB, and kindred strophic designs) and the rhetoric – whereby a script is slowly revealed – seem inextricably linked with the nature of the scripts. Form, pragmatics and rhetoric are so intricately interconnected that to ask which came first seems a chicken-or-egg issue. This intimate interrelation between the main aspects of poetic composition (leaving aside the music, about which we know very little) also seems to underwrite the thesis, argued more than a century ago, that *Amigo* is rooted in native folksong from the north-west of the Iberian Peninsula.

But what about the other two genres? While there has been much debate about *Amigo*, most scholars blithely assume that *Amor* comes from France. The considerable formal debt of *Amor* to Occitan and Old French lyric is undeniable, and many scholars have pointed to clear thematic parallels. It seems likely that parallelism, certain strophic forms, and at least some of the thematics of *Amor* existed before any Occitan or French influence, but it is difficult to go much beyond that, since the genre has been so tinged (or tainted) by foreign sway that we cannot trace its stemma.[27]

The genre that has been left almost untouched by arguments over origins is *CEM*. Only Lang, among the pioneers, seems to have understood that the poetry of insult must also have had deep roots in Iberia.[28] The question is, how deep? Since the topics are nearly all contemporary (though some might

---

[27] Cesare De Lollis, 'Dalle cantigas de amor a quelle de amigo', *Homenaje a Menéndez Pidal*, vol. I (Madrid: Hernando, 1925), pp. 617–26, posits two erotic genres in Galician-Portuguese before the first written texts, thus accepting as beyond question a pre-existing *Amigo*.

[28] Lang, p. ciii.

seem 'timeless') and the forms as complex as those in *Amor* (though there are more aaB in *CEM* than in *Amor*), how can we address the problem? There is no comparably large body of verse in Occitan, Old French, or Italian; and *CEM* are certainly not, as Tavani has suggested, a kind of deformation of the Occitan *sirventes* by a people whose ethical and political intelligence was not up to that of those beyond the Pyrenees. The Galician-Portuguese poetry of insult has nothing to do with the *sirventes*, and can legitimately be seen as a continuation of the Roman customs of *convicium* (insult) and *reflagitatio* (public dunning).[29]

In medieval Iberia, both Visigothic and Hispanic law provided examples of insults and set down punishments for them. How could Alfonso X, and other monarchs and magnates, not only have tolerated but encouraged and enjoyed songs of insult? How could they themselves have composed them? (In the case of Alfonso X, most of his secular output is in this genre, and among them are some of the most brilliant in the corpus.) The only answer I can see that makes sense is that a deeply rooted Roman tradition of comic insult had made this genre an important part of the culture of Iberia, and of the north-west quadrant in particular.[30] But if that is true, then this custom must go back roughly a millennium before 1200. Possible? The social and poetic matrix of an oral tradition is by definition deep. And even if rhymed strophic forms could hardly have existed in the time of the Roman Empire, the rhetoric of insult (*psogos*, *vituperatio*, *convicium* etc.) must have.

The final question, then, is this: if *CEM* has roots that deep in time, what about *Amigo*? To which we can only say: if, in its forms, rhetoric and pragmatics, *Amigo* seems older than *CEM*, how can its roots be more shallow?

The *Cantigas de Santa Maria* (Stephen Parkinson)

The secular lyric is complemented by a body of religious poetry, the *Cantigas de Santa Maria* (= *CSM*; *Songs for the Blessed Virgin Mary*). Their distinctive properties – a unified (devotional) subject matter, a single dominant poetic form, an apparent single author, an exemplary manuscript tradition with an independent tradition of iconography, and an unbroken musical tradition – derive from the special circumstances in which they were commissioned,

---

[29] Catullus, 42 (Peter Bing and Rip Cohen, *Games of Venus: An Anthology of Greek and Roman Erotic Verse from Sappho to Ovid* (New York and London: Routledge, 1991), pp. 205–6), a poetic example of *reflagitatio* (an ancient institution of Roman Law) in which the speaker demands the return of his writing tablets by insulting the woman who took them, has formal and rhetorical similarities with *Amigo*.

[30] The poetic *agon* (contest), found in Greek drama and in Theocritos, was picked up by the Romans (e.g. Catullus, Virgil), sometimes with mutual insults.

composed, collected and compiled in the royal manuscripts that preserve them. The existence of music for all but three of the 420 pieces, by comparison with the survival of a mere thirteen melodies for secular lyrics, has given the corpus a central position in the medieval music repertory (where they are known as 'the Cantigas').

The *CSM* are perhaps the most personal of all the cultural projects of King Alfonso X of Castile, later known as Alfonso el Sabio (Alfonso the Learned or Alfonso the Wise), a testimony of his devotion to the Virgin Mary, and a conscious attempt to portray himself as the troubadour, confidant and ward of the Queen of Heaven, at a time when his power and competence to rule were under threat. Their unity is a matter of design rather than essence, and conceals an enormous variety of authors, origins, content, styles, and techniques; the apparently perfect manuscript tradition points to a highly developed workshop system and a reluctance to release these royal treasures to the wider world.

The *CSM* fall into two main types: devotional and narrative. The devotional songs are known as *cantigas de loor* 'songs of praise', and include hymns, lyrics on the names and virtues of the Virgin Mary, litanies, and songs for her Feast Days, which are sometimes grouped together as festal songs, *cantigas de festas*. In a very real sense, however, all the *CSM* are 'in praise of the Virgin', and what distinguishes the *loores* from the remainder is that while the *loores* are brief lyrics, the narrative songs, 'cantigas de miragre', tell of miracles of the Virgin, from which they draw a devotional or exemplary message. The predominant poetic form is a precursor of the French *virelai*, known by its Arabic name *zajal* (Sp. *zéjel*). Each *zajal* has a refrain which is thematically and metrically central to the poem: the refrain states the theme or message of the poem, which is thus reiterated after each narrative strophe, and it dominates the poem's metrical design, as it sets an initial pattern (usually a rhyming couplet AA) which is replicated as the second half of each BBAA or BBBA strophe, heralding its return as the refrain proper. The music implements this pattern, so that the piece begins with the melody for the refrain, generally a repeated AA phrase; different melodic material (BB, often of a different tessitura, suggesting a soloist rather than a chorus) accompanies the new narrative material, before the refrain music returns for the end of the strophe and is then repeated for the refrain proper. This gives a continuous cyclic musical progression AA BB AA AA BB AA which sustains the often quite lengthy narratives. (The parts of the *zajal* are traditionally labelled with terms borrowed from the later Spanish *villancico*: refrain or *estribilho*, *mudanzas* (lit. 'variations') and *vuelta* ('return').) What stamps this collection as a lyric corpus is the use of a markedly Galician form of the Galician-Portuguese poetic *koiné*, with all the verbal flexibility of the *cantiga de amor* and *cantiga de escarnho*, and a metrical virtuosity all of its own, as in a lengthy poem the poet had to find new rhyming words for the repeated rhyme of the refrain and *vuelta*, and different unique rhymes for the new material of the *mudanzas*.

The 353 miracle stories are one of the largest collections of Marian miracles of the Middle Ages. The corpus can be seen to have grown organically as Alfonso realised the potential of the project, in clear contrast to the process of accretion by which the secular *cancioneiros* were assembled. The first nucleus of *CSM* was a collection of 100 poems, organised in a regular, rosary-like progression of *miragres* and *loores*, with every tenth poem a *loor*. A poetic prologue precedes this structure, and a dedication, in the form of a *petiçon* (petition), in which Alfonso asks the Virgin for a reward for his devotion, seals it. Most of the early narratives are taken from the Latin collections of miracles of the Virgin which proliferated in the eleventh and twelfth centuries, and vernacular collections such as the *Miracles de Nostre Dame* of Gautier de Coinci; even at this stage, however, miracle stories from Iberian shrines such as Montserrat and Salas are included, and Iberian locations are provided for others. Santiago (St James) is emblematically bettered by the Virgin in a version of the miracle of the revival of a pilgrim (*CSM* 26).[31]

At the time the collection was expanded, a splendid decorative scheme was devised in which every poem, with its music, would be set out on one or more complete manuscript pages, followed by a full page of six illustrative panels which set a visual narrative alongside the textual–musical one. For greater visual effect, the fifth *cantiga* of each decade would be illustrated by a double-page spread of twelve panels. As the prospect of completing the project in the king's lifetime waned, a minimally decorated reference collection of four hundred poems was separately compiled.

The expanded collection has progressively more poems from Iberian shrines, including tales from Portugal (Évora, Estremoz, Terena). Other stories relate miracles associated with the royal family, including Alfonso himself, tales of Reconquest skirmishes, and finally, a cycle of poems narrating miraculous events associated with the town of Porto de Santa Maria, which Alfonso himself established on the Andalucian coast, in the former Arabic town of Al-Quanat. While the earlier poems show some evidence of personal involvement by Alfonso himself, and show the metrical and linguistic innovation which characterise his outrageous *cantigas de escarnho*, the later poems show the extension of production techniques in which commissioned writers produced poems of a standard metrical pattern, relatively easy to set to music.

Many of the poems have roots in folktales and popular traditions of the miraculous, and are narrated to amuse as well as to instruct. A cut of meat stolen by an innkeeper from pilgrims bounces up and down in a chest to

---

31 Stephen Parkinson and Deirdre Jackson, 'Collection, Composition and Compilation in the *Cantigas de Santa Maria*', *Portuguese Studies* 22 (2006), 159–72.

reveal the theft (*CSM* 159). A priest who dares ban his flock from going to a church of the Virgin is left bleating like a goat (283); another, who steals an altarcloth to make underclothes, is bent double by night cramp until he confesses (327). In one pair of stories (222, 225), hapless chaplains are each confronted by a spider which has fallen into the communion chalice, and have no option but to swallow it; the Virgin's power results in the spider traversing the men's bodies and emerging intact from an arm and a fingernail. Every refrain reinforces the message that if you serve the Virgin, as Alfonso has done so emblematically, she will look after you. Alfonso died in 1284, deposed and rejected, worn out by fighting cancer and his son. The *Cantigas de Santa Maria* remain as a monument to his hope.

Texts and translations

Alvar, Carlos, and Vicente Beltrán, *Antología de la poesía gallego-portuguesa* (Madrid: Alhambra, 1984)

Cohen, Rip, *500 Cantigas d'Amigo. Edição Crítica / Critical Edition* (Oporto: Campo das Letras, 2003)

Gonçalves, Elsa, and Maria Ana Ramos, *A lírica galego-portuguesa: textos escolhidos* (Lisbon: Comunicação, 1983)

Kulp-Hill, Kathleen, *Songs of Holy Mary of Alfonso X the Wise. A Translation of the Cantigas de Santa Maria* (Austin, Texas: MRTS, 2000)

Lapa, Manuel Rodrigues, *Cantigas d'escarnho e de mal dizer dos cancioneiros medievais galego-portugueses*, edição crítica, 2nd edn. (Vigo: Galaxia, 1970; 1st. edn Coimbra: Galaxia, 1965) = *CEM*

Mettmann, Walter, *Alfonso X 'el Sabio'. Cantigas de Santa María*, 3 vols (Madrid: Castalia, 1986–89)

Michaëlis de Vasconcellos, Carolina, *Cancioneiro da Ajuda: Edição critica e commentada*, 2 vols (Halle: Niemeyer, 1904; reprinted with Glossary, Lisbon: Imprensa Nacional–Casa de Moeda, 1990) = *CA*

Nunes, José Joaquim, *Cantigas d'amigo dos trovadores galego-portugueses. Edição crítica acompanhada de introdução, comentário, variantes, e glossário*, 3 vols (Coimbra: Universidade, 1926–28; reprinted, Lisbon: Centro do Livro Brasileiro, 1973)

—— *Cantigas d'amor dos trovadores galego-portugueses*, Edição crítica acompanhada de introdução, comentário, variantes, e glossário (Coimbra: Universidade, 1932; reprinted Lisbon: Centro do Livro Brasileiro, 1972)

Further reading

Asensio, Eugenio, *Poética y realidad en el cancionero peninsular de la Edad Media*, 2nd edn (Madrid: Gredos, 1970)

Brea, Mercedes, and Pilar Lorenzo Gradín, *A Cantiga de Amigo* (Vigo: Edicións Xerais, 1998)

Cohen, Rip, *Erotic Angles on the Cantigas d'Amigo*, Papers of the Medieval Hispanic Research Seminar, 64 (London: Queen Mary University of London, 2009)

Duffell, Martin J., *Syllable and Accent: Studies on Medieval Hispanic Metrics* (London: Queen Mary University of London, 2007)

Ferreira, Manuel Pedro, *Cantus Coronatus: 7 Cantigas by King Dinis of Portugal* (Kassel: Reichenberger, 2005)

Fidalgo, Elvira, *As Cantigas de Santa Maria* (Vigo: Edicións Xerais, 2002)

Jensen, Frede, *The Earliest Portuguese Lyrics* (Odense: Odense University Press, 1978)

Katz, Israel J., and John Esten Keller, *Studies on the 'Cantigas de Santa Maria': Art, Music and Poetry* (Madison, WI: Hispanic Seminary of Medieval Studies, 1987)

Lanciani, Giulia, and Giuseppe Tavani (eds), *Dicionário da Literatura Medieval Galega e Portuguesa* (Lisbon: Caminho, 1993)

O'Callaghan, Joseph, *Alfonso X and the 'Cantigas de Santa Maria': A Poetic Biography* (Leiden: Brill, 1998)

Odber de Baubeta, Patricia, *Anticlerical Satire in Medieval Portuguese Literature* (Lampeter: Mellen, 1992)

Parkinson, Stephen (ed.), *Cobras e Son. Papers on the Text, Music and Manuscripts of the 'Cantigas de Santa Maria'* (Oxford: Legenda, 2000)

3

Fernão Lopes and Portuguese Prose Writing
of the Middle Ages

STEPHEN PARKINSON

Medieval Portuguese prose writing is dominated by a small number of genres: historical writing, sapiential and memorialistic writing, hagiography and devotional tracts, and romances of chivalry, the latter two firmly rooted in imported and translated materials. Historical writing has a long Iberian lineage, with native Iberian historians such as Lucas of Tuy (*Chronicon Mundi*, 1232) pre-dating the emergence of Portuguese historiography. The historical compilations of Alfonso X of Castile, notably the *General Estoria* which Pedro, Count of Barcelos, reworked as the 1344 *Cronica Geral de Espanha* (*General History of Spain*), beside his own *Livro de Linhagens* (*Book of Lineages*), fed into an ongoing cumulative process of incorporation and reworking of earlier chronicles which had its highest point in the chronicles of the dynastic change of the late fourteenth century, by the first official Royal Chronicler, and keeper of the Royal Archive, Fernão Lopes (?1380–1459).[1]

The first or Burgundian dynasty, descended from Henry of Burgundy, made Count of Portugal under King Alfonso VI of Castile and León in 1097, proceeded largely by direct male succession for nearly three centuries.[2] The only major disturbance had been the civil war of the late thirteenth century in which Afonso III, with Papal support, deposed his brother Sancho II. (The resonances of this conflict, and the many acts of disloyalty or betrayal associ-

---

[1] The *Tombo* or archive of the royal family was established in St George's Castle (*Castelo de S. Jorge*) in Lisbon under King Fernando in 1378, occupying part of what is now the *Torre de Ulisses* (Ulysses Tower). When transferred to the Parliament Building in S. Bento in 1755 it officially became the *Arquivo Nacional da Torre do Tombo* (National Archive of the Archive Tower), a name it retained in its move to a purpose-built archive complex in the University of Lisbon in 1990.

[2] Henry's son Afonso Henriques was followed by his son Sancho I, grandson Afonso II, and great-grandsons Sancho II and Afonso III; the latter was succeeded by his son the poet-King Dinis, grandson Afonso IV, and thence by Pedro I and Fernando I.

ated with it, left their mark in satirical lyrics of the period. 'Not even King Sancho of Portugal was betrayed as I was', exclaimed Alfonso X in a poem cataloguing the wrongs done to him.[3])

The events narrated by Fernão Lopes were in many ways a turning point for Portugal. The crisis of succession generated by the premature death of Fernando I in 1383, leaving a ten-year-old daughter betrothed to the King of Castile as part of a peace treaty forced on him by the failure of his last campaign to extend Portuguese territory, led to civil war, invasion by Castile and intervention by English forces, and ultimately the election of Fernando's illegitimate half-brother João of Avis as João I.[4] João's marriage to Philippa of Lancaster, daughter of John of Gaunt, as part of the 1386 Treaty of Windsor which has linked England and Portugal for over six centuries, created a dynasty from which the next ten Portuguese monarchs descended. João's son Duarte and his grandson Afonso V were responsible for commissioning chronicles of the two dynasties: Duarte employed Fernão Lopes to write chronicles of all the monarchs up to and culminating in João I, while Afonso renewed the mandate, and the pension accompanying it, and officially nominated a successor, Gomes Eanes de Zurara, to chronicle the deeds of João I and his son Prince Henrique, prime mover of the Portuguese discoveries.[5] Zurara was followed by Rui de Pina and Damião de Gois, before historical writing moved its focus from monarchy to Empire, and João de Barros and Diogo do Couto gave more expansive histories of the Portuguese in Asia.

Remarkably little is known of Fernão Lopes's life and origins. The tradition which has him born in 1380, just in time to witness the upheavals of the 1380s, has no firmer basis in documented fact than the tradition identifying him as a dour figure in the *Painéis de S. Vicente*.[6] Lopes's family ties indicate him to have been of humble origins, but he must have been well educated and distinguished himself early as an administrator, to be appointed keeper of the royal archive in 1418, chancery scribe in 1419 and in 1423 private secretary to Prince Fernando (the Holy Prince who would die in captivity after the failed assault on Tangier in 1437, and whose will he drafted in his

---

3   'Nunca assi foi vendudo | rei Don Sanch' en Portugal' (*CSM* 235 st. 11). Lisa Jefferson, 'Use of Canon Law, Abuse of Canon Lawyers in Two *Cantigas* Concerning the Deposition of D. Sancho II of Portugal', *Portuguese Studies* 9 (1993), 1–22, studies the legal contortions found in the *cantigas de escarnho*.

4   Son of Pedro I and his mistress and putative secret wife Inês de Castro, whose murder at the behest of King Afonso IV led to her being enshrined in poetry and drama by Garcia de Resende, Camões and Ferreira (see chapters 1 and 5).

5   Known to the English-speaking world as Henry the Navigator, to the Portuguese simply as O Infante D. Henrique (Prince Henry).

6   A group of six panels from the late fifteenth century, formerly in the Church of S. Vicente de Fora, now in the Museu de Arte Antiga, Lisbon, presumed to depict the Aviz dynasty and its retinue around the figure of S. Vincent, patron saint of Lisbon.

official capacity as Notary General). Lopes's royal commission required him to 'set down as a chronicle' (*poer em caronyca*) the history of Portugal up to the reign of João I, which he interpreted as a twofold task, of narrating chronologically the events of past centuries, and of tracing the sequence of interacting events leading to the dynastic and social changes of the 1380s. It is the skill with which he constructed a large-scale causal account, and the literary qualities which he brought to his description of historical events, that distinguish him above his Portuguese and arguably his European contemporaries. This is not to say that his account is correct or impartial, or that he is in some sense a 'modern' historian, while others are 'mere' chroniclers.

The known chronicles of Fernão Lopes begin with the short *Crónica de D. Pedro*, which follows on from and frequently refers back to chronicles of the first seven monarchs, extant in sixteenth-century versions (the *Crónica de Sete Reis*) incorporating some material from the early fifteenth century. Whether or not Fernão Lopes himself composed these or other chronicles of the early kings, it is clear that he located the origins of his dynastic story in the reign of Pedro I. The dimensions of the chronicles show a clear progression of intensification; the ten-year reign of Pedro I (1357–67) merits forty-four short chapters, Fernando I's turbulent sixteen years are covered in 178 chapters, approximately the same space given to the two years (1383–85) leading up to the accession of João I. The clear division of the *Crónica de D. João I* into two parts, one where he becomes Regent (*Regedor*) and finally king, the other of his defence of the realm as its king and his marriage to Philippa of Lancaster, reveals the chronicle as a narrative culminating in the survival of an independent Portugal under the house of Avis. After further conflict and peace treaties with Castile, the narrative ends with the marriage of João's daughter to the son of his Constable Nun' Álvares, whose ennoblement typifies the Lopean paradigm of social change, while sowing the seeds of the conflicts of the minority of Afonso V. The changes brought about by the next generation of princes, in particular the overseas expansion begun with the capture of Ceuta in 1415, were beyond Fernão Lopes's perspective, if not his comprehension, and must have been officially left to other chroniclers long before Lopes himself, 'so old and frail that he cannot perform his duties', was relieved of his charge in 1454.[7]

Each one of Fernão Lopes's chronicles (including each of the two halves of the *Crónica de D. João I*) begins with a prologue. In the chronicle of King Fernando, and part II of the chronicle of King João, the prologues consist of thumbnail sketches of the monarch; the prologue to Pedro is a reflection on Justice, introducing a pen-portrait of the monarch in the first chapter.

---

[7] 'Tam velho e flaco que per ssy nom pode bem serujr do dito offiçio' (document of 1445 cited in Braamcamp Freire, *Crónica de D. João I*, Parte I, lviii). All translations from Old Portuguese are by the author.

By contrast, the prologue to the second part of the Chronicle of João I is programmatic. It starts with a carefully positioned disquisition on impartiality and the importance of document, not so much a *captatio benevolentiae* as a preemptive strike against accusations of apologism, and then identifies the key stages and components in the irresistible rise of João, which would be developed over the whole chronicle. In this way Lopes signals that he is marshalling historical materials, not just retelling them.

Lopes's extensive and explicit use of the documentary sources (legal documents, Papal bulls, letters) to which he had direct access as archivist, is a prominent feature of his approach. Less obvious, and only slowly being uncovered by current research, is the extent of his overall debt to other historical narratives, and the extent to which he reproduces, paraphrases, abbreviates, expands, and rewrites them. Much of his coverage of the long-running civil conflicts in Castile is based on the Castilian chronicler Pero López de Ayala, and the *Crónica de D. João I* incorporates much of a life of Nun' Álvares Pereira, the *Chronica do Condestabre*, completed shortly after the death of Nun' Álvares in 1431. Other sources included a lost Latin chronicle by a Dr Christophorus and a memoir by the noble Martim Afonso de Melo. Some of these sources are clearly identified, some alluded to in positive or negative terms, some dismissed as old wives' tales. Much of Fernão Lopes's account of the relations between King João and Queen Philippa and their sons is taken directly from King Duarte's *Leal Conselheiro*. Lopes is disarmingly candid and often robust and trenchant in identifying and usually resolving questions of disagreement between his sources:

> If at this point you read that the Castilians cut their lances and made them shorter than was their custom, know it to be true and doubt it not ...[8]

> There was no advantage to the Portuguese in their choice of battleground, nor hills or valleys to confuse the enemy, as some ill-meaning writers narrate in their books.[9]

Not all his preferred accounts, it must be said, have been borne out by subsequent historical research. In many cases it is not possible to identify all his sources, and Peter Russell has drawn attention to the significant numbers of independent and possibly conflicting sources which do not seem to have survived Lopes's appropriation of them. (Lopes's work suffered similar treatment at the hands of Rui de Pina, whose chronicle of Afonso IV, including the narrative of the death of Inês de Castro, is assumed to incorporate, but certainly not improve upon, Lopes's own account of that reign.) Where Lopes

---

[8] *Crónica de D. João I*, II, ch. 42.
[9] *Crónica de D. João I*, II, ch. 38.

impresses, however, is in his appreciation of short- and long-term causality, and his knowing introduction of events, personalities and factors that he knows will be significant at later stages. At the time when Pedro makes his bastard son, the future King João I, Master of the Order of Avis, Lopes has him recount a dream in which the young João quells a fire which threatens to engulf the whole kingdom, a clear prophesy of the events of 1385. Lopes equally excels in expressing the complexity of chronological sequence and of interacting forces, which his sources typically reduce to a monotone chronological sequence, in order to pursue simultaneous narratives:

> Now the King of Castile is on his way to Portugal; at the same time Nun' Álvares is on his way to Lisbon; and the Master together with the people of Lisbon is engaged in taking the Castle [...]; many things are taking place at the same time, so that each one confuses the others, and they cannot be narrated day by day.[10]

Whereas the dramatic climax of the chronicle is the triumph of João and Nun' Álvares at the battle of Aljubarrota, forty chapters into part II of the Chronicle, the political endpoint is the lengthy speech by the legist João das Regras at the Parliament (*Cortes*) held in Coimbra; at the end of part I of the chronicle, in which the case for the legitimisation of João as King is made at great length and with apparent total success (Lopes giving no weight to the continued support for Prince João, the eldest son of Inês de Castro and Pedro). Here the ethico-political and juridical considerations which Fernão Lopes has carefully developed are combined in one grand justificatory argument which in part recapitulates the summary of part I of the chronicle, that the only person with a claim of inheritance, D. Beatriz, had disqualified herself by marrying a foreigner who had waged war on the Portuguese people; that the sons of Pedro and Inês were no more legitimate than the Master of Avis; that the Mestre had been freely chosen by the people, and had defended Portugal against the invader. The third strand in the literary argument, the prophetic, is not stated: the Messianic suggestions, such as the reference to the victims of the siege of Lisbon as martyrs, and the prophesies and magical goings-on with which Lopes's narrative has been laced have done their work, and are not recalled. The earlier narrative of King Pedro's obsessive pursuit of the murderers of Inês de Castro and his opulent translation of her remains to Coimbra brings no favours to her sons, particularly Prince João, exiled in Castile and himself guilty of the murder of his first wife.

---

[10] 'Porque el-Rei de Castela vem pera entrar em Portugall; NunAllvarez outrossi veem-se a Lixboa; desi o castello da çidade trabalha-se o Meestre com o poboo de o tomarem [...]; fazem-se outras muitas cousas em hũa sazom, de guisa que hũas torvam as outras, a se nom poderem comtar nos dias que acomteçerom.' *Crónica de D. João I*, I, ch. 29.

In a passage of measured ambiguity, placed immediately after the abandonment of the siege of Lisbon and the end of the first Castilian campaign, Lopes half seriously, 'as it were in jest', presents the virtual accession of the Master as a Seventh Age, marked by the capture of social and political power by 'the sons of men of such low estate that it should not be spoken of'.[11] Fernão Lopes likens the change of dynasty to a seventh age of man, not because of the coming of the promised kingdom but because of the change of social order and the replacement of the old nobility. This is added to the emergence of the common people, the *povoo*,[12] as a political force: it is the people of Lisbon who elect him Regedor, and who withstand the Castilian siege to protect him; it is popular unrest, either spontaneously triggered by the threat of Castilian rule, or carefully manipulated by Álvaro Pais, mastermind of the elevation of João to popular hero, when he sends around a rumour that the Master is in danger, at the moment when he prepares to assassinate the Queen Regent's favourite. Lopes's descriptions of crowds, and their violent conversion into a mob, are among the most memorable of medieval Portuguese prose.

> The noise of the tumult resounded through the city, as on all sides there were shouts that the Master's life was in danger; [...] everyone came out with weapons, running speedily to where they were told it was happening, to save his life and prevent his death. Álvaro Pais kept leading them, shouting to all around 'Let us aid the Master, my friends, aid the Master who is in peril for no reason!' The crowds began to gather behind him, and there were so many that it was wondrous to see. The main streets were too small for them, and they went by alleys and byways, each one trying to be the first.[13]

These acute perceptions of social forces should not be confused with sympathy for the popular cause, let alone a covert socialism in advance of its time, or a thinly disguised support for the populist Prince Pedro in the civil wars of the 1440s. Lopes expresses wonderment and revulsion at the violence meted out to perceived enemies (a bishop, an abbess, even a notary). The rise of the new class, just as the new type of warfare practised by Nun' Álvares, is a mystery to this deeply conservative royal servant. The same observation and literary force is deployed in the descriptions of Oporto preparing to welcome the Master, and of Lisbon awaiting news of the final battle.[14]

[11] *Crónica de D. João I*, part I, ch. 163.
[12] Lopes catalogues the names thrown at them by the nobility: *arraia miúda* ('common throng'), *ventres ao sol* ('bare bellies').
[13] *Crónica de D. João I*, part I, ch. 11.
[14] *Crónica de D. João I*, II, ch. 41: 'Of those who prayed to God for the good fortune of those Kings'.

Even in his prologue, it can be seen that João, while receiving the praise due to the monarch, is presented as the beneficiary rather than the mover of events: 'the great and memorable deeds of the most famous King João I while Master, how he killed Count Joam Fernandez, how first the people of Lisbon and then others in the Kingdom took him as their Regent and Defender, and how and for how long he reigned thereafter'. Lopes emphasises João's worthiness, his royal blood, his destiny, and the affection in which he is held, but does not conceal his vacillations and failures of judgement (suppressing only the most damaging claims of other writers, such as Ayala's account of the Master initially subscribing to the invitation to the King of Castile). His great achievement is to satisfy his patron's desire for a commemorative chronicle of João I while portraying him as less than perfect. The truly heroic figure of the chronicle is Nun' Álvares Pereira, Galahad to his Arthur, whose importance is recognised when Lopes interrupts the narrative at precisely the point at which civil unrest gives way to military campaigning, to insert what is in practice a prologue to the chronicle of Nun' Álvares. While João is destined to be King, Nun' Álvares is his 'psychological double in action and resolve'.[15] The relationship between them, several times described as a 'gentle rivalry', underlies much of the action leading up to the elevation of João as King.

Not all of Fernão Lopes is high seriousness. In a memorable comic moment, the defeated captain of the castle of Portel takes his wife into exile in style, prefacing a parodic song with a bawdy gloss:

'Come hither, my lady, and we shall dance, you and I, to the sound of these trumpets, you for a wicked old whore and I as a poor villein buggered as you wanted me to be. Even better let us sing this song ...'[16]

[15] Teresa Amado, *Fernão Lopes, Contador de História* (Lisbon: Estampa, 1991), p. 59.

[16] 'Amdaae per aqui, boa dona, e hiremos balhamdo, vos e eu, a ssoom destas trombas; vos por maa puta velha e eu por villaão fodudo no cuu ca assi quisestes vos. Ou camtemos desta guisa, que será melhor', *Crónica de D. João I*, I, ch. 158. The text continues

> Pois Marina bailloou
> tome o que ganou
> melhor era Portell e Villa Ruiva
> que nom Çafra e Segura
> tome o que ganou
> dona puta velha

E esto dezia porque perdia Portell e Villa Ruiva, e davamlhe em Castela Çafra e Segura.

(Marina has danced, so let her have her pay; I would rather have had Villa Ruiva than Çafra and Segura; take your pay, old madam whore. He said this because he was losing Portel and Villa Ruiva, and was being given Çafra and Segura in Castile.) The verse scans much better if 'Portell e' is removed; it was probably inserted by a copyist of the original chronicle, anticipating the text of the explanation. This passage was brought to my attention by Josiah Blackmore.

The episode is found in the *Cronica do Condestabre*, with a garbled version of the song, but Lopes enhances the scene to make it truly theatrical and consciously preserve a late flourish of the *cantiga de escarnho*, which by most tokens had been dead for half a century. Other snatches of verse are fired from the ramparts of Lisbon while it is besieged by the Castilians, and *bons mots* are tossed between disputing courtiers. João I is distinguished by his joviality, whereas the one defect of the knightly paragon Nun' Alvares is an absence of humour (or the suppression of the youthful high spirits which have him casually bring down a dinner table when other guests at a banquet left him no room[17]). The mechanics of a change of narrative become a personal change of view: 'Nun' Álvares then put out his campfires, to catch up on the sleep he had lost, and so good night to him: meanwhile, we will return to see in what state poor beleaguered Lisbon is to be found ...'[18] When the Castilians are finally and definitively defeated at the battle of Aljubarrota, the rout is described with an ironic satisfaction: 'the Portuguese stableboys [...] began to shout *they are on the run, yes they are on the run*. And the Castilians, not wishing to contradict them, ran all the more.'[19] In chapter 163 of part I of the chronicle, immediately after his barbed discussion of the Seventh Age, Lopes indulges in a slyly double-edged Biblical joke:

> Just as the Son of God called his Apostles, saying he would make them fishers of men, so many of these people whom the Master elevated fished so many men for themselves by their high and noble estate that some were always attended by twenty or thirty horsemen ...'[20]

In these and other ways Lopes reveals himself as a deliberately personalising, quietly humorous, and at times intentionally comic writer.

Gomes Eanes de Zurara (?1410–73/4) was a man of a different era. Son of a cleric, brought up at the court of Afonso V, he was groomed for royal patronage, and chosen as chronicler for his rhetorical skills. For Zurara the writing of history was a humanistic literary enterprise, deploying rhetoric for the noble end of recounting glorious deeds and ensuring the abiding fame of the great and those who served under them. Though much of his rhetoric and learning seems over-conscious and laboured to modern readers, his work achieved greater international prominence than Lopes's, being translated into Latin by the humanist Mateus Pisano. His two royal chronicles, *Crónica da*

---

17 *Crónica de D. Fernando*, ch. 166.

18 *Crónica de D. João I*, I, ch. 147.

19 'Os moços portugueses que tijnham as bestas, e muytos dos outros que eram com elles, começarom altas vozes braadar e dizer: Ja fogem! ja fogem! E os castelaãos, por nom fazer deles mentirosos, começaram de fugir cada vez mais.' *Crónica de D. João I*, II, ch. 42.

20 *Crónica de D. João I*, I, ch. 163.

Tomada de Ceuta and *Crónica dos Feitos da Guiné*, both have a clear hero (Prince Henry) and a number of co-stars (the other princes of Avis in *Ceuta*, the captains of the Discoveries in *Guiné*). There is an interesting progression in the laudatory portrayal of Prince Henry, from *Ceuta*, where he is seen as the main advocate and warrior of the campaign, to *Guiné* (completed after his death in 1460) where he is directly addressed in introductory chapters, before being characterised as 'our Prince' (*o nosso príncipe*), a powerful, charismatic and at times frightening power behind the voyages of exploration. The captains now take the role of valiant warriors: their adversary is no longer the traditional Castilian foe faced by King João or the Moors of Reconquest narratives, but is the fear of the unknown, and the essence of otherness, the African, whether it is the redoubtable defenders of Ceuta or the markedly less ferocious natives of Guiné. Zurara must nevertheless take the credit for recognising the common humanity of the Other, in his portrayal of the pathos of the separation of families in the first recorded slave market in Lagos.[21]

Zurara wound down his narrative of the exploration of the African coast with the observation that trade had replaced feats of arms as the main activity. He transferred his attention to theatres of war closer to home, in his lengthy accounts of the careers of the governors of Ceuta, Pedro de Meneses and Duarte de Meneses. Historical writing no longer has a role for Fernão Lopes's studied concern with document, balance and the appearance of objectivity. The emerging Portuguese empire needed no justification or apology, only an unequal distribution of the glory and the credit for its inspiration.

The Arthurian narratives collectively known as the *matéria de Bretanha* (Fr. *matière de Bretagne*, *Tales of Britain*) are assumed to have been transmitted to Iberia through Norman French works, carried by the retinue of Queen Philippa of Lancaster. They survive in translated form in *A Demanda do Santo Graal* (*The Quest of the Holy Grail*) and the *Livro de José de Arimateia* (*Book of Joseph of Arimathea*), as well as inspiring the two enigmatic *lais de Bretanha* ('lays of Britain') appended to the medieval lyric.[22] The importance of these texts is not so much in their literary value as in their influence, shown by the value ascribed to chivalric virtues in the medieval chronicles, and their continuation in later romances, and their role in the wider transmission of Arthurian material, as the Spanish version of the Grail legend is assumed to be a retranslation of the Portuguese text, just as the romance *Amadís de Gaula* (*Amadis of Gaul*), extant only in fifteenth-

---

[21] *Crónica de Guiné*, ch. 25.

[22] A recently discovered translation of Gower's *Confessio Amatis* (Antonio Cortijo Ocaña, 'O Livro do Amante: The Lost Portuguese Translation of John Gower's Confessio Amantis (Madrid, Biblioteca de Palacio, MS II-3088)', *Portuguese Studies* 13 (1997), 1–6) does not seem to have revived fifteenth-century courtly poetry.

and sixteenth-century Spanish versions, is assumed to have been written in Portuguese in the fourteenth century.

Similarly influential were the saints' lives (*Vidas de Santos*) compiled by Bernardo de Brihuega from the Latin hagiographical tradition which had sustained the early compilation of the *Cantigas de Santa Maria*. Among devotional texts the *Orto do esposo* (*The Bridegroom's Garden*), based on a multitude of *exempla* but probably not, as previously thought, a translation, stands beside the translated *Castelo perigoso* (*Castle Perilous*), *Boosco delei-toso* (*Forest of Delights*) and *Virgeu de consolaçom* (*Grove of Consolations*).

The unexpected modernity of the personal reflections of King Duarte's *Leal Conselheiro* (*Loyal Counsellor*) and the less formally organised materials of his *Livro dos Conselhos* (*Book of Good Counsel*) are perhaps the most notable product of a tradition of memorialism in which the House of Aviz complemented the historical writings it commissioned. Duarte also left reflections on translation, and narratives of family life (some of which undoubtedly coloured the accounts of Fernão Lopes and Zurara). He also produced a guide to equestrianism, *Livro de bem ensinança de cavalgar toda sela* (*Guide to Riding all Mounts*), following his father King João's *Livro de Montaria* (*Book of Hunting*). Not to be outdone, Prince Pedro translated Cicero's *De Beneficiis* as *Livro da Virtuosa Benfeitoria*, which was one of Zurara's fundamental references. Recent linguistic research shows that the writings of King Duarte were in the vanguard of changes in the language.[23] In many ways, the house of Aviz modelled the literary landscape of the Portuguese late Middle Ages.

Texts and translations

Fernão Lopes

Chronique du Roi D. Pedro I / *Crónica do Rei D. Pedro I*, ed Giuliano Macchi, introd and tr. Jacqueline Stenou (Paris: CNRS, 1985)

Crónica de Dom Fernando, ed. Giuliano Macchi (Lisbon: Imprensa Nacional, 1975)

Crónica del Rei dom João I da boa memória, Parte I, ed. Anselmo Braamcamp Freire (*Archivo Historico Portuguez* (1915), repr. Lisbon: Imprensa Nacional, 1977)

Cronica del Rei Dom Johan I de boa memoria e doz Reis de Portugal o decimo Parte II, ed. William Entwistle (Lisbon: Imprensa Nacional, 1968)

Crónica de D. João I de Fernão Lopes, selected and ed. Teresa Amado, 2nd edn (Lisbon: Comunicação, 1992)

---

23 Esperança Cardeira, *O Português Médio* (Lisbon: Imprensa Nacional, 2005).

Gomes Eanes de Zurara

Crónica dos feitos notáveis que se passaram na conquista da Guiné por mandado do infante D. Henrique / por Gomes Eanes de Zurara; introd. and ed. Torquato de Sousa Soares (Lisbon: Academia Portuguesa da História, 1978–81)

Chronique de Guinée (1453) de Gomes Eanes de Zurara; introd. Jacques Paviot, trans. Léon Bourdon (Paris: Éditions Chandeigne, 1994)

Crónica do Conde D. Pedro de Meneses, ed. Maria Teresa Brocardo (Lisbon: FCG-JNICT, 1997)

Crónica do Conde D. Duarte de Meneses, ed. Larry King (Lisbon: Universidade Nova, 1978)

Others

Castelo perigoso, ed. Elsa Maria Branco da Silva (Lisbon: Colibri, 2001)

Crónica de Portugal de 1419, ed. Adelino de Almeida Calado (Aveiro: Universidade, 1998)

A Demanda do Santo Graal, ed. Joseph-Maria Piel, completed by Irene Freire Nunes (Lisbon: Imprensa Nacional, 1988)

Estoria de Dom Nuno Alvarez Pereyra. Edição crítica da 'Coronica do Condestabre', ed. and introd. Adelino de Almeida Calado (Coimbra: Universidade, 1991)

Leal conselheiro: o qual fez Dom Eduarte, Rey de Portugal e do Algarve e Senhor de Cepta, ed. Joseph M. Piel (Lisbon: Bertrand, 1942).

Orto do esposo, ed. Irene Freire Nunes (Lisbon: Colibri, 2007)

Further reading

Bullón Fernández, María (ed.), *England and Iberia in the Middle Ages, 12th–15th Century* (New York and Basingstoke: Palgrave Macmillan, 2007)

Deyermond, Alan (ed.), *Historical Literature in Medieval Iberia*, Publications of the Medieval Hispanic Research Seminar, 2 (London: Queen Mary and Westfield College, 1996)

Lomax, Derek W. and R. J. Oakley, *The English in Portugal 1367–87* (Warminster: Aris & Phillips, 1988) [includes extracts from the Chronicles of D. Fernando and D. João I, with translations and notes]

Russell, Peter, *Portugal, Spain and the African Atlantic: Chivalry and Crusade from John of Gaunt to Henry the Navigator* (Aldershot: Variorum, 1995)

—— *Prince Henry the Navigator: A Life* (New Haven and London: Yale University Press, 2000)

4

Portuguese Theatre in the Sixteenth Century: Gil Vicente and António Ferreira

JULIET PERKINS and T. F. EARLE

Gil Vicente (Juliet Perkins)

On the night of 7 June 1502, the royal apartments were invaded by a rumbustious figure, a herdsman sent on behalf of his village to find out whether it was true that the Queen of Portugal, Maria of Castile, had given birth. Indignant but not cowed by the strong-arm tactics of palace servants to stop him entering into the Queen's presence, amazed but not speechless at the luxurious surroundings, he addresses the young mother, jumping with joy at her safe delivery and radiant pride. He showers warm praise on the baby heir to the throne and his lineage before ushering in his companions to present their gifts of eggs, milk, honey and cheese, but not without muttering that they too will have to run the gauntlet of the pages at the door. The Spanish verse monologue delivered by this yokel signalled the beginning of Gil Vicente's career as author, and probably as actor too. It contains, in a nutshell, the blend of forthrightness, religious devotion, loyalty to the sovereign, sly humour and satire that would be repeated in Gil Vicente's subsequent *autos*. It allows also a fleeting glimpse of the gulf that had opened up in sixteenth-century Portugal between courtier and peasant, palace and countryside, conspicuous consumption and subsistence diet, leisure and unremitting toil. It identifies the author as someone sympathetic to rural life and people, yet at ease and of some standing at Court.

That standing can be explained by documentary evidence that the playwright of 1502 had been for some time a goldsmith in the service of Queen Leonor, Dowager Queen since 1495.[1] Belonging to the aristocracy of craftsmen but of humble birth, his early life and education are undocu-

---

[1] The two major studies, with comprehensive documentation, are Anselmo Braamcamp Freire, *Vida e Obras de Gil Vicente 'Trovador Mestre da Balança'*, 2nd edn (Lisbon: Revista Ocidente, 1944); Carolina Michaëlis de Vasconcelos, *Notas Vicentinas* (Lisbon: Revista Ocidente, 1949).

mented. Most likely born in rural northern Portugal (there is evidence for the town of Guimarães, and for a goldsmith father), he could have come south to Lisbon around 1490. In his capacity as poet, he contributed several pieces to Garcia de Resende's compendium of palace poetry, the *Cancioneiro Geral* (*General Songbook*) of 1516. During the 1520s and 1530s he received various pensions from King João III. In a letter to his king, written from Santarém after the earthquake that devastated the Tagus area in 1531, Gil Vicente refers to himself as being close to death.[2] It is assumed that he died in Évora, not long after his last play was performed there in 1536. Certainly, a document of 1540 in respect of his second son, Belchior, refers to him as no longer living.

If this biographical information is sparse, even more unclear is exactly when he started to write and what prompted him. We do know that the monologue of June 1502 was his own initiative. It pleased the Dowager Queen so much that she asked for more, and from then on he became an indispensable furnisher of plays for the Court. His transition from craftsman to playwright under her patronage may be more easily envisaged if we regard him as a 'deviser of stage entertainments for which he wrote original compositions'.[3] When Queen Leonor retired from Court around 1518–19, Gil Vicente passed into the service of her brother, King Manuel. His appointment to organise and direct the January 1521 festivities marking that king's entry into Lisbon with his new queen, Leonor of Austria, did but confirm his *de facto* position of court playwright.[4] It also marked a significant shift from religious to secular subjects, a burst of creative energy that replaced succinct asceticism with vibrant expansiveness, still later to give way to a certain pessimism. Under King João III, he continued to provide plays for every royal event, and at his command started to prepare his plays for publication. In the prologue addressed to his patron, he stated he would not have thought to publish them had he not been so commanded; if his works were worth remembering it was because many of them were devotional pieces directed to the service of God, and nothing of virtue should be left undone.[5] Whether through humility or

---

[2] Gil Vicente, *Copilaçam de Todalas Obras de Gil Vicente* [1562], ed. Maria Leonor Carvalhão Buescu, 2 vols (Lisbon: Imprensa Nacional–Casa da Moeda, 1983), vol II, p. 645. This letter is significant for demonstrating not only his authority and courage in censuring the superstitious friars of Santarém who saw the punitive hand of God in the earthquake, but also the respect in which he was held by the monarch.

[3] T. P. Waldron (ed.), *Gil Vicente. Tragicomedia de Amadis de Gaula* (Manchester: Manchester University Press, 1959), p. 3.

[4] Full details of King Manuel's communications and of the festivities are given in João Nuno Sales Machado, '1521: *Per Ordenança* de Gil Vicente', *Gil Vicente 500 Anos Depois*, ed. Maria João Brilhante *et al.*, 2 vols (Lisbon: Imprensa Nacional–Casa da Moeda, 2003), pp. 475–97.

[5] *Copilaçam*, I, 14.

infirmity, Gil Vicente was unable to complete the revisions before he died. It was left to his son and daughter by his second marriage, Luís and Paula, to do so. The task came to fruition only in 1562, with the publication of the *Copilaçam de Todalas Obras de Gil Vicente* (*Collection of all the Works of Gil Vicente*). This is the only source for all but a fraction of his work.[6]

A virtuous action the compilation may have been, but the works had to be submitted to Inquisition censorship. There is no mention of them in the first Index of prohibited books of 1547, but in that of 1551 seven plays, all of which were circulating in chapbook or broadsheet form, were found wanting. The *Copilaçam* in preparation for the press was subject to the Index of 1561, which maintained the stipulations of 1551 but did not offer any fresh prohibitions; indeed, four of the seven works mentioned in 1551 were printed.[7] The other three have been lost (*Jubileu de Amores* (*Love's Jubilee*), *Auto da Aderência do Paço* (*Play of the Would-Be Courtier*), *Auto da Vida do Paço* (*Play of Court Life*)). It is widely held that the protection of the Queen Regent, Queen Catarina, was vital to ensuring that his work passed unscathed and that the Inquisition relented a little between 1551 and 1562. This was not the case for the second edition in 1586, a severely mutilated version of the works, displaying a Counter-Reformation mentality in full spate.

Gil Vicente's *captatio benevolentiae*, 'my poor little works', was taken literally by his editor son, who set about certain improvements. As he declares, 'I took it upon myself to refine them [the works].' Since no Vicentine manuscripts have survived, the literary damage wreaked through his refinements to style, tone and, especially, to coarse language, may be gauged by collating the *Copilaçam* version of the *Auto da Barca do Inferno* (*Play of the Boat of Hell*) with the chapbook edition, probably dated 1518 and revised by Gil Vicente's own hand.[8] Luís Vicente's editing was also unreliable in terms of the stage directions he introduced, and inaccurate about the dates, places and circumstances of performance. Despite the corrections produced by the best efforts of scholars such as Braamcamp Freire and Vasconcelos, the chronology of the works remains tentative.

---

6 In 1949, I. S. Révah, *Deux 'Autos' de Gil Vicente restitués à leur auteur* (Lisbon: Academia das Ciências de Lisboa, 1949), published his case for the attribution to Gil Vicente of two anonymous plays, *Obra da Geração Humana* and *Auto de Deus Padre e Justiça e Misericórdia*. Not all scholars have accepted this. A further play, *Auto da Festa*, extant in chapbook form but omitted from the *Copilaçam*, was discovered by the Conde de Sabugosa and published in 1906: Conde de Sabugosa, *Auto da Festa. Obra desconhecida com uma explicação prévia* (Lisbon, 1906).

7 Stephen Reckert, *Espírito e Letra de Gil Vicente* (Lisbon: Imprensa Nacional-Casa da Moeda, 1983), pp. 243–54, untangles the complexities of the censors' judgements.

8 Anthony Lappin (ed. and tr.), *Gil Vicente. Three Discovery Plays* (Warminster: Aris & Phillips, 1997) gives both versions.

A preoccupation with genre has been a feature of Vicentine studies from the outset. In his preface to *Don Duardos*, c.1522 (addressed to King João III, and published in the second but not the first edition of the *Copilaçam*), Gil Vicente categorises works composed while in the service of the Dowager Queen as comedies, farces and moralities. For the new play being offered, however, he realised he must 'crowd more sails onto my modest foist', and accordingly would apply the rhetoric and style appropriate to the love story of its elevated protagonists.[9] Therefore, it is in terms of style and tone, not genre, that he embraces change. In the *Copilaçam*, however, the works are divided into five categories: devotional pieces; comedies; tragicomedies; farces; lesser works.[10] The different understandings of these genres, and the suspicion that it was Luís Vicente who imposed them, have caused extensive critical debate. António José Saraiva, for example, found the five categories unsatisfactory and subdivided them into nine.[11] Laurence Keates regrouped the plays according to the function they fulfilled: religious plays, entertainments, satires.[12] Paul Teyssier opts for Gil Vicente's three categories, whilst acknowledging that towards the end of his career, the tripartite division breaks down. He is also suspicious of the tragicomic category, holding it to be an artificial one, and absent from the playwright's vocabulary.[13] However, the Vicentine mixture of serious and comic action, high and low characters, is at least as old as Plautus, whose tragicomedy *Amphitruo* was translated into Spanish in 1515. Also, Gil Vicente was well acquainted with Ferdinand de Rojas's *Celestina*, the third edition of which (1502) bore the title *Tragicomedia de Calisto y Melibea*.[14] He was also entirely aware that the comedy began in turmoil but ended happily. For the modern reader, however, it is not clear where his comedies and farces diverge, nor does it help that Gil Vicente used the term *autos* ('plays') indifferently for farces and devotional works. The moralities, too, have a looser meaning than do their French and English

---

[9] Thomas R. Hart (ed.), *Gil Vicente. Casandra and Don Duardos*, Critical Guides to Spanish Texts, 29 (London: Grant & Cutler, 1981), p. 31.

[10] The lesser works include personal exchanges of poetry with courtiers, occasional pieces such as lyrics on the death of King Manuel and on the acclamation of King João III, a letter to the King written in the aftermath of the 1531 earthquake, a sermon 'preached' to the Dowager Queen in Abrantes, and the comic 'Lament' of the dypsomaniac Maria Parda, in despair at the dearth and dearness of wine in Lisbon.

[11] António José Saraiva, *Gil Vicente e o Fim do Teatro Medieval* [1942], 3rd edn (Lisbon: Livraria Bertrand, 1981), pp. 71–8.

[12] Laurence Keates, *The Court Theatre of Gil Vicente* (Lisbon, 1962), p. 114.

[13] Paul Teyssier, *Gil Vicente – o autor e a obra*, Biblioteca Breve 67 (Lisbon: Instituto de Cultura e Língua Portuguesa, 1982), pp. 42–3.

[14] Of interest to this debate on genre is José I. Suárez's Bakhtinian reading, *The Carnival Stage: Vicentine Comedy within the Serio-Comic Mode* (London and Toronto: Associated University Presses, 1993).

counterparts, often embracing satirical pieces. Understandably, given his Christian faith in redemption and salvation, the one genre missing is tragedy.

Another critical concern has been the lack of unified action, whether real or perceived. Many of the plays are episodic in structure, reflecting the processional nature of proto-theatrical representations, religious and secular, liturgical and courtly, with which Gil Vicente would have been familiar. A fruitful comparison may be with the law court, where witnesses are called, questioned and heard, and then leave the room rather than linger to take part in a generalised discussion. The plays that feature group interaction and dialogue are naturally those with a developed plot, for example, *Auto da Índia*, *A Farsa de Inês Pereira*, *Comédia de Rubena* and *Don Duardos*.

In common with his contemporaries, Gil Vicente wrote for a bilingual court, at which Spanish poets and dramatists were well known and highly regarded. The four Queen Consorts who spanned his literary lifetime were all Spanish. Out of his forty-seven plays and dramatic monologues, fifteen are totally in Portuguese, twelve are totally in Castilian, and the rest are a mixture of both. Within each language there are various registers, such as *sayagués*, the literary version of the Leonese dialect spoken by his shepherds. The speech of Portuguese gypsies, Jews, Moors and Africans is also characterised, and comic mileage is gained from foreign characters speaking their respective languages.

A major element in Vicentine theatre (itself totally in verse) is its lyric poetry. Songs permeate the plays, whether as extracts or in full. Many were pre-existing, but some were composed expressly by him. They develop both the argument of the plays and the psychological characterisation of the personages.[15] Dancing is equally prevalent, to mark entrances and exits, or integrated into the action in the form of rustic dances such as the *chacota* or *folia*, or the courtly *basse-danse* and galliard.[16] In the allegorical fantasy *Frágua d'Amor* (*Forge of Love*), for example, the beating of hammers to forge a succession of characters is enacted to music and song.

In Gil Vicente's time there were no theatres in Portugal. The *autos* were almost all performed on royal premises, whether in chamber or chapel, in Lisbon or wherever the king was residing. It is likely that the royal members of the audience sat on a dais, their ladies-in-waiting perhaps on cushions whilst other spectators stood. A good deal of information about staging and scenery is contained in stage directions or is embedded in the dialogue,

[15] Stephen Reckert, *From the Resende Songbook*, Papers of the Medieval Hispanic Research Seminar 15 (London: Department of Hispanic Studies, Queen Mary and Westfield College, 1998), pp. 86–97, analyses lyrics from plays written before 1516, giving many insights into plot and characterisation.

[16] José Sasportes, *Trajectória da Dança Teatral em Portugal*, Biblioteca Breve 27 (Lisbon: Instituto da Cultura e Língua Portuguesa, 1979), pp. 25–6.

and indicates that Gil Vicente had available to him, at least at some of the locations where his plays were put on, elaborate scenery and sets, a raised stage, and some means of control of lighting, to allow the performance of the numerous scenes which take place at night. For indoor performance he would have used torches or candles, to be dimmed at will; outdoors, curtains could have been positioned to allow or exclude light.

As court playwright, Gil Vicente was obliged to reflect royal policy and power, its overseas enterprises in military, religious or colonising spheres. Where panegyric and propaganda are evident, they are expressed with subtlety. Within the enclosed and competitive world of the palace, where the desire for advancement was not always veiled with courtesy, Gil Vicente's mockery served a function similar to that of court jester, where individuals are named and shamed with impunity. This intimate circle, however, was not a water-tight compartment. In much the same way that the Dowager Queen was a pivotal figure between the reigns of João II and Manuel, Gil Vicente was also an intermediary beyond his ideological positioning between the Middle Ages and the Renaissance. He was a conduit of knowledge, presenting a cross-section of society that Court and courtiers might choose to ignore, whether or not it was meant to constitute a source of amusement. His plays kept in view also the countryside from which many had recently gravitated to Lisbon, left depopulated by the peasantry and undirected by the landowners and gentry. In return, the chapbook editions of his plays bear witness to their wider reception by the populace.

For today's reader, Gil Vicente's plays present difficulties other than linguistic because of their specific allusions to people and events of which we have lost sight. All the texts repay close attention, not the least for their inexhaustible source of information and insight into sixteenth-century Portugal. The following discussion of plays (which makes no pretence at being comprehensive) will be grouped under three broad categories: religious plays, comedies, and occasional plays.

Religious, devotional and morality plays

Gil Vicente's early Nativity works are clearly modelled on the eclogues of the Salamancan poet Juan del Encina.[17] The *Copilaçam* rubrics tell us that Queen Leonor asked for the *Monólogo do Vaqueiro* (*The Herdsman's Mono-logue*, also known as the *Auto da Visitação*, *Play of the Visitation*) to be repeated the following Christmas, but seeing that its subject matter was not appropriate to the occasion, Gil Vicente wrote another play.[18] However, the

---

[17] The influence of Encina, Lucas Fernández and Torres Naharro is traced by Keates, *Court Theatre*, pp. 83–9, and Neil Miller, *O Elemento Pastoril no Teatro de Gil Vicente* (Oporto: Editorial Inova, 1970), pp. 45–67.

[18] *Copilaçam*, pp. 22–3.

Dowager Queen's request was apt. Apart from the combination of secular and biblical in the presentation of gifts to the newborn baby (the shepherds' homely offerings replacing the Three Kings' gold, frankincense and myrrh), there is a clear reference to the Christian topos of Nature responding with excitement to the birth of the Saviour. In the new play, *Auto Pastoril Castelhano* (*Pastoral Play in Spanish*), Gil Vicente introduced the contemplative and somewhat mystical Gil Terrón, a shepherd with a difference: he tires of the games and levity of his worldly fellows; he is tuned to his inner self so that he alone can hear the angels sing. When the shepherds go to the Manger, it is Gil who senses that the child must be feeling cold, and recognises the young maiden as Solomon's beloved, citing from the Song of Songs and the Old Testament prophets. His sudden access of erudition amazes his companions, an erudition that he accepts as the God-given gift of tongues. This opposition between the contemplative and active life is sketched out in the next play, *Auto dos Reis Magos* (*Play of the Wise Men*), with the additional hint of class differences when the shepherds come across the page attending the Three Kings on their journey to Bethlehem.

Gil Vicente's focus on the Nativity and the poverty surrounding the birth of Christ undoubtedly reflected and served Queen Leonor's own religious inspiration, that of the reformed Poor Clares (for whom she founded the Madre de Deus convent in the outskirts of Lisbon in 1509), who interpreted the birth of Christ through the radical nature of the poor manger.[19] With poverty comes humility, a quality in which the shepherdess Cassandra, in *Auto da Sibila Casandra* (*Play of Cassandra the Sybil*), is singularly lacking. In this play, performed at Madre de Deus, she asserts her refusal to marry on the grounds that it is a form of captivity. She rejects the shepherd, Salomão, and cannot be shifted from her stance by the other sibyls and the Old Testament prophets. On the other hand, she rejects the idea of becoming a nun. Her head is turned by her conviction that it is she who will bear the Messiah. Though spiritual enough to receive a divine message, she fails to understand that her presumption disqualifies her from being the Blessed Virgin. Gil Vicente, himself imbued with Franciscan values and a devotee of the Virgin Mary, weaves in here the ethos of the Poor Clares, a combination of mystical awareness, profound humility and obedience to God's will. During the action, Cassandra progresses from resistance to the good advice given by the Old Testament prophets and the sibyls of Classical Antiquity, through her refusal of the truth, towards acceptance of the reality when faced with the Virgin and Child, and finally her joining in worship and hymn singing, urging on the soldiers of Christ. Thus we are to understand the submission of the pagan to

---

[19] Ivo Carneiro de Sousa, *A Rainha D. Leonor (1458–1525): Poder, Misericórdia, Religiosidade e Espiritualidade no Portugal do Renascimento* (Lisbon: Fundação Calouste Gulbenkian–Ministério da Ciência e do Ensino Superior, 2002), pp. 62ff.

Christianity. Two opposing facets of women's lives run through this play: the praise of motherhood (already seen in the *Monólogo*) and the blessedness of the married state; the preference for the single life or, rather, its superiority in the eyes of the nuns who had professed in the Poor Clares.[20] Gil Vicente would return many times to the themes of birth and motherhood, the single versus the married life, the choices and fates of women.

For all their apparent simplicity, the pastoral *autos* contain ambiguity and irony. The two ignorant Castilian shepherds of the *Auto da Fé (Play of Faith)*, who stumble into the Royal chapel during the celebration of Christmas Matins, are amazed at the numbers of priests, and the air of great activity. Such is the ornateness of a cross, that they fail to recognise it as such. It is left to Faith (speaking Portuguese) to enlighten these rustics. However, the last laugh is not on her, nor on the congregation at Matins. We have, in embryo, the dichotomy that Gil Vicente would raise more than once, between the lost simplicity of the early Church and its sheepskin-wearing pastors, and the over-elaborate and empty ritual of his day. Given the ostentation of King Manuel's court and chapel, this broadside from an adept of the *Devotio moderna* (as Gil Vicente most certainly was) indicates not only the respect in which Queen Leonor and those whom she patronised were held, but also a relaxed monarchical attitude to criticism of the contemporary Church. Putting allegory at the service of the Nativity story in the *Auto dos Quatro Tempos (Play of the Four Seasons)*, Gil Vicente brings together angels, the four seasons, Jupiter and the shepherd boy David. This fantastical work, based on a series of monologues by the various characters and personifications, is another illustration of universal homage to the Christ Child.

His talent for sweetening the bitter pill of dogma comes to the fore in the *Auto da Barca do Inferno*, the first of three satires in which the dead face judgement and are sent on their way to Hell, Purgatory or, very rarely, to Heaven. In this evergreen morality, a series of characters traipse to and fro between the ships of Hell and of Heaven, learning from a garrulous devil and a laconic angel why they are condemned to eternal damnation. A nobleman, a usurer, a cobbler, a friar, a bawd, a Jew, a magistrate, an advocate and a hanged thief have all sinned according to the opportunities their station in life or occupation have allowed and have failed to earnestly repent. The only characters to escape damnation are a simpleton, pure in intention if not in speech, and four knights who have died defending the Faith in North Africa.

---

[20] For this reason, an overly secular and feminist reading of the play misrepresents Gil Vicente's intentions. Since Cassandra also rejects the veil, she is not seeking the independence and autonomy that the religious life was able to give. See Jorge A. Osório, 'Solteiras e casadas em Gil Vicente', *Península. Revista de Estudos Ibéricos* 2 (2005), 113–36, for a comprehensive treatment of single and married women in Gil Vicente.

The entirely solemn *Barca da Glória* (*Boat to Heaven*) is distinguished from the *Barca do Inferno* and *Barca do Purgatório* (*Boat to Purgatory*), both of which feature rural characters, not only because all the sinful dead are of the highest rank, secular and religious, but also because they escape damnation. It would be insufficient to read this salvation of the elite as Gil Vicente's kowtowing to his social superiors. What distinguishes these souls is that they are penitent, albeit only at the last minute. At their piteous tears, Christ arrives to bear them off, rather as if he were harrowing Hell, except that He is already risen. Whether they go directly to Heaven or have to pass through Purgatory is not specified.

For his most elevated religious play, the allegorical *Auto da Alma* (*Play of the Soul*), performed for Maundy Thursday, Gil Vicente eschews damnation and punishment as he tracks the path of a Soul along the journey (of life) to an inn (Mother Church), alternately urged on by an angel and delayed by a devil. Eventually drawing up enough strength of will to resist the latter's blandishments, she reaches the refuge of the inn where a sustaining supper (the Instruments of Christ's Passion) awaits her, served by the Doctors of the Church. This beautiful and serene play combines wit, compassion, theology and optimism.

In the late 1520s, this serenity had disappeared. Some of Gil Vicente's severest criticism of the lax clergy and the religious lethargy of their congregations is expressed in the *Auto de Mofina Mendes* (*Play of Mofina Mendes*) and the *Auto da Feira* (*Play of the Fair*), which was probably written in the wake of the Sack of Rome. In the latter play, Rome, personified as a young girl over whom her friends are fighting, can bring nothing to the Christmas exchange-fair that will allow her to acquire peace, truth and faith. Into this picture of religious discord are integrated two farmers, discontented with their respective wives, epitomising the disharmony of the world. The last part of the play features a lively band of country lads and lasses who raise spirits with their flirting chit-chat and exchanges with the Seraphim. From him, they learn of the true purpose of the Fair and its patroness, the Virgin, to whom they sing a beautiful lyric of praise.[21] For his late play, *Romagem dos Agravados* (*Pilgrimage of the Aggrieved*), Gil Vicente again uses the processional structure, and shows a certain fatalism, to present a selection of aggrieved folk coming to terms with their lot. The details of their complaints reveal harsh lives, blows of fate and injustices. Gil Vicente suggests, through the blaming of God voiced by the struggling farmer, João Mortinheira, and the useless advice given by Frei Paço, that the Church is at fault for offering empty rhetoric instead of social action.

---

[21] For a different view, see T. F. Earle, 'O eclipse dos serafins: contactos entre homens e anjos no *Auto da Feira* e no *Auto da Barca do Purgatório*', *Românica* 8 (1999), 109–19.

Comedies and farces

Gil Vicente's first comic success was the tightly-plotted *Auto da Índia*, a treasure-chest of succinct characterisation, drawing on stereotypical figures of farce (the cuckolded husband, the unfaithful wife, the slyboots maidservant, the braggart lover), set against the historical canvas of Tristan da Cunha's voyage to India in 1506, bearing the renowned Afonso de Albuquerque to his governorship. Juggling Portuguese and Castilian lovers with skill while her husband is away on this voyage to get rich – though against a seemingly illogical chronology – the wife is a born survivor. Barely forewarned of her husband's return, she rapidly orders the maid to restore the house to a dreary state with no sign of convivial meals in male company. Both accept at face value the account that each gives of their lives during their separation. Reunited in fact, if not in confidences, the couple dance off, along with the rest of Lisbon's inhabitants, to see the returned fleet, bedecked in bunting.

The farce of the *Velho da Horta* (*The Old Man and the Garden*) is pitiless in its mockery of an old man lusting after a pretty young girl. His cupidity leads to his penury, since he falls into the clutches of a rapacious procuress, Branca Gil. The girl warns him at the outset that his folly will bring his downfall, but he will not be deterred. He even tries to court the maiden in the language of palace poetry, which the courtiers in the audience would recognise as theirs. In part, a victim of love when taken out of its appropriate framework, the old man brings his wife and four children down with him, for they are left penniless.[22] The contrast at the end of the farce between the young girl marrying a fine, upstanding young man who has eyes only for her, and Branca Gil, flogged and exiled for her part in the affair, could not be starker.

Quem Tem Farelos? (translated as *Who Has Bran?*) concerns the wooing of a lively but fatherless girl, Isabel, by an impoverished, guitar-playing, minor nobleman, Aires Rosado. His serenade at her window is interrupted by dogs, cats and cockerels, as well as the insults of Isabel's old mother. Most acutely observed is the argument that ensues between the two women. For the mother, it is important that her daughter looks nice and behaves prettily but she doesn't want this to attract admirers. Isabel furiously points out the inconsistency of presenting an elegant, leisured face to a suitor, whilst having to do the household chores. The gap between the ideal (marriage to money) and the reality (modest domesticity) is echoed by that between a nobleman's appearance and the reality of the feather-brained and improvident Rosado.

Gil Vicente treated courtship and marriage seriously as well as humorously. The *Comédia do Viúvo* (*The Widower's Comedy*), an ostensibly

---

[22] José Augusto Cardoso Bernardes, *Sátira e Lirismo no Teatro de Gil Vicente*, 2 vols (Lisbon: Imprensa Nacional–Casa da Moeda, 2006), vol. I, p. 243.

disunited play about a widower with two marriageable daughters, presents
a situation that many have seen as modelled on Gil Vicente's own. It opens
with the widower lamenting the death of his beloved wife, with whom he
had lived a harmonious existence. A local friar tries to console him, begging
him to accept God's will and to turn his attention to his daughters' needs.
But he only accepts his loss after being visited by the grumpy Compadre,
who envies his bereavement since he is shackled to a difficult, ugly woman,
the antithesis of the widower's partner. His neighbour's diatribe makes the
widower realise that a good marriage, ended prematurely by death, is preferable to long-lasting enmity between husband and wife.

The farcical situation of the impoverished nobleman and the sprightly
daughter at odds with her mother is developed in the anti-romantic *Farsa
de Inês Pereira*. The modestly born and indolent Inês is the fantasist here,
resenting her enforced seclusion and its corollary, sewing. Her mother's
friend, the go-between Lianor Vaz, has found the best solution: a rich and
stupid husband who will give Inês security and freedom, an ideal combination. Through obstinacy or lack of experience, she prefers good looks and
sweet talk from an impecunious squire, who turns tyrant on marriage. With
his fortuitous death – and Gil Vicente puts the knife in this unworthy character by having him die fleeing from a Moorish shepherd in North Africa
– Inês turns to the stupid and complaisant Pero Marques, whom she had
rejected first time around. The last scene shows her riding on his back to a
meeting with a former admirer, now a hermit. Critical opinion has had a field
day debating Gil Vicente's moral intentions in this farce, and the extent to
which Inês is a liberated woman.

Courtship and comedy are combined with patriotism and allegory in the
Farsa chamada Auto da Fama (*Farce called the Play of Fame*), a textbook
illustration of genre anarchy, to use Keates's phrase.[23] Fama, a Portuguese
shepherdess from the Beira region so favoured by Gil Vicente, is courted by
a Frenchman, an Italian and Castilian. The first two are comic characters but
the Castilian is presented seriously (no doubt in deference to the importance
of that country in relation to Portugal). Fama treats her suitors to a history
and geography lesson, turning them down on the grounds that Portuguese
conquests, commerce, military power and defence of Christianity against
Islam, render insufficient anything that they can offer. As she is crowned
with laurel by Faith and Fortitude and borne away in a triumphal car, the
message is made clear: Christian Portugal has achieved superiority over the
Ancient World.[24]

---

[23] Keates, *Court Theatre*, p. 114.

[24] The play was most likely performed in early or late 1510 (Queen Leonor being absent
from Lisbon between March and September), although reference to later historical events
such as the subjugation of Malacca by Afonso de Albuquerque in July 1511 indicates that

Gil Vicente's lyric peak was reached in *Don Duardos*, derived from an episode in the chivalric romance, *Primaleón*. Duardos, an English prince, disguises himself as a gardener in order to gain the disinterested love of Princess Flérida. The action traces the delicate growth of her love for this supposed commoner, counterpoised by Duardos's soliloquies on love uttered alone at night. An image of mature and contented married love is given by the actual gardeners, Julián and Constanza. As a contrast to the main action, a parody of courtly love is supplied by a wild man, Camilote, and his ugly lady, Maimonda. The tragic event in this 'tragicomedia' is Camilote losing his life in a duel with Duardos. If the *Comédia do Viúvo* could be accused of a forced dénouement in the form of Don Gilberto's convenient arrival, *Don Duardos* needs no *deus ex machina* to resolve the progression to mutual love and trust. In its theme and structure, it is an organic whole, where love grows as surely as the trees and flowers in Flérida's garden, a force of Nature that has no time for disparity in rank.

Occasional, festival and allegorical plays

These spectacular entertainments, to mark royal betrothals, births, ceremonial entrances, and so forth, allowed Gil Vicente free reign to his fantasy. They have never proved the most popular texts for analysis, and it is all too easy to relegate them as examples of superficial flattery and propaganda.[25] As with his devotional plays, these draw on the processional and allegorical format of the *momos*. The delightful *Cortes de Júpiter* (*Jupiter's Parliament*) formed part of the magnificent festivities to mark the Infanta Beatriz's departure to join her new husband, the Duke of Savoy. Providence, acting as God's messenger, directs Jupiter to convoke a parliament of the winds, planets and gods, to ensure safe passage on the voyage. The play is famous for conjuring up (most probably in the audience's imagination rather than in reality) the transformation of the courtiers, and inhabitants of Lisbon, into many kinds of sea creatures to accompany the flotilla out of harbour. Equally important is the text's emphasis on hierarchy and power, on Portugal's religious hegemony and maritime domination at a time of nuanced political relations with the Holy Roman Emperor and the King of France.

The *Frágua de Amor* is particularly interesting for its combination of allegory and social comment. Performed to celebrate the mariage of King João III with Catarina of Austria, it begins with a rather laboured allegory of

---

it was reworked for a later performance. Aubrey Bell (ed. and tr.), *Four Plays of Gil Vicente* (Cambridge: Cambridge University Press, 1920), p. xxi.

[25] More recently, however, critical examination has revealed their many-layered references, and the appropriateness with which Gil Vicente used his cultural, literary and iconographic knowledge. The studies by João Nuno Alçada, *Por Ser Cousa Nova em Portugal: oito ensaios vicentinos* (Coimbra: Angelus Novus, 2003), are exemplary in this respect.

the Queen as a castle of Castile being captured by Captain Cupid. In accordance with the spirit of regeneration that the love match will bring to Portugal, a Forge of Love is set up in which a succession of characters are transformed. If the crooked figure of Justice is a predictable candidate, the most touching individual is a black African from Guinea. He enters the forge with the desire to emerge white. This he does, but his speech remains that of a black African. Comedy moves into pathos as Gil Vicente sketches the isolation and dismay of a man with a split racial identity, rejected by both white and black women.

Gil Vicente was very far from being the only Portuguese dramatist of the sixteenth century to put a black man on stage. They figure in the work of other playwrights, and the traffic was not all one way, because it is very likely that one writer of religious *autos* had an African mother. He was Afonso Álvares, the author of four plays commissioned by the Augustinian canons of the church of St Vincent in Lisbon. His work, and the *autos* of many other popular dramatists of the sixteenth century, are only now beginning to appear in modern editions. Their study and appreciation will be a task for future generations of scholars.

When it comes to the classically learned drama of the Renaissance period, one writer, and indeed one play – António Ferreira's *Castro* – dominate all others. Yet Ferreira himself wrote two comedies with classically inspired plots, and so did Sá de Miranda a generation earlier. When we add to these the experiments in humanistic comedy of Jorge Ferreira de Vasconcelos we have another body of work which remains for the most part hardly known. The best of Gil Vicente's *autos* and the *Castro* are masterpieces which can hold their own against anything in the European drama of the first fifty or so years of the sixteenth century, and yet they represent only a small fraction of what was produced in that period in Portugal.

António Ferreira, *Castro* (T. F. Earle)

Castro and *Os Lusíadas* are the two greatest achievements of Portuguese classicism. Ferreira and Camões proved that the Portuguese language could be used for the literary genres regarded as the most noble and the most difficult, tragedy and epic. Unlike *Os Lusíadas* (many Portuguese composed epics besides Camões), *Castro* seems to be unique in sixteenth-century Portugal. It owes nothing to Gil Vicente and it had no immediate successors. It belongs to a brief period in the 1550s in which a fully developed classical aesthetic could blend with a Catholic world view to produce a play of the highest literary and human quality. That blending will be the theme of this brief account.

Ferreira was probably aware of contemporary Italian tragedy, and he certainly had before him the Roman tragedies of Seneca. There were neo-Latin models for him to follow also, by his friend Diogo de Teive and, perhaps, by the Scot, George Buchanan.[26] The conventions and the structure of Ferreira's tragedy derive from these sources. These are: the lack of action, the use of *tiradas*, long and highly rhetorical soliloquies (sometimes delivered in the presence of a confidant); sticomythia, or the exchange of metrically parallel units of dialogue; and finally, the presence of a chorus. The chorus intervenes in the dialogue, as the friends of the heroine, Inês de Castro, and after each of Acts I to IV comments on what has just taken place, in an ode. Ferreira uses the two-part structure of these odes to emphasise the ambiguities latent in the play's subject matter.

The play's structure is also classical. It concerns an event which had taken place in the mid-fourteenth century in Portugal, the judicial murder of a young woman, Inês, the lover of the heir to the throne, Pedro, on the grounds that she posed a threat to the security of the state. Some of Seneca's plays about the events following the fall of Troy have a similar pattern.[27] Ferreira did not, however, know Aristotle's *Poetics*, nor was he aware of the three unities, a convention which only began to operate in the seventeenth century.

Ferreira approached this material with the sensibility of a sixteenth-century Catholic. One of the features of classical, and of all tragedy is a sense of fate. Inês is fated to die, as the the king, Pedro's father, more than once tells her. But Seneca's pagan fate, transcendent and determining, is impossible in a Catholic context, in which human free will is paramount. The king could and should pardon Inês, who is innocent of any crime, and in the climactic Act IV he does so, only to allow himself to be over-ruled by his councillors afterwards. The king tries to absolve himself of responsibility, but cannot. The fate of which he speaks is not the pagan *fatum* but his own weakness and his failure to control his son. It is also his son's disobedience – a trait of the royal family, as the Chorus makes plain (ll. 872–903) – so the attribution of ultimate responsibility in this surprisingly modern play is not easy.

The *Castro* is also a political play, and its message is a clear one. It is that an immoral act – the execution of an innocent woman – cannot have favourable political consequences. Portugal is not more stable after Inês's death, as the king's councillors had predicted, but less, and in Act V, Pedro announces a civil war against his father. But though the message, ultimately deriving from Cicero's *De Officiis*, is clear, putting it into practice is not easy. One might ask why the councillors persist in advising the king that the only solution is the death of Inês. They are not wicked, and are willing to take

---

[26] George Buchanan, *Tragedies*, ed. and tr. Peter Sharratt and P. G. Walsh (Edinburgh: Scottish Academic Press, 1983); Diogo de Teive, *Ioannes Princeps*, ed. and tr. into Portuguese by Nair Castro Soares (Lisbon: Fundação Calouste Gulbenkian, 1977).

[27] Seneca, *Four Tragedies and Octavia*, translated by E. F. Watling (Harmondsworth: Penguin: 1966), especially *Troades* (*The Trojan Women*).

personal responsibility for their actions (ll. 1345–9). It is the political situation following Pedro's refusal in Act I to abandon Inês that makes it impossible for them to give any other advice. They reason that if Pedro cannot be persuaded to obey his father voluntarily then force is the only solution. Once again Ferreira shows how events seem to lead inevitably to tragedy, but could nevertheless have been different if the right human decisions had been made.

Inês's surname gives the tragedy its title, and she is its heroine. She is the only character to develop on stage, from the innocent girl of Act I, who allows her man, Pedro, to think for her (ll. 158–75), to her temporary triumph in Act IV, when she dismisses the councillors' arguments and persuades the king to pardon her. This is a moment of true empowerment, as the king is forced to admit:

> ... Ó mulher forte!
> Venceste-me, abrandaste-me. Eu te deixo.
> Vive, enquanto Deus quer. (ll. 1421–3)
>
> (O strong woman, you have conquered and tamed me. I shall leave you. Live, while God is willing.)

Inês is powerful because she knows that she is innocent of any crime and is faced by a human judge. Her growth in stature as the play progresses is an indication of Ferreira's Renaissance belief in human perfectibility. Yet in the end the king, for the reasons we have seen, is not strong enough to bear the burden.

Ultimately Inês perishes, and Portugal is plunged into chaos. Ferreira leaves the audience in no doubt about what should have happened, but is much less certain whether what is desirable is possible, given the vagaries of human nature, and the multiple pressures that those in positions of responsibility have to bear. The political uncertainties of the tragedy are the product of the unsettled period when Portugal was governed by a regency during the minority of King Sebastião. *Castro* is a tragedy. But its perfection of structure, and consistently beautiful language are also a sign of Ferreira's self-assurance, his confidence that the Portuguese language and Portuguese subject-matter can be used to produce work of the highest quality.

Texts and translations

Gil Vicente
As obras de Gil Vicente, ed. José Camões, 5 vols (Lisbon: Imprensa Nacional-Casa da Moeda, 2002)
Gil Vicente, *Copilaçam de Todalas Obras de Gil Vicente* [1562], ed. Maria Leonor Carvalhão Buescu, 2 vols (Lisbon: Imprensa Nacional-Casa da Moeda, 1983)

Gil Vicente. Farces and Festival Plays, ed. Thomas R. Hart, 2nd edn (Eugene: University of Oregon Press, 2001)

For other translations of Gil Vicente's plays, see chapter 16.

António Ferreira
António Ferreira, *Poemas Lusitanos*, ed. T. F. Earle (Lisbon: Fundação Calouste Gulbenkian, 2008) contains an edition of *Castro* with notes. There is a translation: *Castro*, tr. John Martyn (Coimbra: Universidade, 1987).

Modern editions of plays by other sixteenth-century dramatists

Álvares, Afonso, *Obras*, ed. José Camões (Lisbon: Imprensa Nacional–Casa da Moeda, 2006)
Camões, Luís de, *Teatro Completo*, ed. Vanda Anastácio (Oporto: Caixotim, 2005)
Dias, Baltasar, *Autos, romances e trovas*, ed. Alberto Gomes Figueira (Lisbon: Imprensa Naciona–Casa da Moeda, 1985)
Miranda, Francisco de Sá de, *Comédias*, ed. José Camões and T. F. Earle (Lisbon: Imprensa Naciona–Casa da Moeda, forthcoming)
Prestes, António, *Autos*, ed. José Camões (Lisbon: Imprensa Nacional-Casa da Moeda, 2008)
Teatro Português do Século XVI (5 anonymous plays), ed. José Camões (Lisbon: Imprensa Naciona–Casa da Moeda, 2007)

Further reading

Garay, René P., *Gil Vicente and the Development of the Comedia*, North Carolina Studies in the Romance Languages and Literatures 232 (Chapel Hill: University of North Carolina, 1988)
Parker, Jack H., *Gil Vicente*, Twayne's World Authors Series 29 (New York: Twayne, 1967)
Stathatos, Constantine C., *A Gil Vicente Bibliography (1995–2000)*, Teatro del Siglo de Oro, Bibliografías y Catálogos 36 (Kassel: Reichenberger, 2001)
——, *A Gil Vicente Bibliography (2000–2005)*, Teatro del Siglo de Oro, Bibliografías y Catálogos 45 (Kassel: Reichenberger, 2007)

5

The Lusiads and the Literature of Portuguese Overseas Expansion

CLIVE WILLIS

The new age of the Renaissance was characterised by three important factors: the systematisation of existing Western learning and aesthetics, the emergence of a canon of literary doctrine and the growing recognition of Europe's coming role in a wider world. Linked to these was the demand, which in the sixteenth century grew to a noisy clamour, that the great realities of man's achievements should be immortalised in verse. It is within this vast context that we shall examine the contribution of Luís Vaz de Camões (1524–80) in *Os Lusíadas* (*The Lusiads*, i.e., the Portuguese). This late-Renaissance or Mannerist epic of 1572 celebrates Vasco da Gama's discovery of the sea-route to India in 1498, itself one of the major events of the new age, especially in that it achieved what Columbus had failed to do, namely to reach the Orient by sea. That contribution is particularly relevant under four headings: (i) literary theory, (ii) Neoplatonism, (iii) the humanism of reform, and (iv) political thought.

The literary theory of the fifteenth and sixteenth centuries was dominated by a conflation of the precepts of Aristotle's *Poetics* and Horace's *Ars poetica* (*The Art of Poetry*), though the former was not truly understood till the seventeenth century, and though its influence on the composition of *Os Lusíadas* may legitimately be doubted. There were, however, two significant modifications: the first was a firmly stated preference for epic poetry over tragedy; the second was a preference for the modalities of Virgil's *Aeneid* over those of Homeric epic. The primordial expression of this consensus came from the pen of an Italian cleric, Girolamo Vida, in his *De arte poetica* (1527, *The Art of Poetry*). We have no idea whether Camões had resort to this manual, but, if he had not, then the end-product in *Os Lusíadas* is a remarkable coincidence. Certainly, the overall structure of the work and the nature and sequence of the episodes are closely modelled on the recommended *Aeneid*, with flashback narrations of Portuguese history corresponding to Virgil's account of the Trojan War. Just as Aeneas relates those events to Dido in Carthage, so, in Cantos III and IV, Gama recounts his nation's past to the friendly Sheikh of Malindi in East Africa.

As Vida prescribes, therefore, Camões opens his epic with a Proposition: 'I sing of the renowned courage of the Portuguese' (I. 3. 5).[1] To this he adds an Invocation of the Muses, in his case the Nymphs of the Tagus. Moreover, as Vida recommends, he regularly re-invokes them, and this device signals at various stages in the epos that he has carried out the appropriate research. Furthermore, Camões was well aware of the need for the Platonic 'divine fury' and entreats the Muses to give him 'a grand, resounding fury' (I. 5. 1).

After the Invocation Camões supplied a Dedication to his patron, King Sebastião, though this was optional and not stipulated by the theorists. In his Dedication Camões makes his first reference to Vasco da Gama, mentioning him by name. Vida had insisted that the hero should *not* be named at the outset, that his identity should grow obvious by allusion. But Camões at this stage merely embeds Gama's name in a list of other past worthies who generally and collectively illustrate what the poet means by the 'renowned courage of the Portuguese'; he has not yet turned to revealing *who* is to be the particular representative of that concept (I. 12–13). Indeed, it is not till stanza 44 of Canto I that Gama's name is individualised as the hero most representative thereof.

As to the expression of moral maxims, the poeticists differed. Aristotle's celebrated catharsis was essentially aesthetic, whereas for Plato poetry was solely justifiable when morally edifying. Horace, for his part, insisted that poetry was at its most effective when combining *both* the aesthetic *and* the moral principles, emphasising, in the second poem of the first book of his *Epistles*, Homer's value as a moral teacher. Vida recommended that the poet should slip maxims of his own into the fabric of his epic, and this Camões does, particularly in the closing strophes of his cantos.

On the resort to the 'marvellous' and 'fictions', Aristotle, Horace and Vida were united. Verisimilitude and truth had to be preserved; nothing must assault the reader's credulity or affront his imagination; if anything appeared to take place by divine agency, it must also be susceptible to a natural interpretation; on no account must the irrational or the absurd govern the action.

On that point Ludovico Ariosto's Italian epic *Orlando furioso* (1516) was to be faulted, and Camões adroitly dispatches its 'fantastic' episodes in the eleventh stanza of Canto I (though he was probably more influenced than he would care to admit by Ariosto's varied action). Indeed, in *Os Lusíadas* timely interventions by Venus or Mercury or sea nymphs are but the poet's transcript of the propitious elements, usually countering the stormy efforts of Bacchus to thwart the progress of Gama and his mariners. These incidents

---

[1]   All translations are original. References to the text will indicate canto, stanza and line.

receive their natural parallels in the poet's sources in the chronicles of João
de Barros and Fernão Lopes de Castanheda. Bacchus, indeed, plays a role
similar to that of Juno in the *Aeneid*. At first sight that role seems rather odd:
Bacchus was the father and close companion of the god Lusus, who had given
his name to the Roman province of Lusitania (essentially Portugal) and to
the sons of Lusus, the 'Lusiads', the Portuguese. Twice Camões recognises
this point (I. 39 and III. 21). The family rift is explained by the fact that in
Greco-Roman mythology Bacchus had supposedly grown up in the hills and
vineyards of western India and there had founded the legendary city of Nysa
(I. 31; VII. 52). Consequently, the landfall of Gama and his mariners at Calicut
on the Malabar coast of western India was grimly to be prevented. Bacchus
thus becomes an allegory for Camões's notion of Oriental and particularly
Muslim guile, on occasions disguising himself as some kind of holy man.
To this is added a deft suggestion of a more diabolical and Satanic role.
When Mercury appears to Gama in a dream, Gama's reaction on waking is to
conclude that he has been warned by an angel against an ambush (II. 61–5).
That trap had been earlier prepared by Bacchus by deceiving two convict
mariners who had been sent ashore at the Muslim-ruled island of Mombasa:
there they had come upon Bacchus who had disguised himself as a Christian
priest worshipping at an altar, thus leading them to believe that Mombasa
offered a safe haven (II. 10–12). Here Camões intrigues us with the closing
line 'the false God worships the true one' (II. 12. 8).

Bacchus had failed with his arguments at the Council of the Gods on
Mount Olympus in Canto I (20–41) and had gone on to suffer setbacks at
the Muslim-ruled islands of Mozambique, Kilwa and Mombasa. In Canto VI,
therefore, he descends into the realms of Neptune, turning the aquatic gods
and Aeolus the god of the winds against the mariners. He is, however, once
more foiled by Venus and her nymphs as they scurry to respond to Gama's
prayers for rescue by Divine Providence. Here, however, there is poetic
licence, for the tempest in question, according to the chroniclers, took place
in the Atlantic and not the Indian Ocean. Finally, in Canto VIII, Bacchus,
again in the guise of a holy man, seeks to thwart Gama's trading objectives
in Calicut but is countered by Gama's growing astuteness, as the latter shows
that he now no longer needs divine intercession.

The episode of the giant Adamastor (V. 37–60) – itself an inspired on-graft
to Greco-Roman mythology – is an allegory of the ferocious seas as the
mariners round the Cape of Good Hope. The role of Adamastor was doubt-
less suggested by that of the Homeric and Virgilian giant Polyphemus, the
Cyclops. The foregoing use of the pagan 'marvellous' or 'fictions' was by
no means out of place in a typically Renaissance work. However, the French
critic Voltaire, with his eighteenth-century neoclassical taste, criticised the
episode of the Isle of Love in Canto IX in that it was to him absurd and did
not tally with the precept of natural explanation. This Neoplatonic episode,

however, is an allegory of Reward and Fame (so cherished by Renaissance man), a poetic and rhetorical statement of historical reality, and was fully consonant with Renaissance literary and aesthetic values. In many other regards too, in elaborate diction, in epic similes and epic epithets, in historical flashbacks and rhetorical flourishes, Camões's poem amply complied with Renaissance literary theory.

The current of speculative humanism had survived from antiquity and by the early sixteenth century had developed into the Neoplatonic theories of the celebrated Florentine school led by Marsilio Ficino. To these Camões was no stranger, as his lyric poetry repeatedly reveals. He was attracted, like so many Renaissance figures, by the concepts of the soul's reminiscence of Heaven, of its imprisonment in the body and of its final swansong when death brings release and reunion with the Absolute. Moreover, the soul in life, yearning to recapture the divine and the perfect, sought it in love, particularly via the ascending scale or ladder of love, as outlined by Diotima in Plato's *Symposium*. Such a scale, for the Neoplatonists, involved physical love, spiritual love, love of country, and, via these, the love of and for the Godhead: in theological terms the receipt of Divine Grace.

These various rungs, 'amor baxo', lowly, physical love, as in the case of Adamastor; spiritual 'amor puro', pure love, as with Inês de Castro (III. 118–35); selfless 'amor da pátria', love of country, as with Gama's mariners, are all amply charted in *Os Lusíadas*. All converge and are transfigured in the episode of the Isle of Love that dominates Canto IX, an episode itself stage-managed by a Renaissance Venus worthy of the brush of a Botticelli or a Raphael. Indeed, Botticelli's *Birth of Venus* and his *Spring* – both of which have analogues in the Isle of Love – were Neoplatonic compositions, consciously painted on the basis of Ficino's prescriptions. The entire episode was itself conceived as a spur to the youthful King Sebastião to show his own patriotism by smiting the Infidel in Morocco.

Cultured Renaissance man was a great syncretist: that is, he saw the potential relationship, at different levels of interpretation, between religious, philosophical, and mythological systems and their utility, in an interchangeable way, in the world of the creative arts:

(i)   direct *religious* presentation of a proposition could mean the introduction of the Holy Trinity, the Virgin and angels;

(ii) a *philosophical* presentation could involve an incursion into the Platonic world of the Ideas, those forms (like Absolute Beauty, Absolute Truth, Absolute Love) which were emanations of the Creator or First Cause or supreme Archetype; and

(iii) a *poetical* presentation could introduce the world of the mythological deities and nymphs, presided over by Jupiter.

This interchangeability of systems is fundamental to a full comprehension

of Renaissance art and literature. It was in this spirit that Camões composed
the Isle of Love episode. Gama's mariners had completed their task and
found the sea-route to India – now came their reward. At the lowest level
they are sailors going ashore in search of the 'amor baxo' of the ladies of
some oriental port; such is the *natural* interpretation. But we also have a
supernatural, mythical level – Venus has arranged that Tethys and her sea
nymphs, whom Camões calls 'deusas', goddesses, shall entertain and mate
with the mariners in 'amor puro'; each mariner thereby receives allegorically
the accolade of Reward and Fame. In a later passage Camões uses the expression 'esposas', spouses, in respect of the nymphs at the subsequent banquet,
in order to indicate the immortality earned by the mariners; at later stages
too, he indicates, through Tethys, that the nymphs are 'secondary causes'
('segundas causas'; X. 85. 1–2); he sets them amid a world orchestrated by
a supreme 'Arquetipo', an archetype (X. 79. 2), the very term exercised by
Ficino (and first coined by the Jewish scholar Philo, the first-century Neoplatonist). Thus, we have four levels:

(i)   sailors seeking out whores;
(ii)   stalwart mariners being rewarded with fame (IX. 89–92) by marriage
       to marine goddesses (their 'esposas', IX. 84. 5) in an erotic utopia;
(iii) noble seekers after truth gaining entry to the world of the Absolute
       Ideas; and
(iv)   righteous vassals of a Christian monarch achieving immortality and
       Divine Grace through their pursuit of 'amor da pátria'.

The separate current of the humanism of reform was neither speculative
nor hypothetical, but down-to-earth and pragmatic. We find it in the classical
scholarship of such Renaissance figures as Erasmus of Rotterdam or Ariosto.
Learning had to be harnessed to effect the regeneration of society and of the
individual. With roots both in classical antiquity and in the Middle Ages, it
was a reforming and essentially Christian adaptation of humane studies, its
more extreme developments culminating in the Reformation and the partial
dismemberment of the Roman Church.

Primary objects of this critical zeal were clerical abuses, warfare and greed.
Prominent examples of its literary expression were the maxims contained
in the *Orlando furioso*, the satire found in so much of the theatre of Gil
Vicente, or the moral exhortations embodied in Erasmus's *Adagia*. Erasmi-
anism indeed had considerable vogue in Portugal, firstly at the Royal Court in
the mid-1530s, and secondly at the University of Coimbra in the late 1540s,
before finally being crushed by the newly formed Jesuits and the clamp-down
imposed by the Counter-Reformation.

None of this was foreign to Camões: although it would be over-zealous
to describe him as an Erasmist, he was certainly heir to similar traditions.
This is nowhere better seen than in his prolonged attack, at the opening of

Canto VII, on the internecine strife and lax moral standards of the European states and on what he perceived as the dubious credentials of the Protestant Reformation. Subject as he was to ecclesiastical censorship, Camões nevertheless succeeded in hinting that the Papacy's lack of humility had earned due nemesis in the 1527 Sack of Rome by the soldiers of Charles V (III. 15). With only the thinnest of veils he uses stanzas in Cantos VIII and IX to lambast the greed of the clergy for earthly wealth and power and to criticise their abuse of that power when won. Official censorship was too stupid to notice this. Moreover, in what he concedes is 'dangerous material' ('matéria perigosa') in Canto X. 120. 1, it is argued by some that he even launches, without naming them, into an attack on those Jesuits (the two Câmara brothers) who held sway over the mind of King Sebastião. Common to his lyrics, his theatre and his epic poem are frequent warnings and exhortations on the duties of both kings and their ministers. Their shortcomings, along with those of the feudal nobility, he regularly condemned, in harmony with so many writers of the fifteenth and sixteenth centuries.

At many points in his lyrics and in his epic Camões takes a pessimistic stance in respect of the wretchedness of the human condition, a common classical, medieval and Renaissance topos. He shows concern particularly for the poor and the lowly, but his pessimism is not one of defeatist acceptance. Rather, he shows a practical concern for the regeneration of society by urging those who seek fame to reverse the trend: 'in peacetime grant just and firm laws and prevent the mighty from gaining what belongs to the poor' (IX. 94. 1–2). Conversely, at the close of Canto VII he rejects from the hall of fame any who use high office to 'strip and rob the poor' and urges that 'the worker be paid for his toil' (VII. 85. 8; 86. 4).

Many if not all of these observations by Camões on contemporary society were classical and/or medieval commonplaces of the kind which knew a remarkable vogue in the sixteenth century; yet many of the maxims of such writers as Erasmus, Ariosto and Camões seem to us today to be trite. But to the reading public, which had naturally and recently increased since the invention of typography, they were of striking novelty and reassurance.

One particular crescendo of demand from this brand of humanism was for the outlawing or limitation of war. The list of protesting voices is formidable: Ariosto, Gil Vicente, the Spanish humanists Vives and Valdés, the French scholars Montaigne and Rabelais, Sir Thomas More, Erasmus and Luther, to name only the most prominent. Some of these, of whom Camões was one, rejected war but made exceptions for Holy War and defensive war. Camões's revulsion at war is evident from some of his longer autobiographical lyrics, but nowhere more than from numerous battle passages in Os Lusíadas, in flashback narrations of national history, where the hideous spectacle of gore and dismemberment is so starkly presented. Although Camões allows himself to glorify acts of individual heroism, his true feelings are evident from stanza

44 of Canto IV in his account of the Battle of Aljubarrota. Here warfare is cursed and reviled, as is the very greed, bent on seizing the property of others, that exposes wretched soldiers to the torments of Hell and deprives so many hapless mothers and wives of their sons and husbands.

The only aggressive war he will countenance, he says, is Holy War waged to promote and spread Christianity (IV. 48). Typical of this was the Christian victory over Muslim forces at the Battle of the River Salado (1340), which Camões celebrates with unedifying exultation at the carnage inflicted on the forces of Islam (III. 115–17). Almost paradoxically, Camões stands alongside the near-pacifist Erasmus and the bellicose Florentine Machiavelli in a related matter, for these three were the sixteenth century's most vigorous champions of Europe's need to develop a collective consciousness. This leads us to consider Camões within the context of Renaissance political thought.

That sixteenth-century Portugal was in no sense on the periphery of political debate is evident from the decision of three prominent political thinkers to spend lengthy sojourns on Portuguese soil. These were the Scotsman George Buchanan and the major Spanish theorists Luis de Molina and Francisco Suárez, both of whom held university chairs in Portugal.

Apart from the question of warfare, the Renaissance theorists concerned themselves with five main issues:

(i)   the source of the sovereign's power to rule;
(ii)   the grounds for disobedience and rebellion against the sovereign;
(iii) the *jus gentium*, the 'Law of Nations' (international law);
(iv)   the question of overseas empire; and
(v)   the relations between Church and State.

This last item, a medieval chestnut dating from the early struggles of the Papacy with the Holy Roman Emperor, was largely ignored by Camões. Its only occurrences we have already noted: his disapproval of the Jesuits' temporal influence on King Sebastião and his oblique comment on the Sack of Rome in 1527 by the soldiers of the Emperor Charles V. In the log-jam of Renaissance opinions on the sources of kingly power we find absolutists, pragmatists, and between them a variety of moderates. The position of Camões was essentially conservative, in that, as sundry locations in *Os Lusíadas* show, he considered that the monarch ruled by divine ordinance ('ordenação dos céus divina', IV. 3. 1) and that the community's role was to recognise and confirm the sovereign's power. Not only did kings have a divine mandate, but the Portuguese kings also had a divine mission, namely to encircle and crush the Infidel. This mission, which Camões describes as a divinely inspired intention ('inclinação divina', X. 155. 8), is lent support in his epic by the concoction of the prophetic vision of King Manuel the Fortunate in respect of his oriental empire (IV. 66–75) and in the grandiloquent flattery of King Sebastião as though he were some divine agent par excel-lence, sent to strike terror into Muslim hearts and win for God vast regions of the earth (I. 6. 5–8).

Though Camões held kings to be God's own vice-gerents on earth, Camões could also conceive of extreme circumstances in which a monarch might be deposed. He was not, therefore, a total absolutist. If only on a consequential basis, he approved of the deposition of Sancho II: his proud countrymen, accustomed to kings who were sovereign in all things, would neither obey nor tolerate a monarch who was not a paragon of excellence (III. 93. 5–8). This is obvious hyperbole. But Camões by his very epithets clearly considered Sancho to be a weak sovereign whose feeble policy could destroy the realm. In urging deposition in such cases Camões anticipated the prominent theories of Francisco Suárez.

The *jus gentium*, the Law of Nations, a major topic for many Renaissance political theorists, was an embryonic universal declaration of human rights and looked forward to the political philosophies of Locke and Rousseau. Certain of its aspects, such as the right to sell, barter and trade, the right of peaceful settlement in other countries and the principle of the safe-conduct of envoys, are implicit in Camões's thinking, as can be seen from the very subject-matter of the basic narrative of his epic, especially in Cantos VII–IX. On other matters, such as the right to private property and the equitability of law, his political thinking is quite liberal.

In regard to private property we have noted his championing of the cause of the poor, their right to enjoy the fruits of their labours and to be protected from unjust taxation. Moreover, equality before the law was of similar importance for him, as is plain from his complaint that 'Laws in favour of the King are established while those in favour of the people simply perish' (IX. 28. 7–8).

The demands of the Gospel and the alleged lack of regard for a *jus gentium* throughout the world was for Camões the justification for the spread of 'faith and empire'. The Heathen to him was usually badly governed and abused. What better justification of Portugal's 'civilising mission'? he argued. This uncomfortable doctrine took until the Portuguese Revolution of 1974 to be abandoned. But doubts about the imperial principle and the practice of slavery could never really be expected to have troubled Camões's Renaissance mind.

Certainly, Camões was well aware that certain major figures in Portugal preferred to restrict the campaign to Morocco, as he reveals in the closing eleven stanzas of Canto IV. In an effort to be even-handed he introduces a symbolic, Cassandra-like figure in the Old Man of Restelo (a Lisbon suburb, close to Gama's point of embarkation at Belém). This venerable figure had warned those about to weigh anchor against the folly of questing for global outreach when the Infidel lay so close at hand in northern Africa: if fame and glory were to be sought, they ought to be found by crushing Islam in

Morocco. This prominent view had already been expressed by Gil Vicente in the *Auto da Barca do Inferno*, the *Exortação da Guerra* and the *Auto da Índia*.[2] Many nobles demurred at financing fleets to be sent to the Orient, and the abandonment by King João III, Sebastião's immediate predecessor, of four of Portugal's eight Moroccan fortresses was vehemently deplored. Camões, it would seem, supported both the imperial adventure and the frontal attack in Morocco.

Rather, for Camões, the unattractive aspect of the imperial enterprise consisted in the corruption and unscrupulous ambition of government officialdom, in the greed of merchants, and in the ruthless commercial racket that the spice trade became in the dog-eat-dog world of Goa and Malacca (now Melaka), a world he himself came to know so well in the years 1553–68. These aspects he hastened to condemn in his last Canto and in his celebrated letter from Goa. Camões's political thought and programme ran as follows: Portugal's divinely ordained monarchy, once it had been confirmed by the people, was meet to be obeyed and to be deposed only in extreme circumstances; it was to be loved and feared, governing with justice and liberality, taking the advice of mature counsellors, tempering its absolutism with a respect for law and liberal principles; it was enjoined to reward the selfless and dedicated servant, to suppress corruption, selfish ambition and greed, to reject all those who (like Machiavelli) subordinated ethics to 'politics'; it was summoned to lead a glorious crusade against the Infidel and the Heathen and to do so on behalf of Europe and with the implicit assistance of Spain. But Philip II of Spain temporised, Sebastião hot-headedly went ahead alone, with insufficient support and insufficient preparation, and all Camões's hopes foundered in the Battle of Alcácer-Quibir in Morocco in 1578.

What then must be our conclusion? Was the work of Camões, in particular *Os Lusíadas*, the very epitome of the Renaissance? That depends...

In one respect, his humanism is slightly disappointing. An essential aspect of humanism was its international brotherhood, as Erasmus and Damião de Góis so evidently saw. Yet the parochial and narrow approach of Camões is clear from the fact that the enterprise of Europe's discovery of the sea-routes of the world is represented, for the most part, as a religious crusade against the Infidel, despite his recognition of the commercial venture that it largely became. He lacked the greater tolerance of Montaigne and, unlike, say, his fellow-countrymen and contemporaries in the Orient, Fernão Mendes Pinto or Gaspar Correia, rarely seems to have seen anything of human interest in the resultant juxtaposition of different cultures: just occasionally it entered his head that Portugal or Europe might have something to learn from the East, from Otherness. But, usually, Camões was too busy flag-waving and

[2]   See the discussion of these plays in chapter 4.

moralising to be aware of the real significance of the encounter with Africa and the Orient. Yet perhaps Camões ought to be excused this one lapse. In the twenty-first century Western thinking is becoming less inwardly eurocentric. Camões may surely be forgiven for not foreseeing the Afro-Asian potential, writing, as he was, little more than half a century after Gama's initial landfall.

There remains one final qualification. Insofar as the Renaissance was not homogeneous, it cannot, truly speaking, be epitomised in its entirety. It produced the Neoplatonist Ficino but also the neo-Aristotelian Pomponazzi, Savonarola but also Rabelais, Pope Leo X but also Erasmus. No age of mankind's history is wanting in such contradictions. No work of art or literature can epitomise the spirit of an age, if it is felt that an epitome must also be a catalogue. On the other hand, it *is* possible for creative work to capture and reflect the exuberance of a period of human history, and this, at the very least, is what *Os Lusíadas* accomplishes with reference to the Renaissance, in common with other works, like Michelangelo's *Last Judgement* or Rabelais's five books.

However, Camões enjoyed a far greater wealth of experience of life and of the world at large than such giants as Michelangelo or Rabelais, experience that would qualify him more fully than most to present a universal theme and to sing the glories of the civilisation that produced him. Scholar, lover, minor courtier, *demi-monde* swashbuckler, disfigured soldier, jailbird, exile, shipwrecked mariner, colonial administrator, recurrent pauper, playwright and versatile poet, his biography alone cannot fail to fascinate and not merely on account of its unsolved mysteries. Nevertheless, and in full accord with the Renaissance cult of patriotism, for all the universality of his learning and of his experience, of his treatment and of his appeal, his theme in *Os Lusíadas* remains stubbornly, fundamentally, patriotically Portuguese. Epic of the Renaissance *Os Lusíadas* may well be, yet first and foremost it is the paean, the national panegyric of the long historical pageant of the stalwart Portuguese of the pre-Philippine era.

Gaspar Correia's *Lendas da Índia* (*Tales of India*), not published until the middle of the nineteenth century, holds a prominent position among the more candid literature devoted to Portugal's overseas adventure, but pride of place among such works belongs to the *Peregrinação* (1614, translated as *Peregrination*) by Fernão Mendes Pinto (1510?–83). Written for his children, this highly successful posthumous work purports to record its author's experiences in the East, where he spent the years 1537 to 1558. It bears the extraordinary claim that he was shipwrecked five times, taken captive thirteen times and sold as a slave sixteen times while, nevertheless, making his fortune. Pinto made repeated journeys from the thriving Portuguese outposts of Goa and Malacca, sailing especially to China, Japan and adjacent lands, and was regularly involved in acts of derring-do. Though no great stylist, he spins an enthralling yarn. There are, however, considerable problems concerning the veracity of certain elements in his story: commentators urge that much was invented, embellished or second-hand. Certainly the intense detail was neither memorisable nor lastingly noted down by one who often lost everything, even his clothes. Moreover, Pinto's dating of some events can be challenged, as also can the sequence of events. Yet modern research has revealed that more of Pinto's narrative is true than once was thought.

Not infrequently the tone of the *Peregrination* is that of a picaresque novel, with Pinto cast in the role of anti-hero, a hardbitten mercenary rather than an honest merchant. He even reports his involvement, along with other Portuguese, in acts of piracy and vicious brutality against harmless Orientals. Recollection of his misdeeds and those of his companions fills Pinto with dismay at the squalid morality of so many Portuguese undertakings in the East and leads him to draw unfavourable comparisons between Western civilisation and morals and those of Japan and China. The latter country emerges as a virtual utopia with many cultural characteristics that Pinto finds superior to those of the West.

It would be inaccurate to describe this work simply as a satire; rather it bears a powerful moral content. Particularly noteworthy is the outburst of a thirteen-year-old Chinese boy in Chapter 55. His father had lost his life and all his possessions at the hands of the Portuguese. The boy contrasts their greed and outrageous behaviour with their belief in God, for they would certainly receive the punishment of God's divine justice: 'blind wretches', they were shameful witnesses to their Christian faith.

Though his claim is strenuously disputed, Pinto presents himself in Chapters 132–4 as one of the three Portuguese who in 1543 (or, arguably, 1542) were the first Europeans to reach Japan. There, on the island of Tanegashima, they introduced the Japanese to the arquebus, the forerunner of the musket. Pinto later established good relations with the *daimyō* (warlord) of Bungo and consequently was, through him, greatly able to assist the saintly Jesuit Francis Xavier, the 'Apostle of the Indies', in his remarkable mission to Japan. As though transformed, Pinto briefly became a Jesuit novice (1554–56) following Xavier's death in China in 1552: his final accomplishment was to act as ambassador to Bungo on behalf of the Portuguese viceroy in Goa, before at last returning, a wealthy man, to Portugal in 1558.

Pinto's experience of shipwreck is a clear indicator of the perils that beset Portuguese endeavours on the high seas. In the sixteenth century almost one in seven of Portuguese carracks and galleons met with disaster. On the return voyage to Lisbon this was often the catastrophic result of greedy overloading of their cargoes, with bitter consequences, especially along the shores of south-east Africa. Cautionary reports, originating from survivors, were sometimes published in ephemeral chapbooks or pamphlets. In his *História Trágico-Marítima* (1735–36; translated as *The Tragic History of the Sea*) Bernardo Gomes de Brito (1688–1759) organised the re-publication of seven such reports, with five more appearing for the very first time. This remarkable collection bears the narratives of certain shipwrecks that occurred in the years from 1552 to 1593. Two reports came from the hands of such distinguished chroniclers as Diogo do Couto (1542–1616) and João Baptista Lavanha (1550?–1624), two others from learned Jesuits. Details abound of events leading to shipwreck, of sailors' unavailing efforts to save their ship, of subsequent struggles to reach land, of uneasy encounters with local tribesmen and of grim treks in search of friendly ports. Lessons were taught through the death and misfortunes of so many. Yet the collection stands also as a sombre metaphor for the gradual decline of the overseas enterprise, as well as being a cherished source for the history of early encounters between differing cultures, particularly in southern Africa.

The most prominent narrative is undoubtedly the one that features the shipwreck of the galleon *São João* on the coast of Natal in 1552. Quite apart from inspiring three stanzas in Adamastor's menacing forecast in Camões's epos (V. 46–8), the report also generated a complete and very able epic poem, *Naufrágio e Perdição de Sepúlveda e Leonor* (1594; *The Shipwreck and Demise of Sepúlveda and Leonor*), by Jerónimo Corte-Real (1540–88). The dramatic fate of the nobleman Manuel de Sousa Sepúlveda, his wife and three children (not to mention most of the ship's company of some five hundred) is the most harrowing of Brito's collection. Through a more literate amanuensis, this moving report is narrated by the boatswain's mate, one Álvaro Duarte Fernandes. Having inadvisedly overloaded his ship with Indian pepper and failed to equip it with adequate sails, Sepúlveda ran into heavy seas as he sought to round Cape Agulhas at the southernmost tip of Africa. Having lost mainmast and rudder, Sepúlveda, passengers, crew and many slaves battled their way ashore and endured the harshest privations in their year-long attempt to reach Mozambique. Physically and mentally ill, Sepúlveda was duped by a Bantu chieftain into surrendering his arquebuses and other weaponry and into dividing his party into groups. They were then stripped of all valuables and clothing, a horrific ordeal leading to an inevitably tragic finale. Sepúlveda's hubris and resultant nemesis was a harbinger of Sebastião's at Alcácer-Quibir.

Texts and translations

Brito, Bernardo Gomes de (ed.), *História Trágico-Marítima*, ed. António Sérgio, 2 vols (Lisbon: Editorial Sul, 1956–57); *História Trágico-Marítima, The Tragic History of the Sea*, ed. and tr. Charles Ralph Boxer, foreword by Josiah Blackmore (Minneapolis and London: University of Minnesota Press, 2001)

Camões, Luís Vaz de, *Os Lusíadas*, ed. with an introduction and notes by Frank Pierce (Oxford: Clarendon Press, 1981)

—— *Os Lusíadas de Luís de Camões*, ed. Álvaro Júlio da Costa Pimpão, foreword by Aníbal Pinto de Castro (Lisbon: Instituto Camões, 1992)

—— *The Lusiads*, tr. with an introduction and notes by Landeg White (Oxford: Oxford University Press, 2001)

Pinto, Fernão Mendes, *Peregrinação*, ed. Álvaro Júlio da Costa Pimpão and César Pegado, 7 vols (Oporto: Portucalense Editora, 1944–46)

—— *Peregrinação*, transcribed by Adolfo Casais Monteiro (Lisbon: Imprensa Nacional–Casa da Moeda, 1998)

——*The Peregrination of Fernão Mendes Pinto*, abridged and translated by Michael Lowery, with an introduction by Luís de Sousa Rebelo (Manchester: Carcanet, 1992)

—— *The Travels of Fernão Mendes Pinto*, with an introduction and translation by Rebecca Catz (Chicago and London: University of Chicago Press, 1989)

Further reading

Alves, Hélio, *Camões, Corte-Real e o Sistema da Epopeia Quinhentista* (Coimbra: Universidade, 2001)

Bowra, Cecil Maurice, *From Virgil to Milton* (London: Macmillan, 1962)

Collis, Maurice, *The Grand Peregrination* (Manchester: Carcanet, 1990)

Duffy, James, *Shipwreck and Empire* (Cambridge, MA: Harvard University Press, 1955)

Ley, Charles David (ed.), *Portuguese Voyages, 1498–1663* (London: Dent, 1947)

Newitt, Malyn (ed.), *East Africa* (Aldershot: Ashgate, 2002)

Willis, Clive, *Camões, Prince of Poets* (Bristol: HiPLAM, 2010)

6

Lyric Poetry in the Sixteenth Century

T. F. EARLE

The sixteenth century is especially rich in poetry of high quality. This was a time when poets were open to a great variety of influences, in several languages, which must have stimulated their ambition. It was also the time when the maritime empire in Africa and Asia reached its peak, and great events have a tendency to inspire great minds.

These were years when Portuguese literary culture was open to the world, but still very much in touch with its popular and medieval roots. A classic example of the presence of the past in the Renaissance period, given in all literary histories, is the *Cancioneiro Geral* (*General Songbook*), a huge compilation in several volumes of the lyric and satirical poetry of the fifteenth century, published by the poet and courtier Garcia de Resende in 1516.[1] It was an important moment in the history of the traditional lyric, but not its end. Many writers of the sixteenth century, including Sá de Miranda and Camões, continued to write using the poetic forms and the five- or seven-syllable metre which had been popular in Portugal and Spain the century before.

However, not long after 1516 the Italian Renaissance came to Portugal, in the sonnets, the first to be written in Portuguese, of Francisco de Sá de Miranda. He spent the early 1520s in Italy, principally in Rome, as a member of the household of the Portuguese ambassador to the Holy See. In the years before the terrible sack of 1527 the city was going through one of its most brilliant periods as a centre of art and literature, and the young foreign poet was in the right place at the right time.

The sonnet was not just a new poetic form for the Portuguese; it also involved a new metre. The decasyllable used in sonnets was based on the Italian model, and had, unlike the medieval metres, a constant stress pattern, with a marked stress on the sixth syllable (or less frequently on the fourth),

---

[1]   Modern edition by Aida Fernanda Dias, 6 vols (Lisbon: Imprensa Nacional–Casa da Moeda, 1990–2003).

as well as on the tenth. The decasyllable greatly increased the musicality of poetry, while the new forms of sonnet, *canzone* (in Portuguese, *canção*), and eclogue made possible much more ambitious literary structures.

Portuguese poets of the Renaissance period were very cosmopolitan, often in their lives, always in their reading. They were multi-lingual. Sá de Miranda, for instance, knew Italian, Latin and Spanish (and is said to have known Greek). Italian gave him access to Petrarch and the sonnet, as well as to many other writers. Like every other educated man in the Western Europe of his day he had a first-hand knowledge of the Latin classics, whose presence can be felt in all kinds of ways in his own writing. And he also knew, and very often wrote, Spanish. He had a great admiration for the work of Juan Boscán and Garcilaso de la Vega, his near-contemporaries who had introduced the Italian taste into the poetry of their country.

António Ferreira, another poet to be discussed in this survey, made a conscious decision not to use Spanish in his own writing, but he was very much the exception. Camões, and many other poets, wrote verse in Spanish. And, in the sixteenth century, Latin was not for reading only. It was as near to being a living language as a dead language can be, and many Portuguese wrote and published Latin verse.[2]

To give an account of all this diversity in the space of a single chapter would be impossible, and in any case the current state of scholarship does not allow definitive judgements to be made. I shall confine myself to three poets, all canonical, whose work is available in reliable editions, Francisco de Sá de Miranda (1487–1558), António Ferreira (1528–69) and Luís de Camões (?1524–80).[3]

Sá de Miranda belonged to an earlier generation than the others, but this is not a chronological history of Portuguese Renaissance poetry. Nor is there here any attempt to define the poets' work in terms of the spirit of the age, classicism or mannerism – not least because this has been done before.[4] Rather the aim is to assist the reader of the poetry of the period by drawing attention to some of the characteristic features of the writing of the sixteenth century which differentiate it from that of earlier periods. Some of the formal innovations of the Renaissance have already been briefly mentioned. I have also touched, very fleetingly, on the enormous impact made on Portuguese

---

2   The best known Neo-Latin poets of the first part of the sixteenth century are probably André de Resende (?1500–73) and Diogo de Teive (1513/14–after 1569) but there were many others.

3   A list is given at the end of this chapter.

4   There is an interesting chapter on Camões the mannerist, by Vítor Manuel Aguiar e Silva, in Miguel Tamen and Helena C. Buescu (eds), *A Revisionary History of Portuguese Literature* (New York: Garland, 1999), pp. 30–57.

poetry by writing in other languages. However, what follows will attempt something rather different.

The writers of the period all shared habits of thought, poetic codes which form the intellectual basis for their compositions. Camões, as might be expected, turns out to have been the most ambitious and successful in giving poetic treatment to the intellectual concerns of the age, but this does not mean that the other poets serve only to point the way to the work of the great master. They each had a strong poetic personality of their own. What follows is an attempt to uncover some of the raw material from which they constructed their personal vision.

I have divided that raw material into four groups, as widely differentiated as possible. They are not intended to be exhaustive, and other preoccupations common to many writers could easily be found. But they give some idea of the range of Renaissance poetry, and at the same time give the reader of this Companion the means to approach other poems of the period, and other writers.

The Rhetoric of Love

> Bem podeis vós, senhora, ajuntar fogo
> a este que n'alma ardendo, aos olhos corre;
> bem me podeis trazer em riso, e em jogo,
> pois Amor contra vós ninguém socorre;
>
> bem vos podeis fazer surda a meu rogo
> e a esta alma, que ante vós de si se corre,
> bem me podeis tornar em cinza logo;
> mas ficará o esprito que não morre.
>
> Este vos chama, e vê, e suspira, e chora,
> este irá dando a vosso nome fama,
> qu' Amor me ajudará, que eu só não posso.
>
> Não apagueis a luz da clara chama
> que de vós nasce, que virá algũ' hora
> qu' em minha morte choreis dano vosso.

(Lady, you may well add fire to the fire that burns in my soul, and streams to my eyes; you may well make a laughing-stock and a mockery of me, because Love protects no one from you; you may well be deaf to my complaints and make ashes of my soul, which in your presence feels shame – my spirit remains, and that does not die. That calls and sees you, sighs and weeps, and with Love's help, for alone I can do nothing, gives fame to your name. Do not put out the light of the bright flame that is born within you, for in my death you will mourn your own loss.)

Here is a love sonnet, one of thousands written in Portugal in the sixteenth century. It is conventional, and depends for its effect on a literary code shared between author and reader, and yet is also wholly typical of its author. It is characteristic of the writing of the Renaissance that a good poet's individuality will be apparent even in a text whose vocabulary and imagery is drawn mostly from the common stock.

The sonnet is by António Ferreira; it is number 16 of the first book of his sonnets, written in 1557, or before, though not published until 1598. What is immediately striking is how this is a rhetorical poem, a sonnet intended to persuade. And what Ferreira wants to persuade his lady to do is, if not exactly to love him, then at least to allow herself to be loved.

The argument, as in many sonnets, is a paradoxical one, and the whole poem is a conceit. In lines 1–7 Ferreira concedes that love is a form of torture, but then, in the dramatic line 8, springs a surprise on the lady: you can do what you like to me, but my spirit (*esprito*) remains, and that does not die. The spirit, the creative, poetic part of the personality (as often in Ferreira) thrives on suffering, which provides the raw material for his art. And so Ferreira can conclude his poem by telling his lady not to throw him over, because only if she encourages him will he produce the verse which will make her famous.

The sonnet only makes sense if you understand the codes. In the first two stanzas, the 'octave' in technical language, Ferreira builds up a standard picture of the suffering lover. At one moment he burns with love, and at the next he weeps. The cliché is so familiar that he can refer to it obliquely as the fire which streams to his eyes. The poet's soul has somehow become detached from the rest of him, and lives only with and for the lady, who treats him cruelly. The god of love, Cupid or Amor, has joined forces with her against him. And behind these lines lies another commonplace, one which sustains much sixteenth-century verse, the equation 'love equals death'. It, too, is paradoxical. The suffering of the lover is like death, and yet it is precisely that suffering which keeps him alive. If he ceased to love he would truly die – and therefore not be able to produce any more poetry, the point of the last line.

Some of these codes derive probably from Petrarch: the fire and tears, the disdainful lady who nevertheless possesses a 'bright flame' which leads the poet onwards and upwards. Others, the love–death equation, the separation of the poet's soul from the rest of his personality, reflect the fifteenth-century tradition, though disentangling the influences from each other is not always easy.

Knowing the codes is necessary if the reader is to understand the sonnet, but not sufficient. This is a poem which takes a pride in proclaiming its own individuality. The key is the dramatic line 8, so carefully prepared for by the rhetorical device of *anaphora* (repetition), the repeated, yet subtly varied, 'bem podeis vós', 'bem me podeis', 'bem vos podeis'. The reader, and the lady, are led to expect a grief-stricken utterance, but Ferreira was, at heart, an optimist. All that suffering is the raw material for a work of art which will last for ever.

Poetic self-consciousness, milking a love affair for its literary possibilities, is itself a cliché, and one much associated with Petrarch. But the confidence of Ferreira's sonnet is the expression of a new age. Here is the graduate of the recently refounded university of Coimbra, not an aristocrat, but convinced of the power of the written word to grant immortality – as well as employment. Ferreira ended his career as a judge. Here too is the humanist, the student of the Greek, Latin and Italian classics, who believes he can do as well or better in his own language. And in Ferreira's choice of the word *esprito* (spirit) to designate his own creative capacity, in contrast to the more obviously religious *alma* (soul), there is at least a hint of a new secularism, a belief in human potential.

Ferreira's sonnet I.16 is not one of the supreme poetic utterances of the sixteenth century in Portugal. But it is a highly effective piece of writing, and an indication of what poetry was capable of.

Camões's *canção*, 'Junto de um seco, fero e estéril monte' (On a dry, wild and barren mountain), is at heart a love lyric like Ferreira's sonnet. Its emotional and rhetorical power depends on the reader's familiarity with the codes which have just been discussed. In the *canção*, which is modelled on the *canzone* (literally, 'song') as developed by Petrarch, Camões represents himself as a suffering lover, but on a scale of suffering unimagined by Ferreira – or, perhaps, by any other poet.

The poem opens with a description, not of the pastoral landscape which is the scene of most Renaissance love poetry, but of a bleak desert landscape in the Horn of Africa, where Camões had been sent on a military expedition in the 1550s. There Camões represents himself as entirely alone, the victim of geographical misfortune but also of a cruel destiny. A sense of epic struggle is given not only by the location – more appropriate for *Os Lusíadas* than for a lyric – but also by a self-quotation. In lines 74–5 Camões refers to himself as 'an earthly body, a vile and tiny creature of the earth', which recalls the famous comparison, in the last line of the first canto of the epic, between man and 'a tiny creature of the earth'. But while in the epic Camões was referring to mankind as a whole, in the *canção* it is the poet himself who is the target of a vengeful fate, as though he meant to ascribe to himself the sufferings of all the world.

Such anguish – which is associated with the love–death equation mentioned earlier – can only be redeemed by poetry of more than normal expressiveness. In lines 76–93 Camões implores his lady to remember him, in an enormously long and elaborate periodic sentence, which forms a kind of syntactic bridge linking Africa to Portugal. The poetic virtuosity achieves its surprise – just as it had, on a tiny scale, in Ferreira's sonnet – and Camões is reunited in his imagination with the lady. He asks the winds and the birds to tell him what she was doing, in language whose conversational simplicity suggests that she was actually present (ll. 106–11).

The vision cannot last, and its vividness is its own undoing, because it reminds the poet of its essentially fictional nature. So the poem ends sadly, with another reference to the 'death in life' theme. But it would be wrong to think of the *canção* as one of unmitigated despair. The suffering of the lover is the spur to creativity, and the whole poem is a virtuosic reworking of the traditional love lyric. The fantastically elaborate verse form contributes greatly to the impression of poetic mastery. Each of the eight main stanzas has fifteen lines, divided, according to a strictly maintained pattern, between lines of ten syllables and six, and seven rhymes. The *tornata*, or short concluding stanza, repeats the rhyme scheme of the last three lines of the long stanzas. The whole is a monument to poetic virtuosity.

Christian Stoicism

From the days of the *cantigas de escarnho* there had always been a satirical and moralistic element in Portuguese poetry. In the sixteenth century that was sharpened by the Christian Stoicism which was an integral part of the outlook of all three of the poets included in this survey. Stoicism originated in ancient Greece, but it was one of the most durable systems of thought and in its passage through the Middle Ages was easily adapted to Christianity. Its classical origin gave it great prestige in Renaissance Spain and Portugal, not least because Seneca, one of the leading Roman Stoics, had been born in Córdoba. But for Francisco de Sá de Miranda, perhaps the first great Portuguese poet to have been conscious of himself as a unique individual, Stoicism was a way of fashioning his self-image.

The Stoic ethical system does not just require the practice of virtue; it also insists that virtue should be practised for its own sake. This means that the Stoic is self-sufficient, refusing to recognise the claims of anything, or anyone, over which he has no control. So the man who follows the path of virtue, reason and nature – to many Stoics virtual synonyms – is a man who walks alone.

Sá de Miranda famously withdrew from court life, around 1530, in order to live on his estates in the northern province of Minho. In biographical fact he was a country landowner, with the human and financial responsibilities which that status involves, but his literary persona is that of the solitary, Stoic sage. As a Stoic, Sá de Miranda projected rectitude and self-possession, a heroic refusal to deviate from his path.

Falemos com a natureza
Andando pelas florestas.
Grande sinal de saúde
É ter tudo à parte posto
Olhos somente à virtude;
Ledo ou triste, um mesmo rosto,
Que não há quem vo-lo mude.

(Let us walk in the forests and speak with nature. It is a great sign
of health to lay everything aside, with eyes for nothing but virtue.
The same expression, whether happy or sad, for there is no one
who can make you change it.)

Here, with epigrammatic terseness, Sá de Miranda brings together the
love of nature and the pursuit of virtue, rejection of the material world and
refusal to yield to outside pressures. The lines quoted, from the dedication
to the eclogue *Basto*, are indications of the poet's temperance and of his
fortitude, two of the four virtues regarded as Stoic. He proclaims the other
virtues, justice and prudence, especially in his famous verse letter to King
João III, imploring him to rule justly and avoid the perils which inevitably
surround a ruler.

Sá de Miranda satirised the follies of the age in lines often of passionate
invective. His targets are injustice and the greed and corrupt practices which
had become prevalent, especially in Lisbon, as the great wealth of Africa and
India began to arrive in Portugal. Virtue, associated with the natural life in the
countryside, had been forgotten in the mad rush to the capital.

Most histories of Portuguese literature leave Sá de Miranda like that, but
his work is more complex than first appears. Even his choice of metrical
form is paradoxical. For his satirical and moral poems he used the seven-
syllable line which had been traditional for centuries in the Iberian Peninsula
in popular poetry, not the new-fangled Italian decasyllable. But the popular
verse form is deployed in unpopular complex structures, based on Horace,
which frequently display great learning.

It was the association of virtue with nature which revealed most clearly
some of the paradoxes of his position. The association implies that simple
people, especially country people, must be virtuous, and Sá de Miranda
was not simple. Nor was he a countryman, except by adoption. He had not
only been educated in Lisbon, where he acquired the title of doctor, but
had also spent around ten years in Italy, the most sophisticated society of
early sixteenth-century Europe. As a consequence all of his satirical poetry
delivers a mixed message.

Basto is the eclogue in which Sá de Miranda had expressed his desire to
'talk to nature'. That was in the dedication, to an aristocratic country neighbour, the owner of the estate which gave its name to the poem. In the eclogue

two rustics, Gil and Bieito, do indeed debate. Gil, with whom the poet explicitly sympathises, is an extremist, who believes that only in solitude can he
preserve his moral integrity. However, the fact that he can have a civilised
dialogue with Bieito, who accepts the need for compromise in human relations, gives the lie to his determination to live alone. And Bieito has the last
word, when he points out that Gil's principles will inevitably give way to
the need for female company. What is more, the complex framing device
used in the poem distances the aristocratic poet from his rustic creations. He
observes Gil, but cannot join him in his simple life which, even for Gil, is
probably impossible.

Sá de Miranda was acutely aware of the ironies of his position. His verse
letter to King João III is full of Stoic precept, but is delivered from the point
of view of a goatherd, one of those who 'ask to say a few words about the
beasts and about the ploughing, and then just go on and on' (ll. 383–5).
This is not just the modesty topos, for three lines later the poet begs the
king's pardon for having wasted half an hour of his time, 'das que chamam
sosessivas/estes que sabem latim' ('which those who know Latin call leisure
hours', or *horae subsicivae*; in this sense the Portuguese word 'sosessiva' is
a Latinism).

The paradox of the Latin-speaking goatherd is entirely conscious. It
expresses the impossibility of being a Stoic in a sophisticated urban society,
from which Sá de Miranda could never entirely disassociate himself. It may
be that simple people have access to wisdom, but the poet needs his Latin
and his classical scholarship.

Camões, too, felt the heroic glamour of the individual's struggle against
an adverse fortune, as the *canção* shows, but he also could never be entirely
satisfied with Stoicism. In a long poem in *ottava rima*, dedicated to Dom
António de Noronha, 'sobre o desconcerto do mundo' (on the confusion of
the world), he criticises the Stoic certainties directly. It is not just that the
world is a place of injustice, ruled by an arbitrary fate. Any Stoic knew that,
and would reply that in those circumstances it was the duty of the wise man
to concentrate only on what lay within his power. The trouble, says Camões,
is that 'There is no one … however philosophical he may be, who does not
desire some part of the world for himself' (ll. 53–6).

Like Sá de Miranda before him, Camões considers the possibility that
wisdom may exist among simple people living in the country, but, again like Sá
de Miranda, he knows that such a life is not for him (ll. 121–36 and 185–232).
He gives an example of simplicity whose cynicism goes much further than Sá
de Miranda. Trasilau imagined that all the ships in the Piraeus (the harbour
of ancient Athens) belonged to him, and was consequently happy.[5] When a

---

[5] According to João Franco Barreto, the author of the seventeenth-century *Micrologia*

kindly brother had him cured of this mania he was extremely indignant and asked to be returned to his previous state for, he says, 'na doudice só consiste o siso' (l. 176; the only sanity consists in madness).Camões could probably only make this challenge to Stoic reason, which implies that the world is absurd, through the mouth of an invented character. The rejection of reason, which is not associated with any statement of religious faith, was perhaps as far as a sixteenth-century Portuguese could go in undermining the rational basis on which the Christian as well as the Stoic conception of man was based.[6]

Classical mythology

Classical mythology was another source of material which could, at least potentially, undermine Christian faith. Greek and Roman myths were well known in the Middle Ages, but medieval writers normally treated them allegorically, as illustrations of vice or of Christian virtue. One of the great achievements of the revival of learning in the Renaissance was an appreciation of the myths for their own sake, as aesthetic constructs, but also as a way of engaging with some of the mysteries of human life.

Most of the most famous myths deal in some way with the interaction between the human and the divine. They were accordingly suspect and had to be handled with great caution. Portugal in the sixteenth century was a profoundly Catholic country, hardly touched by the Reformation. The Portuguese were among the first to welcome the Society of Jesus, founded in 1540, and they adhered enthusiastically to the new dogmas promulgated by the Council of Trent, whose third and final session ended in 1563. The Jesuits played an important role in education in Portugal, and they were firm believers in the value of learning Latin and Greek. But to them the myths were decorative, or allegorical. Lay poets who wanted to use them to explore their private sense of the numinous had to be very careful.

The pioneer of the Portuguese literary Renaissance, Sá de Miranda, was, amongst many other things also the author of the first long mythological narratives of Portuguese literature, the interpolated tales included in the eclogues, *Fábula do Mondego* and *Encantamento*. The *Fábula do Mondego* was written first, around 1538. The centrepiece of the eclogue is the tale of Orpheus and Eurydice, told in a way which recalls the versions of Virgil,

---

camoniana, an extremely useful guide to classical allusion in the work of Camões, published for the first time in 1983 by Imprensa Nacional–Casa da Moeda, the poet came across this tale in the work of the Italian encyclopaedist Geronimo Giglio.

[6] See also the useful studies on both poets treated here in Maria Vitalina Leal de Matos, *Ler e escrever* (Lisbon: Imprensa Nacional–Casa da Moeda, 1987).

Ovid, and Poliziano. It is quite literally a centrepiece, because it occupies lines 252–378 of a poem of just over 600 lines.

The myth of Orpheus was greatly attractive to Renaissance poets. Its celebration of the power of love and poetry over death itself was immensely suggestive. Yet Sá de Miranda prefers to stress its negative aspect. Orpheus's fatal backward glance at Eurydice, by which he lost her, is an allegory of the way a man in love deceives himself. And, rather as in *Basto*, an elaborate framing device distances the poet from the narrative.

The poets of the next generation, born in the 1520s, were bolder. Camões in particular was fascinated by the story of Orpheus, though he often treats it obliquely, partly from fear of a hostile reception, partly because of the humanistic desire to hide mysteries from the ignorant. Camões was not so much interested in Orpheus the lover as in Orpheus the poet and musician, whose songs moved mountains and reversed the flow of rivers, as well as freeing the inhabitants of the Underworld from their torments.

Through Orpheus, half human and half divine (his mother was one of the Muses), Camões could express his sense of difference and his sense of the nobility of the poet's calling. Camões's combination of the two roles of poet and soldier (like the Spaniard Garcilaso de la Vega or the English Sidney) made him a true man of the Renaissance. He was probably the first Portuguese writer to be convinced not just of his own individuality but also of his personal genius, certain, like another Orpheus, that his inspiration was more than human. And if the poet was half divine, then poetry too could span heaven and earth, life and death, and reveal the mysteries of love to those capable of understanding them.

The famous sonnet 'Aquela triste e leda madrugada' (That sad and happy morning) gains greatly in significance if it is read with its mythological dimension in mind, rather than simply as the description of the parting of two lovers. The mythological elements are two. The first is the personification of the Dawn, the only witness to the scene. And then, in the final tercet, there appears the reference to Orpheus:

> Ela viu as palavras magoadas
> Que puderam tornar o fogo frio,
> E dar descanso às almas condenadas.

> (She [the Dawn] saw the sad words which could turn fire cold, and give rest to the condemned souls.)

The last lines of the sonnet refer not so much to the content of the words exchanged by the poet and his mistress but to their effect. They help to explain why the parting was happy as well as sad, and why Camões wanted the emotion it induced to be celebrated for ever, 'para sempre celebrada' (l. 4). It was because the beauty of the scene, to which a goddess was the only witness, gave rise to a poem whose eloquence rivalled that of the divine poet. As we read the musical final line, with its alliteration of /d/, we are in touch with the power that could relieve the torments of the damned.

Neoplatonism

Neoplatonism offered Camões another means of expanding the range of poetry, of spanning heaven and earth. Although it is sometimes said that Neoplatonism was in the air that sixteenth-century poets breathed, only Camões had a knowledge of its technical philosophical vocabulary. However, for him it was not so much a systematic body of thought as another poetic code, another means of developing the rhetorical tools at his command. His most famous Neoplatonic poem is his verse paraphrase of Psalm 137 (in the Roman Catholic tradition it is numbered 136), 'By the rivers of Babylon', known to Portuguese readers as 'Babel e Sião' (Babylon and Zion). He glosses the psalmist's command to remember Jerusalem, vv. 5–6, by the Platonic doctrine of reminiscence, the soul's capacity to recall its experiences of the supercelestial world before birth. So, like many other Christian Neoplatonists, Camões identifies the Platonic supercelestial world with heaven. But here too the emphasis is not so much on the vision of heaven as on the power of poetry to make that vision possible. One of the key moments of the poem is to be found at lines 171–80, with its triple pun on *pena*, which means the pain of an earthbound existence, the poet's pen, and the feather of the wing by which his memory can fly to the heavenly Jerusalem. In this entirely poetic way Camões shows how the poet's revulsion at the things of this world is an indication of his fitness to proclaim the glories of the next.

The psalmist brings 'By the waters of Babylon' to a close with a call for vengeance on the enemies of Israel. This is glossed by the Christian Camões in terms of the struggle with sin. In the course of it the vision of heaven fades, and is replaced by a mood of quiet resignation (ll. 360–5). But the poem remains as a monument to the power of art.[7]

Conclusion

Poets of the Renaissance in Portugal, as elsewhere in Western Europe, were very much concerned to project an individual voice. They may have made use of the same codes, but they tried to find a way of giving them a personal

---

[7]   For an excellent study of the poem and its relationship with other paraphrases of the psalm, see Carlos Ascenso André, '*Super Flumina*: as redondilhas camonianas e outras paráfrases quinhentistas', in *Revista Camoniana*, 3rd series, 17 (2005), pp. 15–37.

twist. What they have in common is an extraordinary regard for the written word, and a sense of the importance of the poet's calling. The Renaissance gave poetry a vastly expanded expressiveness, and the Portuguese poets revel in that. The content of the love poetry and the moralising may be pessimistic, but there is a joy and exultation in the capacity of poetry to articulate feeling.

Texts and translations

Camões, *Camões: Epic and Lyric*, translated by Keith Bosley (Manchester: Carcanet, 1990)

Camões, *Lírica Completa*, ed. Maria de Lurdes Saraiva, 3 vols (Lisbon: Imprensa Nacional–Casa da Moeda, 1980–81)

Camões, *The Collected Lyric Poems*, translated by Landeg White (Princeton, NJ: Princeton University Press, 2008)

Ferreira, *Poemas Lusitanos*, ed. T. F. Earle, 2nd edn (Lisbon: Fundação Calouste Gulbenkian, 2008)

Sá de Miranda, *Poesias*, ed. Carolina Michaëlis de Vasconcelos (Halle: Niemeyer, 1885; facsimile, Lisbon: Imprensa Nacional–Casa da Moeda, 1989)

Further reading

Copenhaver, Brian P., and Charles B. Schmitt, *Renaissance Philosophy* (Oxford: Oxford University Press, 1992)

Earle, T. F., *Theme and Image in the Poetry of Sá de Miranda* (Oxford: Oxford University Press, 1980).

—— *The Muse Reborn: The Poetry of António Ferreira* (Oxford: Clarendon Press, 1988)

Mann, Nicholas, *Petrarch* (Oxford: Oxford University Press, 1987)

Reckert, Stephen, *From the Resende Songbook* (London: Queen Mary and Westfield, 1998)

7

The Seventeenth Century

LUÍS GOMES

In the seventeenth century, Portugal no longer had a place at the forefront of Modern Europe, but lagged behind emerging powers like France, England and the Low Countries. To better understand this situation, and its implications for Portuguese literature, it is necessary to trace its antecedents.

In Portugal, the seventeenth century was dominated by the Iberian Dual Monarchy and its aftermath. For sixty years, from 1580 to 1640, Portugal and Spain shared the same sovereign. This period was not too dissimilar from the 'Union of the Crowns' in Britain, which took place when James VI of Scotland inherited the English crown from his cousin, Elizabeth I of England, in 1603. In the same way, when Philip II of Spain claimed the Portuguese crown as Philip I, Portugal and Spain became two nation states ruled by the same king.

It is undeniable that a feeling of animosity permeated Portuguese literature through the duration of the Dual Monarchy. Supporters of D. António, the Prior of Crato, in 1580 the only other serious contender for the Portuguese throne, resented Philip deeply, and there are many examples of literature against Philip's rule. However, after Philip had taken the throne (partly by right, partly by force and influence), Portugal continued to enjoy some degree of autonomy, a factor that contributed to a fair degree of acceptance of the Dual Monarchy. We find signs of opposition and resistance alongside the eulogies of Spanish rule. On the one hand, there is sorrow for Portugal's loss of complete independence, on the other hand there is celebration of the return of Portugal to a 'United Iberia' (a historical sense of national identity reminiscent of the Roman Empire's single Province of Hispania in the Iberian Peninsula). In a poem to Santa Isabel (St Elizabeth), Queen of Portugal, Vasco Mousinho de Quevedo, a lesser-known poet from the turn of the century, first laments the loss of Portuguese independence and then praises the final return of Portugal to her rightful origins, with a simile of a river (Portugal) flowing to its rightful place, the sea (Castile). This ambivalent historical perspective on the Dual Monarchy has largely been absent from Portuguese historiography.[1]

However, it was under the foreign rule of Portugal's traditional enemy that some of what came to be considered the 'classical canon' of Portuguese literature was published, some of it even dedicated to Philip II himself. Indeed, the last decade of the sixteenth century saw the publication of the lyric poetry of such authors as Luís de Camões (1595), Francisco Sá de Miranda (1595), Diogo Bernardes (1596 and 1597) and António Ferreira (1598).[2] With the exception of Diogo Bernardes's works, these were mostly posthumous publications. Camões had died in 1580 and António Ferreira in 1569, but the admiration for their work was still thriving many years later, and their works finally went into print, at the expense of admirers. This helps to explain how their poetry, particularly that of Camões, came to have an enormous influence throughout the seventeenth century and beyond. Indeed, Camões's lyric poetry continued to inspire poets in the seventeenth century, both in print and manuscript, and his epic poem Os Lusíadas (1572) fed into a myriad of other epic poems, which were always discussed with Camões as a reference point. For instance, Vasco Mousinho de Quevedo's Afonso Africano (1611; Alfonso the African), hailing the patriotic feat of King Afonso V's conquest of Tangier in North Africa, was heralded as the best Portuguese epic poem after Camões's Os Lusíadas.[3]

In the seventeenth century, literature was written in either Portuguese or Spanish (or occasionally in Latin). With the exception of António Ferreira, this had been common practice throughout the sixteenth century, and continued to be so, with the vast majority of authors using both Iberian languages in literary or political works in Portugal. This was the norm, even after the Dual Monarchy. A good example is António de Sousa Macedo's 1643 defence of Portugal's rightful independence – published in London, dedicated to a Portuguese noble and aimed at international diplomatic circles. It is a reply,

[1] One of the better known modern defences of anti-Philippine literature is Hernâni Cidade's A Literatura Autonomista Sob os Filipes (Lisbon: Sá da Costa, 1948), which portrays a country always and constantly resenting the Dual Monarchy from its inception. This view was promptly condemned by the Spanish scholar Eugenio Asensio, in 'España en la épica filipina (al margen de un libro de H. Cidade)', Revista de Filología Española 33 (1949), 66–109. However, it is Cidade's work that is still often used as a reference in present-day Portugal.

[2] Luís de Camões, Rhythmas de Luís de Camões Divididas em Cinco Partes (Lisbon: Manuel de Lira, 1595); Sá de Miranda, Obras do celebrado Lusitano o doutor Francisco de Sá de Miranda ... ([Lisbon]: Manuel de Lira, 1595); Diogo Bernardes, O Lima ... (Lisbon: Simão Lopes, 1596); Diogo Bernardes, Rimas varias flores do Lima (Lisbon: Manuel de Lira, 1597); António Ferreira, Poemas Lusitanos ... (Lisbon: Pedro Craesbeeck, 1598).

[3] Manuel de Faria e Sousa, Epitome de las Historias Portuguesas (Madrid: Francisco Martinez, 1628), chapter XVIII; and also in Lusiadas de Luis de Camões, 4 vols, in 2 (Madrid: Juan Sanchez, 1639), I, fls 540-41, on II.103. For a more thorough list, see Luís de Camões, Os Lusíadas, ed., with intr. and notes by Frank Pierce (Oxford: Clarendon Press, 1973), p. xix.

in Spanish, to a writer who had questioned Portugal's right to independence. At the time, this practice was not seen to lead to a conflict of values.[4]

In the first twenty-five years of the seventeenth century, the acceptance of the Dual Monarchy gradually diminished. At times, particularly in the reigns of Philip III (II of Portugal) and IV (III), there was outright hostility. Several attempts to restore Portugal's autonomy and independence, from the mid-1620s to 1640, culminated in the Restoration of Independence on 1 December 1640, a unilateral act of sovereignty that took twenty-eight years to be formalised by Spain and the Pope. During these almost three decades of war, pursued on the battlefield and through diplomacy, attempts were made to promote a national image of an autonomous Portugal in the main courts of Europe. These diplomatic efforts would sometimes find artistic expression, as in the emblems included in another work by António de Sousa Macedo, this time in Latin, *Lusitania liberata ab injusto Castellanorum dominio. Restituta legitimo Principi, Serenissimo Joanni IV ...* (1645; *Lusitania Liberated from the Castilian Yoke, Restored to its True Monarch his Highness John IV*), a treatise defending Portugal's newfound independence.

Two great literary figures stand out in this scenario, Father António Vieira, SJ (1608–97), and D. Francisco Manuel de Melo (1608–66). Both men experienced swings of fortune, from high offices of diplomacy and court life to persecution by the court or the Inquisition, incarceration or exile. From this rough biographical summary one appreciates the sense of instability and insecurity in Portuguese literature. There seems to be a constant underlying sense of fear and caution, where writers must lead a prudent and sensible life, taking care about what they say and to whom.

Although authors of this period often proclaim a certain simplicity in their ideas, the way these are presented is far from simple. There is a clear preference for wittiness, also known as *agudeza*, similes and elaborate metaphors. Generally these were ways to conceal a true meaning, making it intelligible only to those in possession of a suitable intellect, although it would sometimes be used simply to showcase a kind of mental dexterity. Treatises were even written on *agudeza*, the most famous being the Spaniard Baltasar Gracián's *Agudeza y Arte de Ingenio* (1642).

Francisco Manuel de Melo was no stranger to this fashion, and his literary work is ripe with covert, subtle wittiness. Manuel de Melo had a distinguished military and diplomatic career at home and abroad, interspersed by bouts of prison and periods of exile. He had spent most of his adult life at the service of Philip IV (III), either at sea, in military campaigns, or at the court in

---

[4] *Jvan Caramvel Lobkovvitz, ... Convencido* (London: Ric. Herne, 1642). Macedo was secretary of state in the diplomatic mission to Charles I's court in London, and ambassador to the Dutch court, where he aimed to gather support for the Portuguese cause, using both Latin and Castilian to put forward his arguments.

Madrid, where he developed his gentlemanly education through literature. Indeed, he would count the famous Spanish poet Francisco de Quevedo as a close friend for some time.

Although he began his literary career in poetry, he is best remembered for his prose works, the most popular of which is the *Carta de Guia de Casados* (1651; translated in 1697 as *The Government of a Wife*), an informal letter to a friend about to wed, advising him on marital life. In this short treatise, written towards the end of his life, and whilst battling against a sentence of exile, Manuel de Melo disavows literary pretentions, preferring the simplicity of his personal experience as his inspiration. However, simplicity does not exclude wit, *agudeza*. Manuel de Melo's simple praise of the merits of marriage is hinged on a key piece of lifestyle advice: 'a small weight on a man's back is cumbersome, a much greater one drawn upon wheels is easier. The burden of wedlock is not beyond our strength, it generally wants being supported by Prudence, and therefore appears the heavier.'[5] In spite of its popularity, this work is often dismissed as misogynistic and patronising. However, one must read between the lines, where caution and prudence seem to beckon the shape and form of all things: 'What [age] odds there are, ought always to be on the husband's side, who in all respects must be superior to the woman: yet, the greatest happiness always consists in the greatest equality.'

Although not as well known as the *Carta*, Manuel de Melo's posthumously published *Apólogos Dialogais* (*Apologies in Dialogue*) are ripe with covert wit and subtlety, and at times outright criticism of his time. Of particular note must be his fourth *Apólogo*, also known as *Hospital das Letras* (written in 1657, but published only in 1721; *Hospital of Letters*), where the author sets himself as a character walking through an imaginary Hospital of Letters, seeing all famous authors up to the present times, and commenting on the state of their health (i.e., the merit of their work and the recognition of their merit).

Father António Vieira, too, stood up to adversity but in a humble Jesuit way, which is to say, by intelligent rhetoric in sermons and letters. Vieira was brought up in the colony of Brazil from the age of six, and this gave him a lasting affection for its native (and non-native) peoples. He was ahead of his time in promoting universal human rights, including those of the indigenous Brazilian Indians and African slaves in Bahia, a stand that brought him much disfavour with the ruling elite. As the Royal preacher, he used his elaborate sermons to defend his ideas. Vieira was, ultimately, an exemplary orator, and his work, in particular his theory of the Fifth Empire, came to influence Portuguese literature and thought for centuries to come. Taking up ideas

---

[5]   Quoted from the seventeenth-century English translation by Capt. John Stevens, *The government of a wife, or, Wholsom and pleasant advice for married men* (London: Jacob Tonson and R. Knaplock, 1697), p. 5.

voiced throughout Portuguese literature from medieval times, Vieira argues that Portugal was the nation chosen to lead mankind in the second coming of Christ. These ideas, which permeate Vieira's sermons and correspondence, and are given greater prominence in his unfinished *História do Futuro* (*History of the Future*), were still being discussed at the beginning of the twentieth century by the Modernist poet Fernando Pessoa.

Vieira also condemned the growing excesses of *Gongorism*, a literary style named after the Spanish poet Luis de Góngora, which by then had degenerated into an extremely elaborate language of metaphors, often on insignificant subjects (such as a candelabra, or a lady's shoe). We find many of these compositions collected in the two volumes of *Postilhão de Apolo* (*Apollo's Postilion*) and the five volumes of *Fénix Renascida* (1716–28; *The Phoenix Reborn*), which, although published in the following century, still contain a myriad of poems from the seventeenth century, produced in literary academies or *salons* and circulated in manuscript form for many years.

However, it is also possible that this apparent artistic creation of art for art's sake is a reflection of the fear of saying anything of meaning that might cause concern. The role of the Inquisition in this century should not be underestimated; it caused real fear and hindered the country's development (for instance, it played an important role in bringing to an end the short-lived Company of Brazil, which, at Vieira's instigation, sought to gather funds from the estranged Jewish community for the development of trade with Brazil).

It was only in 1668 that Spain and the Pope finally recognised Portugal's sovereignty. By then Portugal had already invested enormous amounts of resources in repelling several Spanish attempts to invade Portugal, and in efforts to defend and maintain her overseas empire. These were almost always associated with the celebration of multiple treaties that mostly favoured the other parties, and thus placed the country in a weaker position relative to now stronger European nations, such as England, France and the Low Countries, which would lead in the new century.

Texts and translations

Melo, Francisco Manuel de, *Carta de guia de casados*, ed. Maria de Lurdes Correia Fernandes (Oporto: Campo das Letras, 2003)
—— *Apólogos Dialogais*, ed. Pedro Serra (Braga: Ângelus Novus, 1999)
Vieira, António, *Sermões*, ed. Arnaldo Espírito Santo (Lisbon: Imprensa Nacional–Casa da Moeda, 2008) [This is the first volume of a continuing series.]

Further reading

Boxer, C. R., *A Great Luso-Brazilian Figure: Padre António Vieira S.J., 1608–1697* (London: Hispanic and Luso-Brazilian Councils, 1957)

Monteiro, George, *The Presence of Camões: Influences on the Literature of England, America, and Southern Africa* (Lexington: University Press of Kentucky, 1996)

Pires, Maria Lucília Gonçalves, *A Crítica Camoniana no Século XVII*, Série Literatura, Biblioteca Breve 67 (Lisbon: Instituto de Cultura e Língua Portuguesa, 1982)

La Littérature d'Auteurs Portugais en Langue Castillane. Arquivos do Centro Cultural Calouste Gulbenkian, 44 (2002)

8

The Eighteenth Century

VANDA ANASTÁCIO

In the eighteenth century the Portuguese cultural field included colonies in India, Africa and Brazil. Before 1700 the country had lost a significant part of its Indian possessions, but Brazil's weight in the economy had increased since the late 1690s, when large amounts of gold and diamonds were found. Between 1700 and 1800 Portugal had four different sovereigns: João V, José, Maria I and João VI. Though each of these rulers adopted a personal style of government, the country was an absolute monarchy throughout the period. Until 1759, primary and secondary education was administrated by the Jesuits, who taught the same curriculum in all parts of the empire. As the centralized politics of the absolute state did not allow for the establishment of universities or printers outside European Portugal, anyone who wanted to have access to higher education within the Portuguese-speaking world had to go to Coimbra University, and authors willing to have their works published had to send them (or come with them) to the mainland.

As a result of this policy, most members of the cultivated elites had a common educational background, and it is impossible to distinguish the literary productions of someone born in Brazil or in any other Portuguese colony, from the works of someone born in Lisbon or Oporto. Not only had their authors read the same books, but they followed the same trends, moved in the same social circles, participated in the same networks of influence, and praised the same patrons. In this sense, one could speak of a common cultural space, where authors, texts and readers circulated under common constraints.

The strongest constraint imposed was censorship. Up to 1768 the Index of forbidden books in use was still the one published in 1624 during Spanish occupation, and the censorship system had remained unchanged since the mid-sixteenth century. It consisted of three entities: the *Inquisição* or *Tribunal do Santo Ofício* (the Inquisition), responsible for the application of the Pope's directives to the specific case of the country; the *Ordinário* (a council of the local bishops), controlling the works published in each diocese; and the *Desembargo do Paço*, or the King's Censorship, which had the right of precedence over the other two. Without the written approval of these three bodies, no text could be printed or communicated. On average, eighteen months to two years would pass between the moment when an original was sent to the printer and the moment it was available for sale.

In 1768, King José I reformed censorship through the action of his Prime Minister, the Marquis of Pombal, and the three bodies were amalgamated. The new institution was called the *Real Mesa Censória* (Royal Censorship Committee) and depended directly on the State. Afterwards royal attention to text diffusion was renewed whenever there was a major change in government: Queen Maria I created a new censorship structure in 1787 – the *Real Comissão Geral sobre o Exame e Censura dos Livros* (Royal Commission on the Examination and Censoring of Books) – and this *Real Comissão* was reformed in 1792 after her son João took over. In spite of all the reforms, the delay between the delivery of the original to be printed and its appearance in the bookseller's remained very long.

As a consequence, the Portuguese book market of the *ancien régime* was extremely fragile. Printers faced great financial risks, given the small number of readers and the permanent dependence upon the whims of censors. This situation may explain, in part, how it is that between 1700 and 1800 around 50% of the works printed in Portugal consisted of 'occasional literature', commemorative of festive occasions of the monarchy, the Church, the Court, princes or patrons. The renewed vogue of the epic is probably due to the support given to public glorification of power, as much as to the revival of the classics: *Uraguay* (1769) by Basílio da Gama, *Vila Rica* (1773) by Claudio Manuel da Costa, and *Caramuru* (1781) by Santa Rita Durão were epic poems in classical style which praised royal policies and the brave actions of the nobility in the new jewel of the crown that Brazil had become. Basílio da Gama in *Quitúbia* (1791) tried to do the same in an African setting.

The existence of censorship also seems to explain why, in a time when the novel – though criticised as immoral by most Catholic thinkers – was gaining status and readers all over Europe, there were such a small number of novels (either written locally or translated) being printed in Portugal. The same state of affairs can help us understand the proliferation of the *literatura de cordel*, chapbooks which were sold on the streets. They contained a large diversity of texts: prayers, saints' lives, traditional popular literature, plays and the *libretti* of operas by Metastasio and Goldoni, in translation, which were adapted to the 'Portuguese taste', by the introduction of funny characters that could change even the most serious story into a comedy or farce.[1] The itinerant circuits of distribution were more difficult to control, and this is why they were also used to disseminate the anonymous pamphlets which fed

---

[1] For an example, see Juliet Perkins (ed. and trans.), *A Critical Study and Translation of António José da Silva's 'Cretan Labyrinth'* (Lampeter: Mellen, 2004).

polemics over books like *O Verdadeiro Método de Estudar* of Luís António Verney (1746; *The True Way to Study*) – a remarkable work, whose intention was the reform of every aspect of the Portuguese educational system – or the anonymous *O Filósofo solitário* (1776; *The Solitary Philosopher*), about the actions of the Jesuits after their expulsion in 1759. Such pamphlets created space for controversy on the fringes of the system.

To grasp the ways in which texts and ideas were disseminated in the Portuguese Empire at the time, one needs to take into account the fissures of the control system, as well as the resistance to censorship observable in the production, sale and consumption of texts. On the one hand, it was possible for members of the upper layers of society to obtain legal permission to read and possess forbidden works. On the other hand, the interest of readers in the philosophical and scientific ideas circulating abroad allowed for the establishment of commercial networks of distributors of forbidden books, mostly in Switzerland and France, who would smuggle them to dealers in Lisbon and Oporto ready to sell them secretly to anyone interested. Some of these forbidden books naturally ended up in Brazil.

Escaping censorship was easier if intellectuals chose not to publish. In Portugal, Spain and in the Iberian-American societies of the modern period there was always considerable circulation in manuscript parallel to the diffusion of printed books. The advantages of the manuscript were clear: it allowed for a fast dissemination of texts, in a controlled way, among selected groups of people. It was also more likely to elude control. Manuscripts were the ideal means for the spreading of political satire, as two cases illustrate: *O Hissope*, and *Cartas Chilenas*. The mock-heroic poem *O Hissope* (c.1768; *The Holy-Water Sprinkler*) was a satirical attack on the Bishop of Évora by António Dinis da Cruz e Silva (1731–99). It created such interest in the reading audience of the time, avid for the opportunity to laugh at the weaknesses of their contemporaries, that it was copied for more than a decade. Similar success was attained by the *Cartas Chilenas* (*Letters from Chile*), a collection of satirical 'letters' written in Brazil in the 1780s by Tomás António Gonzaga (1744–1810). The target was the Governor of Minas Gerais, who is ridiculed and whose vanities are denounced. The same possibilities enabled the transmission of the various manuscript newspapers created under the initiative of groups of aristocrats in the first half of the century, the so-called *Gazetas*, sent through the mail to a network of subscribers. These 'newspapers' conveyed items of news related to the life at Court unsuitable for publication in the official *Gazeta de Lisboa*, which was printed between 1715 and 1760.

The new philosophical and scientific developments of the Enlightenment made no impact in the University or the institutions devoted to education until the second half of the century. But there is abundant evidence of their circulation among men of letters of the high aristocracy, who had direct access to their sources and discussed them in erudite societies from the late 1690s onwards. Portuguese and Brazilian academies followed the organization of similar institutions in Italy and France and maintained contact with some of them. They were promoted by diplomats and members of the Court aristocracy and the Church hierarchy, who would gather around them a number of men of letters (magistrates, lawyers, civil servants, etc.) linked to them through the invisible ties of services and favours rendered. In the first half of the century there were numerous academies devoted to the progress of Letters and Sciences. Some were short-lived, and in most of them the interest in contemporary ideas ran parallel to the kind of rhetorical discussions that had been popular in the previous century. During the reign of João V, who became a patron of the *Arcadia* of Rome in 1716, leading academics came from the noble houses of Alegrete, Valença, Fronteira, and Ericeira, among others. D. Francisco Xavier de Meneses, 4th Count of Ericeira (1673–1743), was especially active, starting the *Conferências Discretas e Eruditas* (Learned and Judicious Lectures) in 1696 and founding the *Academia Portuguesa* in 1717.

In 1720 João V created the Royal Academy of History with the mission of writing 'Portuguese Ecclesiastical and Secular History'. Soon afterwards, in 1724, the *Academia Brasílica dos Esquecidos* (The Brazilian Academy of the Forgotten) was meeting in Salvador, Brazil, with the purpose of writing the history of Portuguese America. One of the privileges given to the Academy of History by the King represented a blow to the censorship system: their works were exempt from the authorisation of the *Desembargo do Paço*.

Around 1745, Manuel Telles da Silva, Count of Vilar Maior, formed the *Academia dos Ocultos* (Academy of the Occult) but its sessions were interrupted by the Lisbon earthquake of 1755. Some of the most active members of the *Ocultos*, namely Pedro António Correia Garção (1724–73), Fr. Francisco José Freire, also known as *Cândido Lusitano* (The Candid Portuguese) (1719–73) and Manuel de Figueiredo (1725–1801), joined the *Arcádia Lusitana*, a literary society instituted after the earthquake, in 1756, under the joint patronage of King José and Pombal. This society, which followed the model of the Roman *Arcadia* founded in 1690, had as its main objective the reform of 'taste' through the influence of poetry and theatre. The most influential poets of this group were Correia Garção and Cruz e Silva: the neo-classic aesthetic models they praised were still followed by authors like Manuel Maria Barbosa du Bocage, Francisco Joaquim Bingre, and the Marquise de Alorna, born a generation after them.

Pombal was also the patron of a new Brazilian academy which met in Salvador in 1759, the *Academia Brasílica dos Renascidos* (the Brazilian Academy of the Reborn), aiming at reviving the spirit and goals of the *Esquecidos* of 1724. The new interest of politicians and the learned elite in Brazil led to the sponsoring, by governors and viceroys, of local academies, like the *Academia dos Felizes* (Academy of the Fortunate) which met in Rio de Janeiro in the years 1736–40 or the *Academia Científica do Rio de Janeiro* in 1771 founded by the Marquis of Lavradio, again under the protection of Pombal. After the fall of the Prime Minister in 1777, the *Academia das Ciências* was the last erudite society created in Lisbon, on the initiative of the Duke of Lafões with the support of Queen Maria I. It exists still today. In 1789, under the regency of the future João VI, the Police Intendant Diogo Inácio de Pina Manique sponsored the *Academia de Belas Letras* (*Nova Arcadia* as it became known), with the objective of reviving the ideals of the *Arcádia Lusitana*. It lasted until 1801.

From the 1760s onwards it became fashionable in Lisbon to organise and to participate in *assembleias* (gatherings), the Portuguese version of literary salons: periodic meetings of men and women presided over by a woman – married and accompanied by her husband – where people could dance, play music, read aloud, improvise poetry, etc.

Also, as had happened in the previous century, convents continued to be visited by intellectuals, who would participate in their *outeiros*, the social gatherings taking place during religious festivities, which had, as one of their main attractions, the improvisation of poetry on given themes.

Academies, *assembleias* and *outeiros* allowed for the constitution of social networks of men of letters, who moved from one circle to another, disseminating their literary work. Belonging to one particular academy, being an *habitué* of the *outeiros* of certain convents, or of the *assembleias* of a certain lady, was seen not only as a sign of distinction, but also as a certification of talent. A number of male poets who were mentioned with praise by their contemporaries but published very late, like Filinto Elísio (1734–1819) – an author so popular and so revered that he was called the 'Portuguese Horace' by his contemporaries – or who left most of their production in manuscript, such as Domingos Maximiano Torres (1748–1810), Fr. José Botelho Torresão (better known as the *Principal Botelho*) (d. 1806) or, in the following generation, Francisco Joaquim Bingre (1763–1856) and Joaquim Severino Ferraz de Campos (c.1760–c.1813), acquired their reputations in this way. Writers of non-aristocratic origin could make themselves known to patrons in the same way, and find protectors, subscribers or sponsors for the printing of their works, as in the case of Manuel Maria Barbosa du Bocage (1765–1805), considered by literary historians as the best lyric poet of the whole century.

Women had been present in the Portuguese literary field since the seventeenth century, at a time when monastic institutions proliferated as a result of Catholic Counter-Reformation ideals. As dedication to religion was considered a reason to teach women to read and write, as well as some Latin, between 1600 and 1750 most Portuguese female authors were nuns. The best known nun-authors of this period are certainly the politically outspoken Soror Violante do Céu (1602–93) as well as Soror Maria do Céu (1658–1753), who wrote poetry and the interesting edifying novels *A Preciosa* (1731; *The Precious One*) and *Enganos do Bosque e Desenganos do Rio* (1746; *Deceits of the Forest and Disappointments of the River*), but other nuns continued to have their works published.

These social occasions as well as the intensity of manuscript circulation allowed a number of women to be recognised as authors by the cultivated elite. The reputations of the Countess of Vimieiro (1739–after 1793), of D. Joana Isabel Forjaz de Lencastre (1745–after 1775), or the Viscountess of Balsemão (1749–1824), not to mention the famous Marquesa de Alorna (1750–1839), who became known as the 'Portuguese Staël', were mostly a result of the diffusion of their texts in the context of informal social gatherings through reading aloud, distribution of manuscript copies and improvisation.

Texts and translations

Alorna, Marquesa da, *Poesias*, a selection ed. H. Cidade (Lisbon: Sá da Costa, 1960)

—— *Cartas de Lília e Tirse*, ed. Vanda Anastácio (Lisbon: Colibri, 2007) [A selection of letters of the Marquise de Alorna]

Bingre, Francisco Joaquim, *Obras*, ed. Vanda Anastácio, 6 vols (Oporto: Lello, 2000–6)

Bocage, Manuel Maria Barbosa du, *Opera omnia*, ed. H. Cidade, 6 vols (Lisbon: Bertrand, 1969–73)

Gonzaga, Tomás António, *Cartas chilenas*, ed. Joaci Pereira Furtado (São Paulo: Companhia das Letras, 1995)

Perkins, Juliet, *A Critical Study and Translation of António José da Silva's 'Cretan Labyrinth'* (Lampeter: Mellen, 2004)

Silva, António Dinis da Cruz e, *O Hissope*, ed. Joaquim Ferreira (Oporto: Barreira, 1966)

Verney, Luís António, *O Verdadeiro Método de Estudar*, ed. Gonçalves Pires (Lisbon: Presença, 1991)

Further reading

Araújo, Ana Cristina, *A Cultura das Luzes em Portugal* (Lisbon: Horizonte, 2002)

Maxwell, Kenneth, *Pombal: Paradox of the Enlightenment* (Cambridge: Cambridge University Press, 1995)

Rego, Raul, *Os Indices Expurgatórios e a Cultura Portuguesa* (Lisboa: ICALP, 1982)

9

Almeida Garrett:
Founder of Modern Portuguese Literature

HELENA CARVALHÃO BUESCU

João Baptista da Silva Leitão de Almeida Garrett (1799–1854) is one of the undisputed founders of Portuguese Romanticism and one of the earliest Portuguese writers to have a typically modern concept of the intellectual and of his political and civic role. His thorough classical training, under the guidance of his uncle, is visible in much of his work which, as a whole, contains clear evidence of the possibilities for frequently successful cross-over and even reconciliation of the classical and Romantic poles.

In 1816 he matriculated at Coimbra University, and immediately revealed those two aspects of his activities which would persist throughout his life: the social and political, and the aesthetic and literary. His first book, *O Retrato de Vénus* (*Portrait of Venus*) was published in 1821, the year he took his degree and entered public service. But almost immediately, in 1823, following an absolutist *coup d'état*, he had to leave the country, opting for periods of exile in England and in France until the early 1830s, when he joined the Liberal expeditionary force under Prince Pedro. Exile had a profound effect on him, deepening his liberalism and giving him first-hand knowledge of the complex literary and aesthetic movements occurring in Europe, which was by now a Romantic Europe, and of some of the more significant works that they gave rise to. It was in this spirit that Garrett wrote the two narrative poems generally considered to be the earliest manifestations of a Romantic aesthetic in Portugal, *Camões* (1825) and *Dona Branca* (1826). Both these books were published abroad, as was his *Tratado da Educação* (1829; *Treatise on Education*), his first volume of verse, *Lírica de João Mínimo* (1829; *Poems of John the Least*), and another poem, *Adozinda* (1829), his first collection of popular ballads.

Garrett's work changed as he gradually assimilated Romantic techniques. However, his early books have the qualities which were to become dominant later. They reveal the inexhaustible intellectual curiosity and literary experimentalism which remained his most distinctive characteristic. They are in every genre and have many literary aims. The lyric poetry (*Poems of John the Least*) has the Romantic irony and the blurring of reality and literary experience which reappears in *O Arco de Sant'Ana* (*St Anne's Archway*) and *Viagens na Minha Terra* (translated as *Travels in My Homeland*). The Romantic plots (*Camões* and *Dona Branca*) are very typical of Garrett, taking in the creation of a personal myth (*Camões*) and the use of popular material, in the manner of Herder, while his treatise about education reveals questions which preoccupied Garrett as committed citizen and intellectual throughout his life. Finally *Adozinda* is the forerunner of the three-volume *Romanceiro* (1843–51; *Ballads*). Garrett's early period, well studied by Ofélia Paiva Monteiro, is of particular importance to the construction of the figure of Almeida Garrett as Romantic writer and key element in the modernisation of Portuguese literature.[1]

In 1836 Garrett finally returned from exile after the victory of the Liberals in the civil war – in which both he and Alexandre Herculano played an active part – to find the necessary conditions in which to develop and extend his work as writer, intellectual and citizen.

From the mid-1830s on, his role in Portuguese culture broadened and deepened, but always on the lines that had guided him hitherto. He wrote for a number of newspapers and periodicals, often as the principal contributor, sometimes as the only one. He drew up plans for the national theatre – he had had an interest in the stage right from the start, as his early tragedies *Catão* (*Cato*) and *Mérope* show – and became the typical tireless and interventionist man of letters. His plays were written with the Romantic intention of creating a national repertory: *Um Auto de Gil Vicente* (1838; *A Play by Gil Vicente*), *Dona Filipa de Vilhena* (1840), *O Alfageme de Santarém* (1842; *The Santarém Swordsmith*), and especially the great work of his maturity *Frei Luís de Sousa* (1843; translated as *Brother Luiz de Sousa*, 1909). As the poet of *Flores sem Fruto* (1845; *Flowers without Fruit*) and *Folhas Caídas* (1853; *Fallen Leaves*) he succeeded in giving form to a whole host of themes, motifs, and prosodic and rhetorical devices which had clearly nothing to do with the classical diction in which he had been brought up. As a novelist he was drawn to the two great Romantic forms, the historical novel (*O Arco de Sant'Ana*, 2 vols, 1845 and 1850) and the story of contemporary life, intimate and digressive (*Viagens na Minha Terra*, published in book form in 1846, but whose first chapters were published in the *Revista Universal Lisbonense* in 1843). Besides this he was a jurist and an educator, a journalist and a politician, a compiler of the Portuguese oral tradition and an essayist. Garrett undeniably became an institution in the Portugal of the first half of

---

[1]   Ofélia Paiva Monteiro, *A Formação de Almeida Garrett. Experiência e Criação*, 2 vols (Coimbra: Centro de Estudos Românicos, 1971), and 'Garrett, Almeida', in Helena Carvalhão Buescu (ed.), *Dicionário do Romantismo Literário Português* (Lisbon: Caminho, 1997).

the nineteenth century, his name associated with everything meaningful and worthwhile in the intellectual and literary field.

Let us examine in more detail some of the distinctive aspects of the work he produced in the twenty years between his return from exile and his death, bearing in mind always the range of activities and the intense curiosity and concern with experimentation which are Garrett's contribution to the development of a truly modern literature in Portugal. Writers of later decades, like Eça de Queirós and Cesário Verde, could not have existed without the intellectual and discursive breadth which Garrett brought to his writing.

As we have seen, the theatre attracted him from the start. His early classical plays show that public affairs would always be central to his thought and work. But it was in the brief period between 1838 and 1843 that he wrote and staged three plays which form the basis of the nineteenth-century repertory. *Um Auto de Gil Vicente* and *O Alfageme de Santarém* are inspired by Portuguese history, but also create space for self-questioning about art and its purposes (particularly through the leading figure of Gil Vicente, whom Garrett uses rather as he had used Camões). Gil Vicente, the Renaissance dramatist, and the political crisis of 1383–85 (treated in *O Alfageme*) cover Garrett's principal symbolic, political and aesthetic concerns. However, it is in *Frei Luís de Sousa* that he achieves one of the greatest literary successes in the whole of Portuguese drama.

The preface to the play, the *Memória ao Conservatório Real* (*Memorandum to the Royal Conservatory*), is of great importance to Garrett's thinking. In it, he sets out especially clearly the guiding lines of his literary theory and practice, at a period when he was at his prime as a writer and as a citizen. His preoccupation with these roles is reflected in his major work, and it is in that light that the preface should be read. It is not relevant to *Frei Luís de Sousa* only, but to Garrett's other plays, to the history of the theatre in Portugal, and to the understanding of his role as a Romantic. An important aspect of the preface is Garrett's characterisation of *Frei Luís de Sousa* as at once classical tragedy and Romantic drama, which is his contribution to a critical reappraisal of the nineteenth-century theatrical tradition. It was a decisive contribution. Its vision of history is at once poetic and symbolic. The action of the play is set at the start of the seventeenth century, during the period of Castilian rule. Portugal appears on stage like a collective spectre, whose independence is an empty political gesture. There are other spectres, besides the collective one, representing the Shakespearian heritage in its mature form, beginning with Camões, the supreme poet, who reappears here in a way which is both personal and collective. His name and a reading of excerpts from *Os Lusíadas* open the play, while in the second part his portrait presides over the complications and the resolution of the plot. It is hung in a room with two other portraits, also supposedly of dead men, King Sebastião and Dona Madalena's first husband, Dom João de Portugal, both of whom perished in 1578 in the battle of Alcácer-Quibir. King Sebastião and Dom João are two more phantoms, whose ghostly presence becomes more and more obvious. So the unexpected but in every way inevitable return of Dom João de Portugal, more than twenty years after his death in Africa, explains what from the start had given signs of being a story of involuntary adultery and betrayal, whose consequences are felt by all the characters. Madalena and Manuel de Sousa Coutinho, both innocent, are blamed for the adultery; their daughter Maria dies of tuberculosis, and simultaneously of shame; and Telmo, the elderly tutor both of Dom João and of Maria, is torn between the rights of each. All the characters share in the tragic atmosphere, in which adherence to the pseudo-Aristotelian rule of the three unities leads to the punishment of the innocent, in an action which puts into play the relationship between chance and necessity, and which follows closely the convention that tragedy only happens to those whose nobility of character sets them above the norm. The play, then, is a tragedy, but one of great historical significance, since it is a key moment in the debate about Portuguese nationhood, whose values it questions and calls into doubt.

The questioning of history is the link between Garrett's writing for the theatre in the 1840s and his novels. (Besides *O Arco de Sant'Ana* and *Viagens na Minha Terra* he left the incomplete *Helena*, with an exotic Brazilian setting.) *O Arco* returns to the Middle Ages, but with a story whose contemporary relevance is obvious and is alluded to by Garrett himself. Medieval Oporto provides a historical setting for the traditionally Portuguese abuse of political authority, to which is opposed the equally traditional capacity of the people to organise themselves and to rebel. Oporto had had a crucial role in the struggle between liberals and absolutists, and Garrett begins the novel with the topos of the discovery of a lost manuscript as a way of bringing into the novel the civic and political events of his own time, in which he had played an active part. The story is set in the thirteenth century, but is also a nineteenth-century story – this is what Garrett wants us to believe, thereby accentuating reflection on forms of oppression and the right to rebel, in typically Romantic style. The plot involves the kidnapping of a local girl by the bishop, a true representative of the unscrupulous public figure criticised by Garrett. Through Vasco, the Romantic hero who is his bitter opponent, Garrett introduces a potentially tragic familial element, whose persistence in his writing it is important to stress. The struggle between Vasco and the bishop is linked to the gradual revelation that they are father and son, a consequence of illegitimacy – a theme of a number of Garrett's major works. The novel gives a new take on the historical nuclear family, at once stable and disfunctional. Finally, the novel is the expression of a deep religious feeling, combined with an equally deep anticlericalism, which Garrett shared with many of his contemporaries, not least Alexandre Herculano.

Viagens na Minha Terra is a turning-point in the history of the novel in Portugal. It is a synthesis of already existing tradition, but also opens new directions for the novel and the essay. It is set in the present day, and combines a story, which has social, political and love interest, with confessional and digressive writing. This is achieved by an unusual structure. At the widest level, we have a first-person narrator who is supposedly describing a journey from Lisbon to Santarém; within that structure comes the tale of Joaninha and her relationship with Carlos, a soldier in the liberal army who returns after a period of political exile to the Vale of Santarém, where he had spent his early life. The two planes intersect insofar as the first to some degree legitimises and makes plausible the insertion of the second. From the crossing of these two planes there arises profound reflection on the hopes and disappointments which the politically engaged author, barely disguised as the anonymous narrator, reveals to be his own and those of a whole generation whose commitment had come to nothing.

One can say, then, that the title of the novel is symbolic and has more than one meaning, as Garrett himself points out. It refers to the journey of a clearly disillusioned individual who is convinced that the future only exists because 'his homeland' will continue to exist, but who sees that the present is in the hands of 'moneylending revolutionaries', or 'revolutionary moneylenders' (like the baron), whose existence he had thought to be no longer possible. The journeys are at once real and symbolic, because they take the narrator to Santarém, because they pass through the historical memory of Portugal, from the Middle Ages to the present, though with some significant gaps, and because they allow the narrator to present the widest spread of information, interests, reading and attitudes in general. We learn his opinions and judgements about Portuguese politics. About ideologies and their basis, as well as about the possibility, always open, that they may degenerate in practice. About literature, from the popular ballads to Camões, including significant writers and books from the classics to modern European literature. About the Romantic opposition between Don Quixote and Sancho Panza as emblems of the contradictions of contemporary man. About love and friendship. About liberty and democracy, so dear to Romantic ideology and aesthetics, and especially to Garrett himself. About the depths and complexities of human psychology. About architecture, about history … *Viagens na Minha Terra* expresses the depth and complexity of a narrative subject who takes up his position in a world which, as he increasingly realises, is subject to too many other relativities.

The metaphor of the journey is the organising principle of the novel's structure: the book's digressive nature depends on it, and it is the means of access to true intimacy with the narrative subject. It is also on these lines that it is possible to argue that the narrator is the true hero of the text. In a period when the so-called 'poets in time of prose' were forced to conclude that they were out of touch with society, turning to prose or else arguing for a place apart for poetry, Garrett's narrator is also a hero because his is the mirror-opposite of the renunciation which affects Carlos, the supposed hero of the story of the Maiden of the Nightingales (*A Menina dos rouxinóis*). In the hero-narrator there is civic and social engagement, psychological and sentimental depth and contradiction which are not obliterated, as they are in Carlos's case, a wide range of thought and an ability to put a value on the diverse cultural legacy which is both his own and that of 'the homeland'.

There is yet another dimension to this physical, psychological, historical, symbolic and cultural journey, a discursive journey, to use Garrett's own metaphor, which is seen in the importance given to dialogue. The whole text simulates, quite consistently, a dialogue with the potential reader, and especially with the potential lady reader, so that for the first time in the history of the Portuguese novel the literary language is consistently and deliberately close to everyday usage. It is a transcribed dialogue, with every sign of having been spoken, with suspension marks, hanging phrases, syntactic changes, interruptions by one or another of the speakers, exclamations, monosyllables and elliptical sentences. Digression and dialogue interchange with one another, so that the multifaceted figure of the narrator is always the centre of interest. And this interchange between dialogue, digression and intimacy makes it possible to understand the importance of a fourth characteristic, Garrett's irony, of a deeply Romantic kind. In rhetorical terms, this irony permeates every level of the book, every layer of observation, every subject, including even the narrative subject himself ... It also reveals the relativity of the positions that we take up in the world, just as the dialogic element does. Finally, all these factors draw attention to the aesthetic side of Garrett's language. His irony and the expressive use of qualifiers and of repeated rhythmic effects are visible throughout, and can be considered the foundation of a decidedly modern literary prose.

The inner structure of the novel is the story of Carlos and Joaninha, which takes place in the Vale of Santarém and is contemplated by the narrator from the overarching structure. The two are linked by the process of alternation, which enables the relations between them to be equally significant. It is a short 'family novel', which rests on three main questions involving Carlos, the supposed hero. They are his mysterious past, the origin of family guilt (a theme with clear Romantic resonances, and which connects *Viagens* to *O Arco* and especially to *Frei Luís de Sousa*); the complexities of his emotional life (which are one-sided and so have a reductive solution); and finally the historical and ideological betrayal which is connected to that solution.

Let us examine this in more detail. There is a suspicion (which is confirmed) that there is a guilty secret in the family's past, concealed but nonetheless real. That explains the retrospective observations made throughout the book, both in stories (especially in Carlos's long letter to Joaninha) and in allusive remarks, above all in the opening pages of the novel, and involving the blind grandmother and the mysterious and fateful Brother Dinis, both in their different ways cryptic figures. The atmosphere thus created derives from an event in the history of the family and weighs apparently irredeemably on the present. Carlos and Joaninha seem to be innocent but cannot detach themselves from their historic roots: Joaninha, the 'angel of the hearth', dies in remission of her guilt; Carlos lives with his, but disguises it by his social materialism – he becomes a baron and a deputy – so harshly criticised by the narrator. The second question is the complexity of Carlos's emotional life, which he regards as hopelessly paradoxical and which he analyses lucidly in his autobiographical letter to Joaninha. That way we have a retrospective view of his character, which leads him to become nearly a hero. He begins as the innocent lover of Joaninha, passes through a contradictory phase in which he feels attracted ('flirt' is the English word used) to the three English sisters whom he lodges with while in exile, and finally has a relationship with Georgina, the youngest of them, who follows him to Portugal. Carlos's self-analysis is lucid, but does not allow him to live in accordance with its logic. For the narrator, his life choice is a failure: he denies the complexity of his situation and resorts to a social mask which apparently does away with the problem. The emotional journey mirrors the ideological one, and Carlos also embodies the historical contradictions of the liberal ideal. He keeps none of the hopes of the fighter for liberalism, prepared to risk his life in defence of the ideal of liberty, just the formal appearance, visible in the bargain which allows him to become a baron and a deputy. (The early pages of the text contain an explanation of the significance of these two icons of contemporary society.) So, once again, legitimate hope becomes real despair.

A similar process of maturation is visible in Garrett's lyric poetry. *Lírica de João Mínimo* is in the eighteenth-century Arcadian tradition, but right from the start, in the prefatory material, there is an ironic lightness of touch, evidence of a Romantic streak undermining the poet's neoclassical training. The conversational diction is the first step in the gradual process of the incorporation of everyday speech into the language of poetry. Twenty years after Garrett's death, that process reached fulfilment in the work of a great poet, Cesário Verde, and after him, Fernando Pessoa. *Flores sem Fruto*, the second collection, is firmly rooted in the poet's emotional experience, particularly his experience of love, in all its manifestations. The legacy of eighteenth-century neoclassicism is visible in a taste for description and in some aspects of the language used, but there are evident signs of Romanticism in passages of reflection about the poet's emotional situation and, perhaps especially, its contradictions, even paradoxes. Garrett explains in the 'Advertência' (Note), in a way which recalls *Viagens na Minha Terra*, that his 'flowers without fruit' are the expression of the feelings of an individual who feels himself to be out of touch with an epoch given over to the cultivation of beetroot. Conversation, in monologue and dialogue form, between the poet and, most often, the beloved, plays a central role, in this foreshadowing of *Folhas Caídas*. See, for example, 'Tronco Despido' (The Bare Trunk), 'Solidão' (Solitude), which is a Romantic poem in prose, 'Suspiro d'Alma' (A Soul's Sigh) or 'Olhos Negros' (Dark Eyes), in which the poet reverts to the popular tradition, and the popular *redondilha* verse form in a way which, as often in Garrett, recalls Camões.

Garrett's most mature verse is to be found in *Folhas Caídas* where, free from the strait-jacket of traditional taste, Garrett creates a fluid poetic language which gives the illusion of colloquial spontaneity. Love is still the dominant theme, mediated through a discourse which brings together a great variety of themes, symbols and metres, rhymes and rhythms. The lyric subject's passionate eroticism is counterbalanced by contradictions and paradoxical desires, physical and intellectual, and draws some of its character from the natural world, with a typically Romantic feeling for landscape. Among the most successful poems are 'Cascais', 'Estes Sítios' (These Places), 'Não te Amo' (I Love Thee Not), 'Barca Bela' (Pretty Boat), and 'Os Cinco Sentidos' (The Five Senses). In all of these there is a perfect fusion of technique, awareness of tradition and the discovery of an apparently spontaneous personal diction, in which popular poetry plays a crucial role. Here an important contributory factor was Garrett's intense effort as a collector and publisher of popular ballads, an activity in which he was a pioneer in Portugal.

There remains to consider Garrett's activities as an intellectual and a politician and his sharp-witted interventions in literary and cultural affairs. Together with Alexandre Herculano, his companion in many an ideological and aesthetic struggle, Garrett achieved symbolic status as a convinced activist. One only has to recall his role as fighter for liberty during and after the civil war; his remarkable ability as a political speaker; his wide-ranging knowledge of classical and modern literature; his moral and social stature. If we add to this his constant and intense literary productivity, it is clear that Garrett was the Romantic writer *par excellence* of the first half of the nineteenth century: a true intellectual, whose literary work went hand in hand with his capacity for intervention as a citizen. Garrett did indeed intervene in a number of literary and legal polemics, and took a determined stance against critical positions that he considered to be unjust or mean-spirited, as in the prefaces to *O Arco de Sant'Ana* and *Viagens na Minha Terra*. He contributed to the legislation supporting the renewal of dramatic literature and of the performing arts, especially the theatre, while in *Portugal na Balança da Europa* (1830; *Portugal in the Balance of Power of Europe*) he reflects on social and political conditions in Portugal in the wider European context. The *Tratado da Educação* is an up-to-date version of the traditional treatises on the education of the prince. Finally, his role as member of parliament, political orator and even minister make it possible to understand Garrett's interventions in the real world as yet another aspect of an encyclopaedic project undertaken in a Romantic spirit, that is, taking as its starting-point a personal view from which the possibility of social action is not excluded.

Seven fundamental areas of interest remain constant in Garrett's work across genres and the various stages of his career, and could be said to form different parts of his encyclopaedic project.

1. Classicism. This can be found in the materialism of *O Retrato de Venus*, which made him the object of ferocious criticism. It leaves its mark, quantitively and qualitively, in the many references to be found in his verse and prose to the classical tradition, both in its aesthetic aspect and as a source of ethical pragmatism, as, for example, in *Lucrécia* (1819), *Catão* and *Mérope*. In this respect Garrett is the heir of Alfieri, Addison and Voltaire.

2. The descriptive and the exotic. Garrett's immediate sources are Bernardin de Saint-Pierre and Chateaubriand, and an example is the Brazilian setting of *Helena*, left incomplete at the writer's death. However, Ofélia Paiva Monteiro has shown how even in the mid-1820s these themes had aroused Garrett's literary interest, and led him to compose the fragmentary novel *Komurahy, História Brasileira* (*Komurahy, a Brazilian Tale*).[2] A taste for description and topography, deriving from the poetry of the eighteenth century, is present throughout Garrett's work, from *Dona Branca* to *Helena,* particularly so in *Viagens na Minha Terra.*

3. The history of Portugal. This comes to the fore in *Dona Branca*, with the Arab roots of the Peninsula; in *Camões*, which contains the poetic paradigm of political and literary Portuguese nationalism; in *Frei Luís de Sousa*, the emblem of the tragic period of the loss of independence; in *Um Auto de Gil Vicente*, the encounter with the popular roots of a truly national literature; and, associated with these, texts like *Filipa de Vilhena* or the fragmentary poem *Magriço, ou Os Doze de Inglaterra* (*Magriço, or the Twelve of England*), in which there is a constant reappraisal of Portuguese history, as well as innumerable references and allusions to different periods of the national historical memory.

4. Literary criticism. As early as 1820 Garrett was putting forward his individual vision of the literary history of Portugal, in works like *Bosquejo da História da Poesia e Língua Portuguesa* (1826; *An Historical Sketch of Portuguese Poetry and the Portuguese Language*). An outline of a history of poetry in Portugal, contained in an 1828 letter to Duarte Lessa, became the preface to the London edition of *Adozinda*. He also revisited some of the founding names of Portuguese literature, like Camões, Gil Vicente and Sá de Miranda. Another text is the *História Filosofica do Teatro Português*, a kind of literary and historical essay in which, around 1822, he put forward the

---

[2] Monteiro, *A Formação*, vol. 2, pp. 316ff.

bases of his thinking about drama.[3] This was later expanded to become the Introduction to *Um Auto de Gil Vicente* and the *Memória ao Conservatório Real*. A part of this activity is *O Retrato de Vénus*, a polemical history of painting which has obvious connections to the didactic and descriptive poetry of the eighteenth century.

5. Oral and popular culture. This first appears in *Adozinda*, is continued and extended in the *Romanceiro* and can be found in various forms in different works, like the poems dedicated to Santa Iria in *Viagens*. It is the mould into which much of Garrett's lyric inspiration flows, first with *Flores sem Fruto* and especially with *Folhas Caídas*.

6. The poetic encyclopaedia. Garrett's hybrid output is a systematic assembly of many genres: tragedy and drama, essay and narrative, fixed poetic forms and the four-line stanza of popular verse, classical tradition and modern practice. It is worth mentioning his interesting sketch for a picaresque novel, *Memórias de João Coradinho* (*Memoirs of John the Blusher*), begun in 1825,[4] where it is possible to detect, amid the colloquialisms and Garrett's typical humour, disillusioned reflection on the contemporary situation in Portugal. It is a foretaste of more important works like *Viagens*.

7. Historic monuments, in general but especially of Portugal. In the early *Lírica de João Mínimo* there is a description of the Convent of Odivelas and the tomb of King Dinis, and of the Sé Velha (Old Cathedral) in Coimbra, while *Viagens* brings us Santarém, the 'book in stone', and the Monastery of St Francis with the desecrated tomb of King Fernando.

Almeida Garrett's life and career do not just define Portuguese Romanticism, or the first half of the nineteenth century, but make him the founder of modern Portuguese literature. He provides the subject-matter and the rhetoric; he creates a personality beset by insoluble contradictions; and he is a true intellectual, open to many literary influences but also to the call of civic and political duty. What he brought to the history of Portuguese literature goes beyond his considerable achievements, for he opened up the past and paved the way to many future developments.

---

[3] Published by Jose Oliveira Barata in *Discursos. Estudos de Língua e Cultura Portuguesa* 14 (1997), 107–41.

[4] Published by Gomes de Amorim, in *Garrett. Memórias Biográficas* (Lisbon: Imprensa Nacional, 1881), I, pp. 453–68. The fragments were later republished by Teófilo Braga in his edition of Almeida Garrett's complete works.

Texts and translations

Almeida Garrett, *Obras Completas*, 2 vols (Oporto: Lello, 1966).
Almeida Garrett, *Viagens na Minha Terra*, preface and notes by Augusto da Costa Dias, 2nd edn (Lisbon: Estampa, 1983); *Travels in my Homeland*, tr. John Parker (London: Owen, 1987)
Brother Luiz de Sousa, tr. Edgar Prestage (London, 1909)

Further reading

Buescu, Helena Carvalhão (ed.), *Dicionário do Romantismo Literário Português* (Lisbon: Caminho, 1997)
Coelho, Jacinto do Prado, *A Letra e o Leitor* (Lisbon: Portugália, 1969) [contains a number of studies on Garrett]
Lawton, R. A., *Almeida Garrett. L'intime contrainte* (Paris: Didier, 1966)
Lima, H. C. Ferreira de, *Estudos Garrettianos* (Oporto, 1923).
Raitt, Lia Noémia Correia, *Garrett and the English Muse* (London: Tamesis, 1983)
Reis, Carlos, *Introdução à Leitura de 'Viagens na Minha Terra'* (Coimbra: Almedina, 1987)

10

The Transition from Romanticism to Realism: Alexandre Herculano, Camilo Castelo Branco and Júlio Dinis

DAVID FRIER

Although the rise of extensive prose fiction in Portugal lies long before the nineteenth century (with precedents such as Bernardim Ribeiro's *Menina e Moça* and Fernão Mendes Pinto's *Peregrinação*), it is in the nineteenth century that the novel becomes an established literary genre in Portugal, largely (as elsewhere in Europe) due not only to the growth of a leisured and literate middle class with the time and the disposable income to hand for this pursuit, but also to the increasing capacity of publishers to cater to a mass market. At the same time, however, it is this very fluid social and economic context (allied to other historical circumstances, such as the loss of Brazil and the ideological and dynastic disputes of the early decades of the century) which stimulated the urgency of a creative reflection on the state of the nation and the individual within it. These factors may be seen running through the work of the four most notable writers of prose fiction before Eça de Queirós: Almeida Garrett, Alexandre Herculano, Camilo Castelo Branco, and Júlio Dinis.

The historical fiction of Alexandre Herculano (1810–77) has often been compared to that of Sir Walter Scott. Herculano himself referred to 'the immortal Scott' in the notes to his *Eurico o Presbítero* (1844; translated as *Euric the Priest*), and while this and his other major works of fiction – *O Monge de Cister* (1843; *The Cistercian Monk*), *O Bobo* (1848; *The Jester*) and *Lendas e Narrativas* (1851; *Tales and Legends*) – easily lend themselves to such a comparison through their evocation of the nation in its period of formation and the stimulation of an environment of past heroism, they are also marked by an intense preoccupation with historical accuracy and detail, as well as by forceful (if occasionally extreme) psychological portraits of the major characters depicted.[1] This sense of realism even within the context of a Romantic re-creation of an elusive past led to controversy in other contexts,

---

[1]   T. F. Earle, 'Alexandre Herculano and Fernão Lopes', *Portuguese Studies* 1 (1985), 68–81.

as, for example, in Herculano's open letter to the Patriarch of Lisbon *Eu e o Clero* (1850; *My Relations with the Clergy*), where he questioned the legitimacy of one of the foundational narratives of the nation, the veracity of the legend regarding Christ's anointing of Afonso Henriques as King of Portugal before the battle of Ourique in 1139. The very nature of this debate, which pitched his rational analysis against the deep-seated authority of a clerical Establishment, demonstrates an essential modernity of outlook even in a writer purportedly evoking the past glories of a nation now clearly in decline. The focus on the faults and virtues of a bygone era remind the reader that even in the writer's own time the country could not and should not remain static within fixed notions of its identity, one of the cornerstones of absolutist doctrine in nineteenth-century Portugal.

Yet Herculano's role in the growth of Portuguese literature was more deep-rooted than what might be suggested simply by his own creative contribution in prose, significant though this was. After fleeing to exile in Britain in 1831, he moved away from the early national influences of Castilho and Bocage to welcome the works of early Romantic thinkers and writers in northern Europe such as August and Wilhelm Schlegel (with their emphasis on the formative influence of national character on subsequent generations) and Victor Hugo; the influence of the latter, through works such as his *Notre Dame de Paris* of 1831, is most evident in the efforts within Herculano's writing to stimulate a convincing and detailed re-creation of a past ambience. After some early attempts at poetry, most notably in the production of *A Harpa do Crente* (1838; *The Harp of the Believer*), he became editor of the journal *O Panorama* (*Panorama*) in 1837, and it was there that his early historical fictions were published. Their success was to demonstrate the potential of prose fiction and make it possible for later writers to achieve greater success in terms of portraying the nation in a contemporary setting.

In spite of the superficial conservatism of his exaltation of the national past and of his lifelong attachment to what he saw as the true essence of Catholicism, as opposed to the rigid orthodoxy promoted by the official Church, his preoccupation with the spread of literacy and education and his attachment to a less rigid form of Liberal thought than that widespread during the middle years of the century offered the potential for a reconciliation of conflicting sides within national debates (for example, in spite of his criticisms of the Church, he was critical of the abolition of monastic orders in the 1830s). However, rejected for his independent line of thought by both Liberals and traditionalists, in 1859 he retreated in some disillusionment to his estate at Vale de Lobos in the Ribatejo, where he continued his work on national history, most notably in the form of his *História da Origem e Estabelecimento da Inquisição em Portugal* (1864–72; translated as *History of the Origin and Establishment of the Inquisition in Portugal*), and his compilation of the valuable and extensive *Portugaliae Monumenta Historica* (*Monuments of Portuguese History*), a task for which he was originally commissioned by the Academia das Ciências de Lisboa in the early 1850s.

It was Camilo (1825–90), however, who was to transform the novel into a convincing portrait of the nation as it was in the middle decades of the nineteenth century.[2] Although he is largely associated with the northern provinces of Minho and Trás-os-Montes, the city contexts of Lisbon and (more prominently) Oporto also figure strongly in his work. If he has achieved lesser international recognition than Eça de Queirós, this is perhaps because he is reflecting realities more varied in nature and less instantly recognisable to the modern reader than Eça's more familiar novels, whose critique of Portugal is based on models imported from the French novels of Balzac, Flaubert and Zola: it is Camilo's mastery of the diverse social environments of a country still living with quasi-medieval social structures and attitudes (even as it displays the outer trappings of modernity) which provides the peculiar character, the biting satirical content and often the comedy of some of his finest fiction, including *A Queda dum Anjo* (1866; translated as *The Fall of an Angel*) and *Maria Moisés*, from the *Novelas do Minho* (1875–77; *Novels from the Minho*).

Camilo's early career included such melodramatic fictions as the novelette *Maria! Não Me Mates, Que Sou a Tua Mãe* (1848; *Maria! Don't Kill Me: I'm Your Mother!*), based on a violent crime which scandalised Lisbon society in the 1840s, before he moved on to his first substantial novels *Anátema* (1851; *Anathema*), *Mistérios de Lisboa* (1854; *The Mysteries of Lisbon*) and *O Livro Negro do Padre Dinis* (1855; *The Black Book of Father Dinis*), all of them marked by convoluted plots, manichaeistic characterisation, lengthy digressions, and sensational chains of events (this aspect of the texts no doubt being influenced by their initial publication in serial form); yet, all of these works, nonetheless, are developed with a compelling pace and a lively narrative tone which compensate for the excesses of conception and plot. While the influence of Eugène Sue's *Les Mystères de Paris* of 1842–43 is all too evident in the title of the *Mistérios de Lisboa*, the importance of the motifs of frustrated love, of illegitimate birth and of penitence as an essential component of human existence were to become more marked in the author's later writing.

In reality, Camilo could not have been unmoved by French Realism, particularly in view of his aim to write his novels in a spirit of 'TRUTH, NATURALNESS, AND FAITHFULNESS ... until such time as this planet is rebuilt in accordance with the idiotic model used by some to beautify it and by others to deface it',[3] but it is important to note not only that he

---

2 Herculano explicitly acknowledged in 1856 that Camilo had taken the novel a step beyond his own work: *Lendas e Narrativas*, 2 vols (Amadora: Livraria Bertrand, 1974), vol. I, p. 8.

3 From *Carlota Ângela*, in *Obras de Camilo Castelo Branco*, ed. Justino Mendes de Almeida, 18 vols (Oporto: Lello e Irmão, 1982–2002), vol. II, p. 916.

was temperamentally averse to rigid formulaic writing but also that Portugal was a very different country from the French city society in which conventional Realism had matured: the rural society of northern Portugal which Camilo knew best was one where daughters reluctant to enter into marriages arranged as business deals were routinely sent to convents, where property was still passed down from generation to generation on a patriarchal model which effectively transformed daughters into valuable merchandise for those arranged marriages, and where the ignorance and spontaneous violence and yet also the apparent piety and devotion of everyday life were inescapable social realities. Meanwhile, in rejecting the rigid orthodoxy of those who followed Taine's Naturalistic doctrines, Camilo was also effectively recognising the unpredictable aspects of human character, perhaps more readily visible in a rural than in an urban environment, and this aspect of his literary practice is intimately related to the autobiographical strand in his writing.

It is one of the commonplaces of Camilo criticism that his greatest novels are, in fact, representations of the author's own turbulent life, and, even in an era when critical practice is – justifiably – cautious about making such simplistic equations of autobiographical creation with real-life experience, there is no denying that many of Camilo's major works reflect intensely some of the major experiences of the author's personal history: a lonely childhood, distant and uncaring parents, and, above all, turbulent love affairs, often with two young lovers presented in idealistic terms as struggling against the will of paternal authority and a complacent social establishment which closes ranks in its exclusion of those who seek to escape its norms. This is certainly the case of many of what might be termed the 'typical' works by Camilo dating from the late 1850s through to the mid-1860s, such as *Carlota Ângela* (1858), *O Romance de um Homem Rico* (1861; *The Novel of a Rich Man*), *Amor de Perdição* (1862; translated as *Doomed Love*) and *Amor de Salvação* (1864; *Redeeming Love*). In all of these works one can find a certain reflection of the real-life author's own controversial liaison with Ana Plácido, which scandalised Oporto society in the late 1850s: Ana was the young wife of a respected (but much older) businessman, Manuel Pinheiro Alves, who relentlessly pursued Camilo and his lover through the criminal courts after their affair became public knowledge. In the end, the case was resolved in Camilo and Ana's favour (although only on the technical basis that there was no incontrovertible evidence that adultery had been committed), but not before both of them had spent a long period in prison in Oporto. It was there that Camilo claimed to have written his most famous novel, *Amor de Perdição*, 'in two weeks, the most tormented weeks of my life'.[4]

Regardless of the accuracy of this claim, the author's mind obviously cannot help but have been fixed on the possibility that he himself could have

---

[4]   From *Memórias do Cárcere* (1862; *Prison Memoirs*), in *Obras*, XI, 613.

ended up receiving the same sentence for his offence as his (real-life) uncle, the novel's protagonist, Simão Botelho: exile to the African colonies (a fate which was widely regarded at the time as an effective death sentence, given the unhealthy conditions in which convicts had to live and work there). And the intensity of Simão's love-affair with Teresa de Albuquerque (portrayed within the text in a light of idyllic, unconsummated and pure passion, countered by the mean-spirited attitude of an older generation set on continuing family feuds and preserving their material interests) would certainly help to paint an alternative picture of the novelist's own relations with Ana to counteract the negative one circulated within respectable society in Oporto by Pinheiro Alves on the eve of their trial.

In similar fashion, countless other Camilo novels portray young, idealistic couples struggling against hostile family and social structures in order to be able to fulfil their relationships. Yet these plots should not be read as simple one-to-one mappings of factual events, and not only on the obvious grounds of the author's own subjective slant on events: while the standard figure of the *brasileiro* in Camilo's novels (in this context, this word does not mean simply a Brazilian, but a stock figure of the wealthy Portuguese exile returned from Brazil with a fortune to spend and generally with a desire to make a young bride one of his first acquisitions) is a caricature of a gross, ignorant and vulgar materialist (as is the case, for example, of Hermenegildo Fialho Barrosas in *Os Brilhantes do Brasileiro* (1869; *The Jewels of the Returning Exile*) or of Manuel Pereira in *Anos de Prosa* (1863; *Prosaic Reality*), where the physical description of the character is presented in ludicrously but entertainingly grotesque terms), the very plot structure of several novels indicates a much greater tendency on the author's part to engage in creative introspection on his own character than might be instantly evident.

In the case of *Amor de Perdição*, a powerful narrative of frustrated love often compared to Shakespeare's *Romeo and Juliet*, this reflection is achieved primarily through the introduction into the narrative of the quasi-maternal Mariana, who selflessly takes Simão under her wing, promoting the interests of his love for Teresa even in spite of her own feelings for him, and who eventually chooses to seek her own death in the sea after he dies at the start of his journey to exile in Africa. Not only do her actions provide a positive counterpoint to the essentially self-destructive actions of the novel's protagonist (in the cold-blooded killing of his love rival Baltasar Coutinho), but her presence in the novel alongside Teresa's provide us with the two images of women which were to recur in much of the author's fiction: the *mulher-anjo* (in this case Mariana) and the *mulher fatal* (Teresa, as the woman whose obsessive presence in his life eventually leads him to his doom). While contemporary feminist criticism would certainly see this tendency as part of a manichaeistic plot structure (and the author's own treatment of Ana and of other women in other contexts might serve to suggest that he was not entirely free of such assumptions), it is also important to observe the self-ironic dimension introduced into the narrative by the presence of these two female figures: for the beauty of Mariana's devotion exists in a plane above and beyond that of ordinary mortals, and (as is argued at length by Lawton and Sérgio, in readings challenged by Prado Coelho) this level of devotion is surely undeserved by a tempestuous and ultimately irresponsible lover such as Simão.[5]

Part of Camilo's remarkable achievement in a novel such as *Amor de Perdição*, then (and repeated through other ironic narrative structures in *Amor de Salvação* and *O Romance de um Homem Rico*),[6] is to provide the reader with the type of galloping populist narrative, full of well-observed dialogue and dramatic incident, which would guarantee good sales, while also reflecting with some degree of subtlety on the very flaws and lacunae of the discourse provided: in the case of *O Romance de um Homem Rico*, Álvaro's eventual decision to become a Catholic priest, after a life of turbulent emotions, provides a pious ending to a storyline which is essentially much more tragic in nature than this potentially sentimental conclusion might suggest. Once again, the manichaeistic characterisation of the principal female characters, Maria da Glória and Leonor, suggests a potentially awkward reflection on Camilo's part on the role played in his own life by Ana Plácido, while also placing the perception of their characters within the subjective vision of the narrating subject, Álvaro himself, who is presented to the reader at one remove from the novel's principal narrator through an encapsulated narrative structure.[7] In this way the temptation to cast Leonor (the *mulher fatal* in this novel) in the negative light attributed to her by a superficial reading of the embedded narrative is counteracted by the ironising effect of the framework narrative, while the adoption of this technique also casts some doubt on the traditional categorisation of Camilo as a fundamentally religious writer, suggesting instead that this dimension of his work consists of an agonising search for an elusive panacea rather than a settled vision of an indisputable truth.

After the death of Pinheiro Alves in 1863, Camilo and Ana moved to her former husband's estate at S. Miguel de Ceide (near Vila Nova de Famalicão), which was to become the author's home for the remainder of his life,

[5] R. A. Lawton, 'Technique et signification de l'*Amor de Perdição*', *Bulletin des Études Portugaises*, new series, 25 (1964), 77–135; António Sérgio, 'Sobre o *Amor de Perdição*', in *Ensaios* (Lisbon: Publicações Europa–América, 1954), vol. VII, pp. 119–25; Jacinto do Prado Coelho, 'O *Amor de Perdição* – Romance de Pundonor?', in *A Letra e o Leitor*, 2nd edn (Lisbon: Portugália Editora, 1977), pp. 103–6.

[6] Frier, David G., 'On Autobiography and Fiction: The Case of Camilo's *Amor de Salvação* and *O Romance de um Homem Rico*', in Charles M. Kelley (ed.), *Fiction in the Portuguese-Speaking World: Essays in Memory of Alexandre Pinheiro Torres* (Cardiff: University of Wales Press, 2000), pp. 3–14, at pp. 8–10.

[7] Frier, 'Autobiography', p. 11.

and where he was to find the inspiration for many of his works in coming years from the dramatic personal narratives taking place in that area. With the passing of the years and the resolution of his conflict with Oporto society, then, the intensity of the level of reflection on his own personal experience within Camilo's novels waned somewhat, and his finest novel of the late 1860s is undoubtedly the comic masterpiece *A Queda dum Anjo* of 1866. This work, compared by some to a nineteenth-century version of Cervantes's *Don Quijote*, plays with the traditional dichotomy of the corruption of city society in conflict with the virtues of the traditional bedrock of the nation, its conservative rural heartland, which had so recently entered into conflict with more progressive forces in the dynastic disputes between D. Miguel and D. Pedro in the 1830s and the 'Maria da Fonte' uprising of 1846. Yet the devastating analysis offered of the nation here is one where village life is as corrupt as that of the more blatantly self-serving city elite and where no real prospect is envisaged for the redemption of the nation within existing socio-political structures.[8] At the same time, however, the comic potential of the presence of unsophisticated country people in Lisbon and Sintra, allied to the deliberately pseudo-dramatic presentation of parliamentary debates in a manifestly ironic reflection on the falsehood of the spectacle offered by the affairs of state, contrives to produce a deeply engaging and lively depiction of the rotten state of Portugal at the time, in a manner somewhat different from, but similar in its overall effect to, Eça's more systematic analysis of national life.

This was also a period in which Camilo turned in a certain respect to the historical novel. He was interested in history throughout his life, and the later *Eusébio Macário* (1879) and *A Corja* (1880; *The Rabble*) (subtitled respectively *História e Sentimentalismo* and *Sentimentalismo e História*) include a number of historical essays alongside the fiction. However, Camilo's writing as a historian lacked the rigour of the systematic scholar, and works such as his *Perfil do Marquês de Pombal* (1882; *A Portrait of Pombal*) are marked by the same type of unashamed partiality as characterised large sections of his novels or his open polemics such as *A Senhora Rattazzi* (1880, *Madame Rattazzi*), which sought to refute what the author regarded as the superficial observations of Portugal by the visiting Princess Maria Letizia Rattazzi. Even his novels with a contemporary setting often have a certain flavour of historical background to them, most notably in the treatment of the question of the false D. Miguel who dominates large parts of *A Brasileira de Prazins* (1882; *The Maid of Prazins*). Yet in general, while there is a certain presence of history in the setting of those of his works which are located in the

---

8   João Camilo dos Santos, 'Os Malefícios do Amor, da Literatura e da Civilização – Leitura de *A Queda dum Anjo*', in *Os Malefícios da Literatura, do Amor e da Civilização* (Lisbon: Fim de Século Edições, 1992), pp. 49–120.

nation's past, the protagonists are very much akin to those of the author's own time, and the narrative patterns conform to the same outline as most of his contemporary fiction: *O Judeu* (1866; *The Jew*) (based around the life of the eighteenth-century playwright António José da Silva, who was eventually tried and executed by the Inquisition) displays some interest in the external trappings of Jewish life, but the dominant themes of exclusion and the denial of fulfilment in love mirror the more familiar patterns of countless other works by the author. In similar fashion, *O Santo da Montanha* (1866; *The Saint on the Mountain*) is a tale of thwarted love which simply happens to be set in the late seventeenth century, with only the occasional narratorial comment on the passage of time serving to remind the reader that the setting is not a contemporary one. In this sense, then, while Camilo often uses history as a setting, his attempts at the historical novel certainly do not fit the classical Lukacsian expectation of this genre: they revolve very much around the individual in conflict with his or her environment rather than around the great movements of the historical process.

The author is, however, very much aware of the passage of time, and increasingly in his later work, there is a sense of the need to recuperate the personal past. The series of short novels *Novelas do Minho* of the mid-1870s displays a regular structure of expiation and return, both a physical return to Portugal from travel to Brazil and Africa, and a revisiting of past emotions. Nowhere is this more ably demonstrated than in the two-part short novel *Maria Moisés*, where the orphaned Maria sets up a home for children who have been abandoned (as she herself was at her own birth) and thus atones not only for the social offence of her mother, Josefa da Laje, in having had illicit sex with her lover but also for the deeper offence of Josefa's father, who had wanted to marry her off to an unwelcome match. Maria's virtue is eventually rewarded by the reunion with her natural father on his return to Portugal after years of enforced exile in Brazil, and it is his wealth which allows her to continue with her valuable work when her charitable ambitions seemed destined to fail. The observations both of social realities and of local speech in this novel are acute, and this work above all others demonstrates Camilo's mastery of the realistic depiction of the environment which he observed.

There has been some controversy regarding the status of his two novels considered to have been written most in keeping with the Realist practice which had gained prominence through the early novels of Eça de Queirós: *Eusébio Macário* and *A Corja*. The opening passage of the former novel in particular, with its intensely detailed physical description, has prompted suggestions that this should be read as a pastiche of Naturalist technique rather than as a serious attempt at indulging in a new style, and this line of interpretation appears to be supported by a closer examination of Camilo's own comments on the matter. While his dedication of *Eusébio Macário* to Ana Plácido alludes to a challenge made to him by her to write in the contemporary style,[9] around the same time, in his preface to the fifth edition of *Amor de Perdição* in 1879, he was to write of his most successful work in a tone of apparent humility compared with the widespread acclaim for Eça's more recent *O Crime do Padre Amaro* (1875) and *O Primo Basílio* (1878), stressing the excess both of expressive language and of melodramatic sentimentality within it and concluding that 'It is said, however, that *Amor de Perdição* made people weep. That was bad, but now, to make up for it, it makes people laugh.'[10] The important point to note in the same passage, however, is the considerable tone of irony added by Camilo's initial observation that the commercial success of his work constitutes 'a phenomenal success-story, without precedent in Portugal': effectively he is declaring that literary trends will come and go but that he continues to see inherent merit in his own style of writing, and this refusal to bow to the demand that he subjugate himself to foreign models is re-emphasised in comments made in his preface to Silva Pinto's *Combates e Críticas* (1882; *Skirmishes and Critical Pieces*) in relation to the function of the Oedipus legend in classical Greece:

> All these killings of parents, killings of children, and incestuous relationships were carried out with the greatest purity of heart and the clearest of consciences. It was the fate which was decreed by the gods. We have race, hereditary transmission, diet, place, environment, natural phenomena, all the irresistible influences which correspond to the destiny of the ancients.[11]

The specific act of name-checking Taine's categories of *race, moment, milieu*, only to dismiss them as offering nothing essentially new, makes the writer's attitude on the latest trends clear: while there is clearly some admiration on his part for the merits of Eça's work, he does not see the ideas underpinning the school that he represented as necessarily bringing greater insights than those which he himself had practised throughout his career. In keeping with Camilo's own reflections on *Amor de Perdição*, then, it is appropriate to remember that his work constitutes a vivid portrait of Portugal (and particularly of rural Portugal) in an era when intellectual attention was focused almost exclusively on the city and on Europe, even at a time when the country as a whole remained largely rural and relatively backward in comparison with the social structures of countries such as France. In this sense the tradition begun by Camilo has had important successors in the twentieth century in writers such as Miguel Torga, Aquilino Ribeiro and Agustina Bessa Luís, while his digressive style might be seen to have had its continuation in the work of José Saramago. While *Amor de Perdição* and *A Queda dum Anjo* are the only two of his novels to have been translated into English, his success may be measured both

---

[9] *Obras*, VIII, p. 461.
[10] *Obras*, III, p. 381.
[11] José António da Silva Pinto, *Combates e Críticas, 1875–1881*, 3 vols (Oporto: Tipografia António José da Silva Teixeira, 1882), I, xx–xxi.

in the continuing high sales of his works in Portuguese-speaking countries and in the number of translations of his work which have been published in languages as diverse as Spanish, French, Swedish, Japanese and German.

Camilo's younger contemporary Júlio Dinis (real name Joaquim Guilherme Gomes Coelho, 1838–71) betrays certain parallels to Camilo in his shrewd observations of life in the rural north and in his discussions of the relative neglect of rural Portugal by the city elites. In his most notable work, *A Morgadinha dos Canaviais* (1868, *The Heiress of the Cane-Fields*), the initially negative impressions of country life made on the novel's protagonist Henrique de Souselas are counteracted by a process of rational debate and slow revelation of the real interests of the community, leading to his marriage to the initially shy and unglamorous Cristina, while the local schoolmaster, Augusto, is rewarded for his own personal merit and growth by marriage to Madalena, the *morgada* (heiress) of the title. This Austen-like progression towards enlightenment, conducted largely through a series of well-constructed dialogues and the gradual revelation through example of the underlying motivations of a variety of characters, feeds into an essentially rational vision of the appropriate actions that are required in a given context. In this sense, the author's perceptive understanding of his society in its time nonetheless lacks the essential force and tempestuous character of Camilo's writing at its finest, so that his novels reflect an altogether gentler vision of the same provincial environment.

It should, of course, be recognised that by the time of his early death, Dinis had already written a number of other fine novels: *As Pupilas do Senhor Reitor* (1867; *The Rector's Wards*), *Uma Família Inglesa* (1868; *An English Family*), and *Os Fidalgos da Casa Mourisca* (1871; translated as *The Fidalgos of Casa Mourisca*), and it is impossible to say how his work might have developed over time. In this sense, the famous judgement made by Eça of Júlio Dinis seems somewhat harsh: 'Júlio Dinis lived gently, wrote gently and died gently.'[12] If one remembers that, of his major works, by the age of thirty-three Eça himself had published only the first version of *O Crime do Padre Amaro* and *O Primo Basílio*, then it is perhaps appropriate to consider Júlio Dinis as a fine novelist whose works display neither the power and individuality of Camilo at his best nor the devastating critique of national life offered by the mature Eça, but whose vision of the potential for the positive construction of a better nation is perhaps more difficult to identify in the works of either of his more famous contemporaries.[13]

---

[12] 'Júlio Dinis viveu de leve, escreveu de leve, morreu de leve', see Eça de Queirós, 'Júlio Dinis', in *Uma Campanha Alegre*, 2 vols (Oporto: Lello e Irmão Editores, 1969), I, 195–7, at p. 195.
[13] Maria Manuel Lisboa, 'Júlio Dinis and History Revisited: What Good is a Dead Mother?', *Portuguese Studies* 19 (2003), 38–50.

Texts and translations

Castelo Branco, Camilo, *Obras de Camilo Castelo Branco*, ed. Justino Mendes de Almeida, 18 vols (Oporto: Lello e Irmão Editores, 1982–2002) [contains all the works mentioned]

—— [*Amor de Perdição*] *Doomed Love: A Family Memoir*, tr. Alice R. Clemente (Providence, RI: Gávea-Brown, 2000)

—— [*A Queda dum Anjo*] *The Fall of an Angel*, tr. Samuel Dennis Proctor Clough (Translator's edition, 1991)

Dinis, Júlio, *Uma Família Inglesa* (Mem Martins: Publicações Europa–América, 1977)

—— *Os Fidalgos da Casa Mourisca* (Barcelos: Livraria Figueirinhas, 1967); *The Fidalgos of Casa Mourisca*, tr. Roxana L. Dabney (Boston, MA: Lothrop, 1891)

—— *A Morgadinha dos Canaviais* (Barcelos: Livraria Figueirinhas, 1979)

—— *Os Novelos da Tia Philomela* [from *Serões da Província*]; *Aunt Filomela*, tr. Luiz Marques (Philadelphia: McKay, and London: Harrap, 1927; reprinted 1943).

—— *As Pupilas do Senhor Reitor* (Oporto: Livraria Figueirinhas, 1964)

—— *Serões da Província* (24th edn, Lisbon: J. Rodriques & Cia, 1922)

Herculano, Alexandre, *O Bobo* (Lisbon: Livraria Bertrand, n.d.)

—— *Eu e o Clero: Carta ao Ex.ᵐᵒ Cardeal-Patriarcha* (Lisbon: Imprensa Nacional, 1850)

—— *Eurico o Presbítero*, introd. and rev. Vitorino Nemésio (Amadora: Livraria Bertrand, 1972)

—— *A Harpa do Crente* (Mem Martins: Publicações Europa–América, n.d.)

—— *História da Origem e Estabelecimento da Inquisição em Portugal*, 11th edn (Lisbon: Livraria Bertrand, n.d.); *The History of the Origin and Establishment of the Inquisition in Portugal*, tr. John C. Branner (Stanford, CA: Stanford University, 1926; republished New York: Ktav, 1972).

—— *Lendas e Narrativas*, 2 vols (Amadora: Livraria Bertrand, 1974)

—— *O Monge de Cister*, 2 vols (Lisbon: Livraria Bertrand, n.d.)

—— *Portugaliae Monumenta Historica*, 7 vols (Lisbon: Academia das Ciências de Lisboa, 1856–88)

Further reading

Frier, David G., *Visions of the Self in the Novels of Camilo Castelo Branco (1850–1870)* (Lewiston, NY: Edwin Mellen, 1996)

Santos, João Camilo dos (ed.), *Camilo Castelo Branco no Centenário da Morte* (Santa Barbara, CA: Center for Portuguese Studies, University of California, Santa Barbara, 1995)

11

Eça de Queirós: A European Writer

TERESA PINTO COELHO

José Maria Eça de Queirós (1845–1900) was among the most cosmopolitan men of his time. He went on the Eastern Grand Tour, taking in Egypt, where he witnessed the opening of the Suez Canal (1869), and the Holy Land (like Disraeli, Nerval and Gautier). In 1873 he travelled to the USA (Philadelphia, New York and Chicago) and Canada. His professional life as consul first took him to La Habana (1872–74), then Newcastle (1874–78) and Bristol (1878–88). His last post was Paris, where he died in 1900.

Having lived abroad, mostly in England and France, for most of his adult life, Eça knew European culture well. Although his readership was Portuguese and Brazilian, and despite the fact that he portrays Portuguese bourgeois and aristocratic society in his novels, he also engages with late nineteenth-century European cultural, aesthetic and political debates and shows concern about the role of Portugal in Europe. The crisis of Naturalism, *fin-de-siècle* fears of cultural and racial decline, the imperial question, reflections on science and progress, and on the debate between culture and nature, are just some of the topics he has in common with European writers of his time. Well-read and well-travelled, with the advantage of having reached maturity as a novelist while living in Victorian England, he was in a privileged position to acquire a broad European view of events and cultural changes.

Critical evaluation of Eça de Queirós's fictional and non-fictional works has often tended to suffer from political bias. He has been appropriated by both the Left and the Right: critics on the Left have celebrated his early novels, especially *O Crime do Padre Amaro* (1880; translated as *The Crime of Father Amaro*) and *O Primo Basílio* (1878; translated as *Cousin Basílio*), for their social and political concerns, while those on the Right praised him highly for what they deemed to be the nationalism of *A Cidade e as Serras* (1901; translated as *The City and the Mountains*) and *A Ilustre Casa de Ramires* (1900; translated as *The Illustrious House of Ramires*). Biographical criticism has underpinned some of these interpretations, by establishing a link between his marriage in 1886, at the age of forty, to Emília Resende, an aristocrat from Northern Portugal, and his later writings. To some critics, marriage (regardless of whether it was a marriage of convenience or a love match) into an influential and relatively wealthy family made him more reluctant to pursue his former social concerns. It is not that simple. His journalism, a life-long pursuit, dealt with social and political issues from the outset, and these do not disappear from his last novels. They are just expressed in a different way. At any rate, his works should not be read solely in ideological and/or biographical terms, or within the context of Portuguese culture and society, but rather should take into account the changes undergone by European thought and aesthetics during the last quarter of the nineteenth century.

Despite this, criticism of Eça's novels is still predominantly francophile: most of his works are still studied within the context of French literature and culture. Although he knew Heine and Poe, among others, in French translations, it is true that his early masters were primarily French (Proudhon, Taine, Stendhal, Balzac, Hugo, Flaubert, Zola), as he himself recognised and later deplored in texts such as 'O Francesismo' (c.1887; 'Frenchification'). This is hardly surprising given the hegemony of French culture in Europe, not least in Portugal, since the eighteenth century. For instance, the influence of Flaubert's *Madame Bovary* or *L'Éducation sentimentale* can be traced in *O Primo Basílio* or *Os Maias* (1888; translated as *The Maias*), while Balzac's *Les illusions perdues* informs *A Capital* (1925; translated as *To the Capital*). In his own time, Eça was famously accused of plagiarising Zola's *La Faute de l'Abbé Mouret* in *O Crime*. Nevertheless, Eça's literary tastes and aesthetic theories evolved, as he became increasingly disappointed with French Naturalism. His long stay in England, to which not enough critical attention has been paid, led to an expansion of his views on European literature, culture and politics.

Beyond French cultural hegemony

Os Maias is the novel in which most references to England (some of them derogatory) can be found, but Eça's fascination with England can be traced in other texts long before that. In 1877 he started writing articles about Victorian society, politics, literature and culture for the Oporto newspaper *A Actualidade*, the so-called *Crónicas de Londres* (April 1877–May 1878; *Reports from London*), and later on, for the Brazilian paper *Gazeta de Notícias*, the *Cartas de Inglaterra* (July 1880–October 1882; translated as *Eça's English Letters*). These texts have been studied as an example of his alleged ambiguous love–hate sentiments towards England. They also show, however, how much he knew about English literature and the extent to which he was fascinated by it. In one of them, entitled 'Acerca de Livros' (17 November 1881, 'On Books'), he praises English intellectual life and the volume of publishing activity, especially during what he calls 'the book season', from October to March:

> A book by Darwin, a study by Matthew Arnold, a poem by Tennyson, a novel by George Meredith will naturally be kept for the 'season'. Besides, throughout the whole year this phenomenal publicity does not cease, with a vast, noisy, flooding torrent of books, spreading, layering the crust of the vegetal earth with a new crust of paper printed in English.

'O Francesismo' should be read in the context of this ongoing reflection on English literature and culture:

> France has never had a single poet who could be compared to the English, to Burns, to Shelley, to Byron, to Keats, men of emotion and passion, as poetic as their poems. And nowadays what French poet could be ranked with Tennyson, with Browning, with Rossetti, with Matthew Arnold, with Edwin Arnold, with Austin, etc.?

He goes on to argue: 'It is time to consider if French literature, as *table-d'hôte*, suits us: I dare say that it does not,' lamenting that: 'English literature, incomparably richer, livelier, stronger and more original than French, is ignored, despite the fact that the English language is widely known.'

Eça is not guilty of such ignorance. Nowadays we know what might have been some of the contents of his library from the books kept in the *Fundação Eça de Queirós*.[1] Works by some of the authors he mentions can be found there: Matthew Arnold's *God and the Bible*, *Essays in Criticism* and *Literature and Dogma*, Tennyson's complete works, Dickens's *David Copperfield*, Meredith's *Diana of the Crossways*, Elizabeth Gaskell's *Cranford*, Hardy's *The Trumpet Major* and *Jude the Obscure*, among others.

When it came to outlining the Programme for the *Revista de Portugal* (1889–92), he declared he was intent on creating a review that would widen its scope

> beyond France (our exclusive school and the only prop of our mind) the source of our ideas and emotions, in order to allow us to make the best of what the great thinking nations – England and Germany (or even others, such as our neighbouring progressive Spain) – so little known among us,

---

[1]   Established in the house and farm which Eça inherited by marriage, the Quinta de Vila Nova in Santa Cruz do Douro (the fictional Tormes of *A Cidade e as Serras*), the *Fundação* was created in 1990. It houses not only the remains of Eça's library but also some of his personal belongings and furniture, as well as his personal archive.

have more recently produced in the field of Letters and achieved in the pursuit of erudition.

The *Revista*, whose contributors include the best intellectuals of Eça's generation, the so-called *Geração de 70*, aimed to be a European project modelling itself on English high quality reviews, like *The Contemporary Review*. It includes articles on European politics, reviews of American, English, French and Spanish periodicals, European literature in translation and book reviews.

The *Revista* reveals a more mature Eça, now living in Paris, who has gone through several stages of cultural and aesthetic evolution. In England, he had started to distance himself from French Naturalism. Several reasons can account for this. On the one hand, he became better acquainted with English literature. On the other, by the 1880s, French writers themselves were moving in other aesthetic directions, as in the case of Joris-Karl Huysmans in his *A Rebours* or Melchior de Vogüé's *Le Roman Russe*, two important manifestos against Naturalist fiction. While in England, Eça could not have missed the outcry about Naturalism, nor could he have been unaware of the trial and conviction of Henry Vizetelly for translating Zola in 1889.

He himself had been heavily criticised by his contemporaries for the realistic coarseness of *O Crime* and the erotic scenes of *O Primo*. But the last version of *O Crime*, although it still contained deterministic chapters like the ones on Amaro's and Amélia's education, was already something personal, innovative, registering an attempt to free himself from literary schools.

Bigotry in a provincial town: *O Crime do Padre Amaro*

Eça wrote four different versions of his first novel, *O Crime do Padre Amaro*, published in 1875, 1876, 1880 and 1889, respectively. The one we read nowadays is the 1880 one, although the Imprensa Nacional–Casa da Moeda critical edition (2000) is based on that of 1889.

The first edition came out in instalments in the *Revista Ocidental* (15 February–15 July 1875) without Eça having read the proofs or given permission for it to be printed. It was rewritten for the 1876 book edition and further remodelled in 1880. A comparison between the latter two shows how he became increasingly distant from the techniques of Naturalism. It is still the tale of an opportunistic, selfish, sensual Catholic priest, living in a gossiping provincial town run by manipulative priests and unscrupulous politicians, who seduces a young girl and makes her pregnant. The portrait of the priests could hardly be harsher. Obese, lustful and scheming, they use their status in every way – personal, political, sexual – to obtain what they want: better posts, privileges, social and political influence, women. Theirs is a religion of fear and terror, persecution and punishment.

The portrait of women is no better. Bigotry, a topic that Eça would exploit in masterly fashion in *A Relíquia* (1887; translated as *The Relic*), is the key word. Surrounded by priests, women both use them and depend on them either psychologically, financially and/or sexually. In fact, sex and religion are generally inseparable in the novel.

However, many important details are changed in the 1880 edition. Some characters are added to the original plot, such as the pious, humble Father Ferrão, or Dr Gouveia, the representative of science, and new episodes are created. Amaro, who does not drown his newly born child, as in previous versions, but sends it to a 'weaver of angels' (*tecedeira de anjos*) to be disposed of, becomes more calculating and cynical and his crime is explained in social rather than individual terms. On the other hand, although criticism of the Church is still devastating, it is simultaneously counterbalanced by the introduction of Father Ferrão. His is a Church of the weak, the poor, the sick, the simple souls; his is a merciful God not a punishing one, the God of Eça's subsequent hagiographical short stories of the 1890s, such as *São Cristóvão* (*St Christopher*), the good giant, already mentioned in *O Crime*.

One of the most important changes in the 1880 edition is to be found in the closing chapter. It is the scene in which Amaro, Canon Dias and the Count of Ribamar meet in Lisbon, with the statue of Camões in the background. The symbolic meaning of the episode has been pointed out by critics. In a decadent, sleepy Lisbon, watched over by the old epic poet, the representatives of Church and Government exchange views on what they see as the promising future of Portugal, the envy of European nations. The ironic contrast between late nineteenth-century Portugal and Camões's time is elaborately and cleverly achieved: on the one hand worn-out, decrepit, degenerate Lisbon; on the other, virile, noble, heroic Camões.

Throughout the drawn-out process of rewriting *O Crime*, Eça had learnt how to use symbolism. From then onwards, he would be able to unite realism and imagination. Together with irony and a masterful use of language, this synthesis would turn him into one of the best nineteenth-century European novelists.

Bourgeois, petty Lisbon: *O Primo Basílio*

Eça was still engaged in the last version of *O Crime* when *O Primo Basílio* was published. From the provincial town of Leiria he moved the setting to Lisbon. From the opening chapter, the Portuguese capital is carefully portrayed as sleepy and dreary (echoing the ending of *O Crime*). In keeping with the deterministic principles of Naturalism, Eça provides the milieu that will explain the behaviour of his characters, mainly Luísa. The atmosphere is suffocating: the hot city, the narrow gossiping street, Luísa's house where the novelist skilfully lets us in from the first paragraph. If the social setting is consciously built, so is Luísa's profile. Again, following the Naturalistic creed, the novelist is careful to provide some details of her past, namely her romantic education. This was not a new topic: Eça had already developed the connection between female education and adultery in his early journalism, in *As Farpas* (1871–72; *Barbs*). In *O Primo Basílio*, he wants to test the validity of his theories by creating a sentimental, bored, lazy Luísa, intoxicated with romantic readings. Nonetheless Luísa is not as empty as most critics claim.

The dramatic story of the fall and death of a middle-class married woman who becomes the lover of her cousin and former boyfriend, Basílio, has led critics to compare the novel with *Madame Bovary*. However, *O Primo* should be read within the broader context of the nineteenth-century novel of female adultery, as shown by Bill Overton: *La Femme de trente ans*, *Anna Karenina*, *La Regenta* or *Effi Briest*.[2]

O Primo Basílio sold better than *O Crime* because of its love scenes. But, in addition, it would withstand the test of time for its incomparable gallery of characters, such as Acácio (nowadays the adjective *acaciano* is still in use), the liberated Leopoldina, and the spiteful maid Juliana. Furthermore, its portrait of Lisbon would have continuity in *A Capital*, *O Conde de Abranhos* (both published posthumously in 1925) and *Os Maias*.

Eça, Oliveira Martins, Portuguese History and *fin-de-siècle* decline

It is useful to compare the endings of *O Crime* and of *Os Maias*. In the latter novel the ending is set ten years after the death of Afonso da Maia and the discovery that the relationship between Carlos and the beautiful, enigmatic Maria Eduarda, newly arrived in Lisbon, is incestuous. Once again, a decadent Lisbon represented by the sad, languid younger generation, metonymically standing for Portugal, is set against a past time of virility, energy and genuineness. The Ramalhete, the Maias' family house in Lisbon, symbolically echoes a similar atmosphere of national decline, as Carlos and his best friend João da Ega walk through a ghostly house on a pilgrimage to the world of the dead. Once full of life, the rooms have become dusty and inhabited by gloomy memories and lifeless objects aimlessly scattered around. There is the chill of death everywhere. Outside, Afonso da Maia's beloved garden, once a lush image of Paradise, has turned into a symbol of the inexorable passing of time, the loss of love and the inevitability of death. The once voluptuous statue of Venus Citereia (a symbol of Maria Eduarda) has become

---

2   Bill Overton, *The Novel of Female Adultery: Love and Gender in Continental European Fiction, 1830–1900* (Basingstoke: Macmillan, 1996).

mossy green and the water in the Elysian cascade is now reduced to a tearful trickle. The sun is slowly setting. In the distance, a windmill has stopped.

Both the epilogues of *Os Maias* and *O Crime* can only be properly understood in a *fin-de-siècle* national and European context. At a broader European level, they express the late nineteenth-century feeling of the end of civilisation, the 'dusk of nations', to use the title of the first chapter of Max Nordau's *Entartung* (1892; *Degeneration*). Influenced by Benedict Morel's *Traité des dégénérescences physiques, intellectuelles et morales* and Cesare Lombroso's *L'uomo delinquente*, Nordau envisages late nineteenth-century Europe as an era of decline and artists as mentally, emotionally and physically diseased. His book is a diatribe against decadent art (the opposite of middle-class values) exemplified by Naturalists, Decadentists and Symbolists such as Zola, Baudelaire, Tolstoy, Wagner, Burne-Jones, Huysmans and Wilde, among others.

From a national perspective, both *O Crime* and *Os Maias* shift the focus away from the story of individuals, or families, towards the wider context of nineteenth-century Portuguese History, as conceived by the historian Oliveira Martins.[3] From then onwards, Eça would borrow from Martins's theories: *Os Maias*, *A Ilustre Casa de Ramires*, and *A Cidade e as Serras* are the most obvious cases.

Drawing on Martins's *Portugal Contemporâneo*, both *Os Maias* and *A Cidade e as Serras* start with a flashback (more concentrated in the latter) in which the story of the fall of an aristocratic family over the course of three generations corresponds to three key periods in Portuguese history: the 1830s, represented by Afonso and D. Galeão (although the former stands for liberal Portugal and the latter for absolutism), the *Regeneração* (Regeneration) of the 1850s, symbolised by Pedro and Cintinho, and late nineteenth-century Portugal, epitomised by Carlos and Jacinto, the last representatives of their families and, as such, symbols of their country's ultimate decline.

Nonetheless, whereas the ending of *A Cidade e as Serras* is redemptive, in *Os Maias* the idea of decadence is tragically emphasised by the incestuous relationship of Carlos and Maria Eduarda, which continues even after Carlos learns that she is his sister. In figurative terms, incest means not only the incapacity of the Portuguese aristocracy to lead the country, but also its moral downfall and genetic degeneracy.

Eça's reflection on Portugal and Portuguese History reaches its climax in *A Ilustre Casa de Ramires*. The opening of the novel reads like a mini-History of Portugal based on Martins's *História de Portugal*. Drawing on both Herculano's *História de Portugal* (1846, 1847, 1850, 1853) and Antero

---

[3]   Joaquim Pedro de Oliveira Martins, *História de Portugal*, 19th edn (Lisbon: Guimarães Editores, 1987 [1st edn 1879]), *Portugal Contemporâneo*, 2 vols, 8th edn (Lisbon: Guimarães Editores, 1976 [1st edn 1881]).

de Quental's 1871 lecture at the Lisbon Casino, *Causas da Decadência dos Povos Peninsulares nos Últimos Três Séculos* (*The Causes of the Decadence of the Peninsular Peoples in the Last Three Centuries*), and furthermore influenced by organicism, Oliveira Martins envisaged Portuguese history as an apocalyptic cycle of birth, progress, decay and death corresponding to four periods of time: the first comprising the first dynasty (1143–1383); the second, the Avis dynasty (1385–1580), considered by Martins the Golden Age of Portuguese history, although the highest praise is for King João I and his sons; the third starting with overseas expansion in the Orient and ending in Alcácer-Quibir (1578), viewed as a watershed in Portuguese history; and the last, the remaining three centuries.

A close reading of the opening of *A Ilustre Casa* reveals how carefully the narrator links the Ramires's saga to selected episodes of Portuguese history and the extent to which Eça borrows from Martins. Older than Portugal itself (the family starts in 967), the first Ramires faithfully and bravely served the monarchs of the first dynasty, helping them in the *Reconquista*. Some of the Ramires connected to the Avis dynasty are highly praised for their bravery. They fought at Aljubarrota (1385) and in North Africa. But things start to change, as announced by the narrator: 'But then Portugal takes to the sea.' From then onwards the Ramires still follow their kings and fight with and for them but the tone is different. Apparently, they are still 'illustrious' (as the title of the novel seems to indicate), but soon Eça's subtle irony dismantles that assumption. Again, Oliveira Martins's theories underlie the Ramires's fate. According to the Portuguese historian, degeneration had started long before Alcácer-Quibir, still during the Avis dynasty, at the peak of Portuguese overseas expansion. This may seem a contradiction. It should be noticed, however, that Martins did not criticise the Discoveries, but rather the conquest of the Orient, which not only brought about luxury and thus moral degeneration, but also encouraged political centralisation and a religious fanaticism that reached its climax with the Braganza dynasty.

'But, as the nation, so did the noble race degenerate', the narrator asserts. And from the seventeenth to the late nineteenth century (as in Martins) the Ramires's saga becomes one of progressive decadence. Instead of distinguishing themselves in battles, they increasingly become as corrupt as the Braganza monarchs.Gonçalo is the last heir of the Ramires's estate (a ruined manor house in Northern Portugal, the original seat of the Ramires's power) and historic name, which he tries to resurrect by writing *A Torre de D. Ramires*, a historical novella about his ancestors, in order to promote himself, get into politics and move to Lisbon. He is idle, bored and as useless as his empty dark Tower, a symbolic space, like the Ramalhete, which echoes the Ramires's decline.

In the closing chapter, Gonçalo is explicitly associated with Portugal. Furthermore, the ending – Gonçalo's departure to Africa after a long dreamt of but surprisingly brief career in politics – brings the imperial debate of the 1880s and the 1890s into the novel, thus emphasising its historical meaning.

The first version of *A Ilustre Casa* was published in the *Revista Moderna* (May 1887–April 1889). As usual, Eça made sweeping changes when revising it for the book version, adding, for instance, several references to Africa to make the ending less unexpected. One of them was a conversation between Gonçalo and Gracinha, his sister, in which the former revealed that he was reading Rider Haggard's *King Solomon's Mines* (1885).

The reference to Haggard's novel, which Eça might have purchased and read (there is a book by Haggard in Tormes, *The Wizard*), is no mere coincidence. Through the introduction of a map drawn by a Portuguese in the sixteenth century, the novel echoes the late nineteenth-century Anglo-Portuguese rivalry in East Africa drawn to a close by the British Ultimatum of 1890, which paved the way for the partition of Africa and British supremacy in South Africa. Eça was aware of the potential impact of the book and published it in Portuguese (some think he might have translated it himself) in the *Revista de Portugal* between October 1889 and June 1890.

The imperial debate was not new to him. He had already written on Portuguese colonialism in *As Farpas*. Once in England, he had followed and condemned British expansion in Africa, in his articles on Egypt (1882) for the *Gazeta de Notícias* for instance. He himself wrote an article on the Ultimatum for the *Revista de Portugal* published in February 1890.

Although some critics claim that he was promoting imperialism, the ending of *A Ilustre Casa* is ambiguous. Ironically, we do not see Gonçalo either departing from or returning to Portugal, the African adventure being told second-hand by another character. And, unlike Amaro, Luísa and even Carlos da Maia, Gonçalo's fate is not hampered by deterministic principles. Ultimately, he is left free to act and the reader to imagine the outcome.

Degeneracy and the dandy

In some of Eça's narratives of the decline of the family and the nation, several characters are dandyish or dandies in the fullest sense: Basílio and his friend Viscount Reinaldo in *O Primo Basílio*, Carlos, João da Ega, Craft, Clifford, Dom Diogo in *Os Maias*; and Jacinto and even Zé Fernandes (although apparently a man of the *serras*, as will be discussed below) in *A Cidade e as Serras*. The ultimate dandy is, however, Carlos Fradique Mendes.

Fradique is a very interesting creation. Invented in 1869 by Eça, Antero de Quental (1842–91) and Jaime Batalha Reis (1847–1935), he reappears in *O Mistério da Estrada de Sintra* (1870; *The Mystery of the Sintra Road*), this time as a joint venture of Eça and Ramalho Ortigão (1836–1915), and is appropriated by Eça from 1888 onwards when he starts publishing Fradique's letters in *O Repórter* and the *Gazeta de Notícias*.

The Fradique of the late 1880s and 1890s is clearly a *fin-de-siècle* character who shows Eça's aesthetic evolution. His *Correspondência*, published in book form in 1900, is an aesthetic statement revealing new directions in Eça's art: fragmented narrative, mixture of narrative genres, the capacity to unite several tendencies in the same individual (Fradique is far removed from pairs such as Carlos/João da Ega or Jacinto/Gonçalo), showing that the 'I' is composed of multiple selves. This literary creation points to the absorption of new narrative methods Eça may have acquired from the Modernist writing of Robert Louis Stevenson. Above all, Fradique is a dandy in the line of Oscar Wilde's or Huysman's dandies, who, in turn, belong to the English–French dandy tradition, dating back to George 'Beau' Brummel (1778–1840).

Eça must have laboriously studied the dandy myth. Having lived in England, he certainly knew about some of the most popular and influential real-life dandies of his time: Disraeli, D'Orsay and Wilde. On the first, he wrote the brilliant obituary 'Lord Beaconsfield' for the *Gazeta de Notícias* on 23 August 1881, in which he evokes Disraeli's beauty, his curly hair, his fashionable clothes, his Orientalism and his friendship with the extravagant Count d'Orsay.

As exemplified by Beau Brummel (with whom Carlos, Ega and Fradique are explicitly compared), dandies are immaculately dressed, and eccentric elements are limited to a single detail: a green carnation as a *boutonnière* (corresponding to Jacinto's or Dorian Gray's flower), a brightly coloured waistcoat or a pair of gloves (Ega). Fradique even writes two letters about tailors and the art of dressing, echoing Carlyle's *Sartor Resartus* (1830–31; literally *The Tailor Re-Patched*).

The dandy partly carries one of the signs of Nordau's degenerate type: effeminacy. Eça's dandies are effeminate. One can compare not only the clothes of Carlos, Ega, Jacinto and Fradique but also their boudoirs, which look more like a woman's with brushes, perfumes, creams, etc. In this respect, Jacinto's is exemplary.

But dandyism is not only about clothes and extravagance. It expresses rebellion against bourgeois utilitarianism: dandies are idle and useless, qualities that stand in direct opposition to middle-class industry. They express boredom with the ethos of the commercial bourgeoisie; they pursue dilettantism, rather than professional activities. Fradique, Carlos, Ega and Jacinto all fit into these categories. They collect exotic objects and books (like Des Esseintes and Dorian Gray), travel to the East and cultivate Eastern exoticism (like Disraeli). In the last part of *Os Maias*, Carlos indulges in the late nineteenth-century fashion for things Japanese. So do Jacinto and Fradique (as Dorian Gray and Des Esseintes).

Wasteful and unproductive, dandies do not put knowledge to productive use. Carlos, Ega, Jacinto and Fradique are good examples of knowledge-for-knowledge's sake. Carlos never practises medicine, Ega never completes his *Memórias de um Átomo* (*Diary of an Atom*) and neither publishes their much-talked-of magazine. Fradique, despite his extensive travels, books and much boasted about worldliness, never publishes a book: all that is left is his letters and some obscure manuscripts which, according to his unreliable biographer, remain in the hands of his mysterious former lover Libuska, unseen by anyone.

Decadent late nineteenth-century Paris is their world. Jacinto's Parisian life occupies half the novel before he moves to the *serras*. It is the Paris of the underworld, portrayed like a disease-ridden body, a huge uncontrollable machine, epitomised by Jacinto's Palace, the mythical 202, in the Champs-Élysées.

Despite all their sporadic activity, Eça's dandies express a feeling of *ennui* (another sign of degeneracy, according to Nordau), the so-called *fartura* of Jacinto. Even Eça's Ulysses suffers from world-weariness. In his rewriting of the *Odyssey*, the short-story *A Perfeição* (1897; translated as *Perfection*), Eça portrays a fat, idle, bored Ulysses, on a languid island, who fits into the concept of late nineteenth-century decadence.

In fact, the dandy is the product of anxieties about cultural decline. Dandies are urbanites and, therefore, linked to the late nineteenth-century debate about cities and progress. They affect disdain for modern, industrial and technical processes, in contrast to their own pursuit of distinction and refined pleasures; nevertheless, the fact that they remain mostly single and childless mirrors fears of race extinction.

The death of the dandy

Eça does not, however, seem entirely happy about his dandies. Fradique dies in 1888. This is his biological death. His fictional life goes on in the *Revista de Portugal*, the *Gazeta de Notícias*, the *Revista Moderna* and the *Correspondência de Fradique Mendes*.

In the meantime, the other dandies become family men, while Ulysses returns home from decadent Ogygia. Eça, therefore, moves away from dandyism, by providing Jacinto and possibly Gonçalo with a family, removing them from urban life, turning them into useful men, erasing their effeminacy. Ambiguity remains, nonetheless. We do not know if Gonçalo is going to marry Rosinha and become useful, while the Parisian Jacinto's conversion to the so-called *serras* is not entirely convincing. He brings urban knowledge to the countryside, as well as culture, sophistication, technical and scientific progress and manners. Compared with his rural neighbours, he is still superior, original and extravagant. The city is still there, providing the *serras* with what is needed for change and improvement.

Even Zé Fernandes, the narrator, who controls events and the narrative, is ambiguous as he makes the reader believe things he will dismiss in the end. Although he seems to abhor the city, he indulges in dandyish pleasures. He is the one (not Jacinto) who goes back to Paris, only to return to Tormes, carrying the trappings of city life – pornographic magazines – which will take root in the *serras*. Besides, the *serras* are not the innocent paradise they seem to be (neither is Gonçalo's Santa Ireneia, for that matter). Even Aunt Vicência's apparently naïve friends and neighbours, although generous, warm-hearted and unsophisticated by Paris standards, are no simpletons. They have ambitions, frustrations and prejudices and do not refrain from playing political and social games.

Hence, the ambiguity of *A Cidade* is that it cannot be read as a simple return to the countryside. It is, rather, part of the late nineteenth-century European debate on the meaning of science and progress, the role of urban life versus rural economy, the future of Man in the twentieth century, themes also explored in the short stories *Civilização* (1892; *Civilisation*) and *Adão e Eva no Paraíso* (1897; *Adam and Eve in Paradise*), in Fradique's letters or in newspaper articles such as 'A Europa' and 'A Europa em Resumo' (published in the *Gazeta de Notícias* on 2 April 1888 and 18 January 1892, respectively).

The so-called 'last' Eça shows serenity, maturity and the capacity of synthesis. Without leaving social and political questions aside, he, like most European writers of his time, is looking for new solutions for his art. Fradique, Carlos and Ega may stand as the ultimate dandies. But Fradique dies in Paris, as he should, and Carlos and Ega are replaced by Gonçalo and Jacinto, the men of a new age who benefit from their wordly experience and, unlike the dandy, put it to profitable use. The dandy also gives way to the Saints, mainly St. Christopher, the good giant, already referred to as a model of humility as early as *O Crime*. As for fat and bored Ulysses, he goes back home to claim his wife, his property and his fatherhood, leaving behind the sophisticated, ultra-perfect island of Calypso.

In the final analysis, the indolent, useless dandy is superseded. Eça, not unlike Gonçalo who undergoes some change as he writes his *A Torre de D. Ramires*, finds fresh solutions for his characters and his writing. Ultimately it may be said that Eça, unlike his dandies and like his Ulysses, 'departed for the toil, for the torment, for the misery – for the delight of imperfect things'.

Texts and translations

[*A Cidade e as Serras*] *The City and the Mountains*, tr. Roy Campbell (Manchester: Carcanet, 1994)
A Correspondência de Fradique Mendes (Lisbon: Livros do Brasil, n.d.)

[*A Ilustre Casa de Ramires*] *The Illustrious House of Ramires*, trans. Anne Stevens (Manchester: Carcanet, 1992)

Cartas Inéditas de Fradique Mendes e Mais Páginas Esquecidas (Oporto: Chardron, 1929)

Eça de Queirós. Correspondência, leitura, coordenação, prefácio e notas de Guilherme de Castilho, 2 vols (Lisbon: Imprensa Nacional–Casa da Moeda, 1983); *Eça's English Letters*, tr. Alison Aiken and Ann Stevens, Introduction by Jonathan Keats (Manchester: Carcanet, 2000)

[*O Crime do Padre Amaro*] *The Crime of Father Amaro*, trans. Margaret Jull Costa (Sawtry: Dedalus, 2002)

[*O Primo Bazílio*] *Cousin Bazilio*, tr. Margaret Jull Costa (Sawtry: Dedalus, 2003)

[*Os Maias*] *The Maias*, trans. Margaret Jull Costa (Sawtry: Dedalus, 2002)

[*A Perfeição*] *Perfection*. A Translation from the Portuguese of Eça de Queiroz by Charles Marriott, with Decorations by John Austen (London: Selwyn and Bount, 1923)

Textos de Imprensa IV (da *Gazeta de Notícias*), Edição Crítica das Obras de Eça de Queirós, ed. Elza Miné and Neuma Cavalcante (Lisbon: Imprensa Nacional–Casa da Moeda, 2002)

Textos de Imprensa VI (da *Revista de Portugal*), Edição Crítica das Obras de Eça de Queirós, ed. Maria Helena Santana (Lisbon: Imprensa Nacional–Casa da Moeda, 1995)

Últimas Páginas (Oporto: Lello & Irmão Editores, 1911)

Further reading

Amann, Elizabeth, *Importing 'Madame Bovary': The Politics of Adultery* (New York and Basingstoke: Palgrave Macmillan, 2006)

Bloom, Harold, *Genius. A Mosaic of One Hundred Exemplary Creative Minds* (Clayton: Warner Books, 2002)

Coleman, Alexander, *Eça de Queirós and European Realism* (New York and London: New York University Press, 1980)

Hemmings, F. W. (ed.), *The Age of Realism* (Harmondsworth: Penguin, 1974)

Mónica, Maria Filomena, *Eça de Queiroz*, trans. Alison Aiken (Woodbridge: Tamesis, 2005)

Overton, Bill, *The Novel of Female Adultery. Love and Gender in Continental European Fiction, 1830–1900* (Basingstoke: Macmillan, 1996)

Pritchett, V. S., *The Mythmakers. Literary Essays* (New York: Random House, 1979)

Seymour-Smith, Martin, *A Reader's Guide to Fifty European Novels* (London: Heinemann, 1980), pp. 309–17

12

Fernando Pessoa and the Modernist Generation

MARIANA GRAY DE CASTRO

When the American critic Harold Bloom included 'the amazing Portuguese poet, Fernando Pessoa' among his selection of the most significant writers in *The Western Canon* (1994), *Time Magazine* was wrong to consider this an example of Bloom's pandering to 'the obligatory academic obscurity'. Pessoa is the inescapable giant of modern Portuguese letters: through his unique feature of writing different character–poets, who author separate bodies of work with distinctive styles and themes, as well as his involvement in the literary circles of the day, he almost single-handedly brought Modernism to Portugal. While some may deplore the way in which his living presence continues to overshadow every other writer in the period, and his transformation into a national icon, used and abused in contemporary culture (the so-called 'Pessoa industry'), few would dispute the significance of his literary achievement. Bloom's championing of Pessoa's work and a recent proliferation of English anthologies has lifted him from relative obscurity in Anglophone countries to the mainstream of twentieth-century literature, placing him on a par with illustrious contemporary modernists like Ezra Pound, W. B. Yeats, T. S. Eliot and James Joyce.

Pessoa was born in Lisbon in 1888. Following the death of his father, his mother married the Portuguese consul in Durban, South Africa, and the family moved there when Pessoa was seven. He had a British education and excelled at school, immersing himself in English literature: Shakespeare, Milton, Poe, Dickens and Carlyle became firm favourites. He would have gone on to study at Cambridge but for a legal technicality to do with residency requirements, and he continued to read and write in English throughout his life. His brand of English, however, the product of a very British education in a then British colony, was always of the nineteenth-century variety: although fluent, it was old-fashioned and affected by the standards of the new century. He only became truly modern when writing in his native Portuguese.

Pessoa returned to Lisbon definitively in 1905, aged seventeen; he never again left the country, and hardly ever left the city. He mostly lived alone, was inconspicuous, and earned a modest living by writing the foreign correspondence of Portuguese companies with commercial interests abroad. The work was undemanding, and it evidently gave him time to write: upon his death in 1935, Pessoa left behind almost thirty thousand manuscripts in three wooden chests. The three have become one in popular mythology, and are referred to as his famous *arca*.

The finer details of Pessoa's biography remain sketchy, partly by his own design. There are surprisingly few anecdotes and stories about the man, the diaries he kept were mostly reading diaries and, although he was active in artistic circles, his public life was otherwise remarkably unremarkable. It has been stated, in reference to Pessoa, that great poets do not have biographies; that their writings are their biography. Pessoa himself would improve on this commonplace by claiming, with characteristic immodesty, that great poets have only their genius. Unlike Oscar Wilde, who channelled his genius into his life at the expense of his writings, Pessoa chose instead to live more fully in the world of literature. His imaginary childhood friends were authors he made up, like a Chevalier de Pas who wrote letters to the six-year-old Pessoa. Pessoa went on to pen works he attributed to Robert Anon and Alexander Search, in pieces that reflect the typical anxieties and existential questions of a sensitive adolescent. Jean Seul was his solitary French collaborator (Pessoa's fictional names, like his own, are loaded with suggestive meanings). As an adult, he continued to people his literary universe with scores of would-be authors: there were poets, prose writers, philosophers, psychologists, astrologists, even a poor hunchback girl and an expert at crosswords. Over seventy of these pseudo-authors have emerged from Pessoa's *arca*, although it is debatable how many represent alternative, autonomous personalities rather than slighter literary experiments. His superabundance of competing voices, who threaten to overpower his own identity, is in part an extreme literary experiment, in part a psychological necessity, and in part an elaborate joke. Does Pessoa contradict himself? Very well, he contradicts himself; as Walt Whitman, one of his major influences, memorably put it, he contains multitudes. His divergent voices, strains and interests should be a cause for celebration rather than concern.

The most developed of his character–poets Pessoa called 'heteronyms' (*heterónimos*), coining the word to distinguish them from the more usual pseudonyms, masks and voices that were common practice in the period. Their difference is one of degree rather than kind: the heteronyms can be thought of as a radical evolution of Pound's *personae* and Yeats's masks. But no previous writer had ever granted his fictional voices such autonomy: Pessoa's heteronyms, which he describes as dramatic constructs, interact with each other as well as with himself; they hold philosophical discussions, write letters, and respond to each other's work. Each has a distinctive poetic idiom, thematic core, and context of literary influence. Pessoa went as far as to describe their physical appearances and their life stories, and provide them with astrological birth charts. The ways in which he directed, differentiated and explained his heteronyms invited early readers to treat them as real people, with thoughts and feelings entirely distinct from his own. Many still do; it is not uncommon to refer Pessoa's heteronyms as poets entirely separate from their *ur*-author.

The modernist crisis of identity, an ongoing ontological meditation on the nature of being or, more usually in the case of Pessoa, non-being, is an omnipresent motif. Perhaps his family name, whose competing connotations evoke *persona* (theatrical mask) in Latin, person in Portuguese, and *personne* (wonderfully, either 'person' or 'no one') in French, was deterministic in this respect. Or perhaps it was a lucky coincidence. Pessoa's writings, and our reactions to them as readers, often hinge on this unsettling balance between the profoundly tragic and the superficially playful, poised as they are between elation and despair.

The poetry of the 'orthonym' (*ortónimo*), or Pessoa writing as 'himself', calls everything we take for granted into question, including ourselves. Like the heteronyms, the orthonym signals a poetic possibility rather than a historical subject, not to be confused with the flesh and blood Pessoa, who in any case doubted his own reality. His poems reveal a constant search for a deeper truth lying beyond the surface appearance of reality, just out of reach. Pessoa's lifelong search for an alternative truth is reflected in the library he left behind upon his death, which contains more occultist titles than works of literature. His esoteric leanings, like those of Yeats, are a rich source of imagery for his orthonymic poetry.

'Isto' (This) and 'Autopsicografia' (Self-Analysis) are two prescriptive poems, concerned with the making of poetry. Direct communication is felt by the modernist generation to be impossible; poetry must therefore involve a conversion of the poet's subjective personal emotions into universal images, capable of evoking a similar emotion in the reader. 'Autopsicografia' opens with the famous line: 'The poet is a faker' ('O poeta é um fingidor'). Pessoa's concept of *fingimento*, or the problem of artistic (in)sincerity, is crucial to his literary enterprise. The difficulty in establishing a consensual English equivalent for *fingir* – the verb has been variously rendered as 'to fake', 'to feign', 'to pretend', even 'to lie' – points to its competing connotations. In Latin, however, *fingere* also means to shape, fashion, form or mould, which points at deliberate construction rather than mere play-acting. The charge of insincerity is one often levied against the self-professed faker, but the point is that Pessoa everywhere denounces the concept of a fixed, knowable self as a fiction. The modernist revelation is that we have no selves, in the conventional sense, to speak of.

Pessoa's theoretical claims for literary impersonality are echoed by those of the English modernists: Eliot states in his seminal essay 'Tradition and the Individual Talent' (1919) that 'the emotion of art is impersonal', because 'the progress of an artist is a continual self-sacrifice, a continual extinction of personality'. Pessoa would have agreed that a text is a dramatic construct, not to be analysed for signs of authorial life; like Eliot, who was labelled 'The Invisible Poet' by one biographer, he is similarly elusive in his writings. Joyce in *A Portrait of the Artist as a Young Man* (1916) describes the ideal artist as the 'invisible God of creation', who 'remains within or behind or beyond or above his handiwork, refined out of existence, indifferent, paring his fingernails'. Pessoa 'himself', in the poem that begins 'I leave to the blind and the deaf' ('Deixo ao cego e ao surdo'), also claims to contemplate his artistry 'from the heights of being conscious' ('do alto de ter consciência'). For all their critical emphasis on intellectual construction and impersonality, however, it is well to remember that the emotion is what comes first, which explains most readers' powerfully emotional response to these writers' works.

The process of transforming the self into art is, for Pessoa, a painful one, as revealed by the anguished existential undertones to many of the orthonymous poems, wherein the 'pain of (over) thinking' ('dor de pensar') is pervasive. In 'Ela canta, pobre ceifeira' ('She Sings, Poor Reaper') the poet expresses a wish to be the unthinking, all-feeling other, in the image of a nameless reaper who is able to burst into spontaneous song, rather than being shackled to his own rational self. In another recurring image, the orthonym describes himself as the contents of a glass that is filled to overflowing; the overflow of personality is what Pessoa channels into his various fictional authors. Pessoa's profound investment, since childhood, in 'persons not his', in the words of Robert Browning, a poet he admired, came to a head in 1914, with his heteronymic explosion into Alberto Caeiro, Álvaro de Campos, and Ricardo Reis, all major twentieth-century poets in their own right.

According to Pessoa, Caeiro had blue eyes and was of fragile health; he eventually died of consumption. He lived peacefully in the Portuguese countryside with a maiden aunt, having received no formal education. Caeiro is the negative image of Pessoa 'himself': utterly uncomplicated and unself-conscious. He simply exists, at one with the natural world around him, and sees things for what they are, without probing any underlying mystical or symbolic content: 'My gaze is as clear as a sunflower' ('O meu olhar é nítido como um girassol'). Álvaro de Campos, in contrast, is the great cosmopolitan and lover of cities: a naval engineer by profession, he trained in Scotland, wrote in English as well as in Portuguese, experimented with drugs, and travelled extensively. Campos was active in public life, arguably more so than Pessoa himself: contrary and provocative, the engineer published articles and manifestos, and even appeared in the place of his creator in front of the latter's friends and girlfriend Ophélia (she grudgingly played along, but preferred the company of Pessoa). One mutual friend recorded, in a muddle Pessoa would have delighted in, that when he was not pretending to be Álvaro de Campos, Pessoa was the most normal and down-to-earth person imaginable.

It was Campos who helpfully informed readers that 'Fernando Pessoa does not, strictly speaking, exist' ('Fernando Pessoa não existe, propriamente falando').

Campos is described by Pessoa as hysterical, a diagnosis in vogue at the time, albeit one more usually applied to women. Campos's thin veneer of madness and natural irreverence make him the perfect mouthpiece for sentiments one feels Pessoa wishes to express but would rather not sign under his own name. He defends Pessoa's friend, the poet António Botto, against charges of literary indecency in a manner less convoluted than Pessoa's, and even takes it upon himself to 'out' his fellow heteronym Ricardo Reis, pointing out that the women in Reis's poems are mere abstractions. Reis, whom Pessoa describes as 'a Greek Horace writing in Portuguese', is a doctor and classicist who pens heavily structured odes featuring the vaporous female muses of antiquity. His poems convey an attempt to live stoically in the face of inevitable mortality, with the least possible amount of suffering, and to make the most of the fleeting moment; they are generally harmonious, but some anxious undertones betray a less than Stoic worry about the future: 'Everything that passes goes so quickly!' ('Tão cedo passa tudo quanto passa!') What he made of Campos's charge is not recorded.

Campos embodies the true modernist poet, from his early engagement with experimental trends to his later belief that modern life is empty and absurd. His professed goal is to 'Feel everything in every possible way' ('Sentir tudo de todas as maneiras') and the furious enthusiasm of his early odes to modernity, progress and civilisation is as contagious as it is exhausting. Their optimistic euphoria eventually leaves Campos drained, and he enters a more decadent phase of apathy and existential unease: 'What is within me is, mainly, tiredness' ('O que há em mim é sobretudo cansaço'). Both he and modernity, seemingly so full of promise, had ultimately failed to deliver. Death, of course, is the only definitive way out – he tries to talk himself into committing suicide in one poem, and finds he lacks the courage – but in the meantime the only thing to do is to dive, body and soul, into experiencing everything to the limit, trying to be 'everyone, and every place' ('toda a gente e toda a parte'), to search for beauty and, of course, to go on writing poetry. The Campos of the second phase, the one we encounter in 'Tabacaria' ('Tobacco Shop'), a poem once featured in a full-page spread of a French newspaper as the most beautiful text ever written, is devastating in his nihilism, its opening repetition of 'nothing [...] nothing [...] nothing' ('nada [...] nada [...] nada') evoking one of the bleakest lines in world literature: Lear's 'Never, never, never, never, never.'

What saves Campos's poems, even late ones like 'Tabacaria', from being merely depressing is his great sense of humour. He is exaggerated and melodramatic, but able to laugh at himself and take some comfort from the fact that he, a brilliant but imperfect individual, is as out of sorts as the world around him: 'Poor Álvaro de Campos, whom no one cares about! Pity him who feels so sorry for himself!' ('Coitado do Álvaro de Campos, com quem ninguém se importa! Coitado dele que tem tanta pena de si mesmo!') Campos delights in weird and wonderful juxtapositions, and alternates effortlessly between the ridiculous and the sublime: a memorable shorter poem begins 'I have a bad cold' ('Tenho uma grande constipação'), goes on to compare sneezing to metaphysical thought, and concludes by asking for truth and aspirin. In another poem, he immediately qualifies a potentially nihilistic image – 'Vast are the deserts, and everything is a desert' ('Grandes são os desertos e tudo é desertos') – with a deflationary aside: 'Unless, of course, I am mistaken' ('Salvo erro, naturalmente').

The Zen-like Caeiro, the still point of Pessoa's turning heteronymic world, is firmly placed at its centre, and praised as the master by Campos, Reis, and Pessoa 'himself'. His vision of the world is the one they aspire to, the one they wish they shared. Thinking too much, probing hidden meanings, is for Caeiro to lose sight of things as they are; it is also ridiculous, unnecessary, and leads to unhappiness, as he implies in poetic digs at the orthonym. Metaphysics, Campos finally comes to agree, is the result of feeling out of sorts ('uma consequência de estar mal disposto'), but neither he nor Pessoa 'himself' can ever escape their rational makeup. Campos is the only one of the three to evolve, and he often seems more believable than Pessoa himself. Someone like Reis could conceivably have existed, but only in an age so distant from our own that he is now difficult to visualise. Caeiro is too flat a character to be psychologically credible, and the state of pure being he promotes is unfortunately untenable; he describes himself, in one poem, as the only poet of his type, and there may be a reason why there are no others. However, while the nature poet is a more controlled experiment than Campos, some of Pessoa's best-loved poems are born of this impossible ideal.

Writing about the genesis of the heteronyms some twenty years after the event, Pessoa explained that they appeared to him, fully formed, in a flash of inspiration on 8 March 1914; it was, he claimed, 'the triumphal day of my life' ('o dia triunfal da minha vida'). He described how he walked over to a chest of drawers and furiously penned the thirty-odd poems in Caeiro's longest collection, *O Guardador de Rebanhos* (*The Keeper of Sheep*) as well as poems by Campos, and finally one in his own name, 'Chuva Oblíqua' ('Slanting Rain'). Pessoa's account has been discredited as something of a fabrication: for one thing, we now know that 'Slanting Rain' was attributed first to Caeiro (with whom it does not sit at all), then to Campos (a slightly better fit), before finally landing on the orthonym; such shifting attributions suggest Pessoa consciously working out the characteristics and poetic ranges of his various literary alter egos. Pessoa is prone to creating his own myth and improving on the bare bones of biography; his numerous self-explanations, always interesting, should be taken as declarations of intent rather than statements of fact.

In one recurrent explanation for his unique mode of literary creation, Pessoa likens it to the making of dramatic poetry. When the heteronyms are not criticising and explaining each other, a favourite habit of the interfering Campos in particular, Pessoa tends to speak of them as dramatic characters, acting out a 'drama in people' ('drama em gente') in the theatre of his mind. Álvaro de Campos, he informs us, is a character in a play; the only thing missing is the play itself. Pessoa, his creator, is thus essentially a dramatist (Pessoa only published a single play, but this does not seem to trouble him). If his descriptions of the heteronyms evoke larger-than-life stage characters like Hamlet, it is no coincidence. Pessoa admired Shakespeare, above all, as the 'greatest expressor' ('maior expressor') of personality who ever was.

Mário de Sá-Carneiro (1890–1916), a fellow modernist and Pessoa's closest friend, also explores in his writings the problems of the divided self, being fascinated by the gulf between what one is in reality and what one is potentially, in dreams. His fictional characters are forever attempting to escape the banalities of everyday life into a higher realm of art and beauty, which appears in his writings as the 'Great Beyond' ('Além'), a plane of existence tinged with the surreal, fantastic atmosphere of dreamscapes. Sá-Carneiro himself spent his final years escaping what he considered to be provincial, slow-paced Lisbon to artistic, cosmopolitan Paris, from where he wrote intimate, heart-wrenching letters to Pessoa that chart the mental anguish of his final years.

Like Pessoa, Sá-Carneiro is obsessed with the splitting of the self, but his literary fragmentation is more limited, in one direction only. His protagonists tend to multiply into doubles whom they often do not recognise as themselves, with disastrous results. The main character of the short story *Eu Próprio – O Outro* ('I Myself – the Other') becomes so entwined with a stranger he meets, a shadowy figure who resembles him more and more by the day, that he decides he must kill the unknown other. Since we are led to believe that the stranger is a part of himself, we sense his own imminent demise. The problematics of alter egos and shadow personalities are potentially explosive, and offer up dramatic possibilities: what happens when you meet your own double? Sá-Carneiro's treatment of the theme is reminiscent of that in Wilde's *The Picture of Dorian Gray* (1890) and Robert Louis Stevenson's *The Strange Case of Dr Jekyll and Mr Hyde* (1886); his writings also contain more or less disguised homoerotic undertones, placing them in the decadent, *fin-de-siècle* tradition despite their more modernist storytelling technique.

The tragic outcome of 'I Myself – the Other' mirrors that of Sá-Carneiro's only novel, *A Confissão de Lúcio* (1914; translated as *Lúcio's Confession*). Lúcio, his friend Ricardo de Loureiro, and Ricardo's wife Marta are caught in an unusual love triangle, and may be on inspection different projections of the same personality. If so, when Ricardo attempts to kill Marta, the event is thus a murder–suicide. Lúcio can be viewed as a modern tragic subject, a product of both internal causes, especially unconscious impulses that Freud would raise an eyebrow at, and external ones in the shape of restrictive, traditional society. His tragedy may be that he is called upon to be responsible for his actions even though he cannot understand or explain them, making him the most slippery of unreliable narrators.

Psychological readings of Sá-Carneiro's writings are often irresistible; unlike the impersonal Pessoa, he is certainly a poet who bleeds, and his writings seem to foreshadow his own tragic end. Of course there is much artifice involved, and fiction is not unmediated autobiography, but there is even a poem in which the speaker desires to die in a circus-like fanfare. The consummate performer, Sá-Carneiro killed himself with terrible theatricality in 1916. He was twenty-five years old. For him as for his creations, there is no way out of the crisis of identity; he is always suspended between one state and another; as he despairs in one poem: 'I am neither myself nor the other' ('Eu não sou eu nem sou o outro').

Beyond embodying, in their splitting of the self into its constituent parts, the pinnacle of the modern sensibility, Pessoa and Sá-Carneiro played a leading role in bringing the Portuguese literary scene up to speed with the best of the European *avant-garde*. At the dawn of the new century, the world was becoming modern: there was rapid industrialisation, cities were growing, and their inhabitants were more nervous than ever, according to their own perceptions and their doctors' diagnoses. The unprecedented complexity of modern urban life began to show in its art scene, which confronted head-on the subject matter of the machine age and of man's predicament in this brave new world. There was a proliferation of experimental currents in Europe, with an array of modernist -*isms* vying to best capture the spirit of the day. In Italy there was Marinetti's aggressive futurism; in France, painters were exploding traditional perspectives with cubism; Germany bred expressionism; in Britain, Ezra Pound and Wyndham Lewis's dizzying vorticism found an outlet in their subversive magazine *Blast* (1914). It was the heyday of the little magazine, full of artistic manifestos and radically innovative texts. In Lisbon, Pessoa and Sá-Carneiro founded *Orpheu* (1915; *Orpheus*), which only ran to two issues.

The *Orpheu* generation, as their circle became known, included also the painter Santa-Rita Pintor (1889–1918) and the immensely versatile Almada Negreiros (1893–1970), among others. In the pages of the magazine, these artists worked their way through a plethora of modernist currents and sub-currents, revived older ones, and invented new ones. 'Intersectionism' (*Interseccionismo*, from 'intersection') was a sort of cubism transposed to literature, with Pessoa's 'Chuva Oblíqua' as its emblematic poem. Sá-Carneiro signed off as an intersectionist poet in letters dating from this time. Santa-Rita Pintor provided cubist paintings and geometric abstractions in the style of Wyndham

Lewis's iconography. A more profound engagement was with futurism, which Marinetti, its Italian founder, claimed had been inspired by a car crash. It is a worthwhile exercise to read Campos's 'Ode Triunfal' ('Triumphal Ode'), first published in *Orpheu*, side by side with Marinetti's first futurist manifesto (1909), tracing the ways in which the latter's directives inform passages of great poetic beauty. Marinetti's ideal of 'words in liberty' was reflected in the innovative visual graphics of the magazine, and was a clear influence on pieces like Sá-Carneiro's poem 'Manucure' ('Manicure').

Pessoa had become friends with Almada following the publication of a review he wrote on Almada's first individual exhibition of paintings a few years prior to their collaboration in *Orpheu*, to which Almada had retorted that he (Almada) knew nothing about art. Almada considered himself an out-and-out futurist, but his impressionistic vignettes contain many other *avant garde* elements, being infused with the surreal and the absurd. He was a prolific, multifaceted artist who participated in futurist conferences, choreographed modern dance, and was a prime caricaturist in addition to being a published author and admired painter; his are the best-known, oft reproduced images of Pessoa. He outlived Pessoa and Sá-Carneiro by many years, and continued to be a major player in Portuguese culture. Looking back to the time of *Orpheu*, he described its unending series of experimental *-isms* as 'hilarious' (*hilariante*), hinting at the magazine's dual intention: ostensibly a serious effort to usher in modernity, it also contained a subversive sense of fun. Its publication predictably caused a public outcry, a sure sign of success. Júlio Dantas, a staunch upholder of tradition and ideal symbol of the establishment (he would a few years later become Minister of Education), was one public figure to denounce its artists as mad and immoral. He and his ilk were promptly counter-attacked by Almada in his aggressive *Manifesto Anti-Dantas* (*Anti-Dantas Manifesto*), published as a leaflet in 1916.

Orpheu paved the way for subsequent modernist reviews. *Portugal Futurista* (1917; *Futurist Portugal*), edited by Santa-Rita Pintor, contained his own paintings, translations of Marinetti and other futurists, poems by Pessoa, letters of Sá-Carneiro, and a prose piece by Almada written as an unpunctuated, uninterrupted flow of words. It also published 'Ultimatum', a programmatic manifesto in which Campos gleefully attacked everything in contemporary culture, from politicians to artists, in the style of the 'Blast – Bless' section of the English magazine *Blast*. The first number of *Portugal Futurista* was promptly seized by the authorities, and the magazine was forced to shut down. The typographically daring but otherwise less provocative *Athena* (1924–5) marked the first public appearances of Reis and Caeiro.

The magazine *Presença* (1927–40; *Presence*), founded by José Régio (1901–69) and João Gaspar Simões (1903–87), was longer lived, running to fifty-six issues. It did much to promote the work of the *Orpheu* group, whom it held in the highest regard. Régio set out to define the main characteristics of the previous generation's modernism in an early issue of *Presença*, in terms relevant to this day: he highlighted its ironic juxtaposition or super-imposition of contradictory subjective experiences, its interest in the uncon-scious as well as the conscious mind, and its treatment of personality as multiple and fluid rather than single and unchanging. Its technical virtuosity and stylistic flights of fancy Régio considered the natural byproducts of such tendencies, when in reality they were an integral component. Gaspar Simões was particularly attracted to modern psychological theories, especially those of Freud, and pioneered psychoanalytical readings of Pessoa's work; Pessoa, who insisted on artistic impersonality and had no wish to be psychoanalysed, resisted the approach.

We have seen how Pessoa, unlike the hapless Sá-Carneiro, found a solu-tion of sorts for his tenuous grip on his own identity, an artistic way out in his fragmentation into alternative selves. Another way in which he escaped disappearing into the vortex of his inner world was by stepping outside his incessant introspection to promote a national cause. This parallel strain, so different from his modernist enterprises – modernist poets being generally little concerned with such trivialities as politics – was also patent from an early age: Pessoa's earliest known poem is often cited as an expression of his affec-tion for his mother, but more unusual in a boy of six is its fusion with a love of his country. In 1912 Pessoa had published two critical articles in Teixeira de Pascoaes's magazine *A Águia* (*The Eagle*), expounding the nationalist ideals of Pascoaes's *Saudosismo* movement (derived from *saudade*, that word of noto-riously problematic translation evoking a melancholic nostalgia for things now lost). *Mensagem* (1934; *Message*), the only book-length collection to be published in Pessoa's lifetime (he had previously self-published two chap-books of poems in English), was the poetic culmination of his patriotism. It gained Pessoa wider public acclaim and, not least, a useful cash reward, by winning first prize in its category in a national literary competition.

The result of a parallel, anti-modernist drive in Pessoa, in its formal struc-ture as well as its subject matter, *Mensagem* was meant to be the great national epic of the future, just as *Os Lusíadas* had been the great national epic of the past. This is the most charitable explanation of why it fails to mention the name of Camões. Other explanations, to do with anxieties of influence, abound; Pessoa was adept at clearing imaginative spaces for himself, and preparing the ground for his own poetic entry. In his articles for *A Águia*, the germ of *Mensagem*, he had opportunely announced the imminent appear-ance of a 'Supra Camões' who would restore Portuguese culture to its former glory; Campos helpfully explained a few years later, in *Ultimatum*, that the greatest artist should have fifteen or twenty different personalities.

Mensagem is ostensibly a patriotic piece, and it was certainly promoted as such in the days of the *Estado Novo*, but it is also infused with Pessoa's trade-mark concerns. In one instance, the poet claims that the charge of madness levelled against King Sebastião is the very proof of the King's greatness. Those associated with *Orpheu* had also been labelled mad (one was 'objectively' mad, writing his contributions from a lunatic asylum), and Pessoa often hinted that his process of heteronymic creation had something to do with his own streak of madness, namely hystero-neurasthenia. Presumably, to be a hystero-neurasthenic was for Pessoa no bad thing: some of Campos's most beautiful poems are anchored in the hysteria Pessoa bestowed upon him. Pessoa also diagnosed his greatest literary idol, Shakespeare, as a fellow hystero-neurasthenic, and even linked it to dramatic poetry, for him the highest form of art.

If *Mensagem*, in its broad contours, can be considered anti-modernist, Pessoa's prose masterpiece *Livro do Desassossego* (1982; translated as *The Book of Disquiet*) has been described as post-modernist. Its putative author is the semi-heteronym Bernardo Soares: 'semi' because his personality is close to Pessoa's own, being a limited version of it rather than a dramatic departure like that of Caeiro, Campos or Reis. Soares's disquieting book of hauntingly poetic prose, which he describes as a factless autobiography, contains the essence of Pessoa's entire literary output, including that of his heteronyms and other fictional voices. Like his creator, Soares lives in Lisbon, has a trivial day job, and only exists fully in literature, claiming that 'literature is the most pleasant way of ignoring life' ('a literatura é a maneira mais agradável de ignorar a vida'). He takes it upon himself to record, with curious detachment, his thoughts and feelings on an enormous variety of subjects, ranging from serious metaphysical examinations to the banalities of everyday life. His book is a disjointed collection of dreams, psychological examinations, observations about man and the universe, aesthetic appreciations, and maxims to live by; an implausible alternation of the profound and the trivial, the pretentious and the tongue-in-cheek. No subject is too great or too small. Soares indulges in narcissistic, introverted examinations of his own boredom and self-pity: 'I write, unhappy, in my quiet room, alone like I always have been, alone like I always will be' ('Escrevo, triste, no meu quarto quieto, sozinho como sempre tenho sido, sozinho como sempre serei'). He discourses on the big questions of religion, literature, the soul, and immortality: 'Death is a release because dying is not needing anyone else' ('A morte é uma libertação porque morrer é não precisar de outrém'); 'God is us being alive, and this not being all there is' ('Deus é existirmos e isto não ser tudo'). In between, he touches on more earthly affairs, as a glance through a few section headings will illustrate: '(Notes on Indifference or something like that)' (in parenthesis, in English); 'Advice for unhappily married women' ('Conselhos às mal-casadas'), and so on.

Livro do Desassossego lacks any narrative action or story in the conventional sense, reading instead like the shapeless diary of a soul; it is a sprawling, unfinished mass of fragmentary texts. Pessoa published a few of these in 1913, and others almost twenty years later, but the vast majority he stuffed into a large envelope or left unclassified among his papers, to let future readers make of them what they would. Due to the great editorial challenges this poses – there is still no definitive, standard text – *Livro do Desassossego* was first published in 1982, almost fifty years after Pessoa's death. In many ways this was a positive turn of events, since it allowed the post-modernist generation to stake its claim to Pessoa, delighting in his book's slippery language and infinitely allusive, ultimately elusive, nature. Some have suggested that its ideal form would be a collection of loose papers, which is probably taking things too far: despite his frantic, compulsive mode of composition and impatience to go back and revise, towards the end of his life Pessoa crafted elaborate plans on how to best organise his works for publication, even if he never saw them through. The inability to finish his writings satisfactorily is also the chief torment of Pessoa's final literary alter ego, the aristocratic Barão de Teive, who finally commits suicide in despair. After burning the bulk of his life's work, he leaves behind a suicide note (also fragmented), and a few manuscripts stuffed into a drawer. Pessoa, who claims he discovered the Baron's papers, takes it upon himself to make his work public. He goes as far as to write a brief introduction, but then seemingly abandons the project.

Pessoa, unlike the Baron, did not destroy his thousands of unpublished manuscripts. Instead, he bet on literary immortality by keeping them in his *arca*. Its depths contain much material that is still awaiting discovery, transcription – Pessoa's handwriting is notoriously appalling – and publication. His *arca*, like Joyce's *Ulysses*, in which Joyce claimed he had put enough puzzles and enigmas into it to 'keep the professors busy for centuries', is a dizzying abyss that throws up new facets of Pessoa's life and work. Of such stuff his legend continues to be made.

Pessoa's influence on Portuguese letters and, increasingly, on world literature is pervasive. Nobel prizewinner José Saramago revived one of Pessoa's heteronyms in *O Ano da Morte de Ricardo Reis* (1984, *The Year of the Death of Ricardo Reis*), taking to its logical conclusion the fact that Pessoa never killed Reis off. There is a poignant scene where Reis stands before his creator's grave. It is the perfect image for the way in which Pessoa's fictions have outlived him, firing the imagination of future generations.

Texts and translations

Negreiros, José de Almada, *Ficções* (Lisbon: Assírio & Alvim, 2002)
Pessoa, Fernando, *Forever Someone Else: Selected Poems*, ed. and tr. Richard
      Zenith (Lisbon: Assírio & Alvim, 2009) [Parallel text edition]
—— (as Bernardo Soares). *Livro do Desassossego*, ed. Richard Zenith (Lisbon:

Assírio e Alvim, 1998); *The Book of Disquiet*, ed. and trans. Richard Zenith (Harmondsworth: Penguin Classics, 2002)

—— *A Little Larger than the Entire Universe: Selected Poems*, ed. and trans. Richard Zenith (Harmondsworth: Penguin Classics, 2006)

—— *Fernando Pessoa: Selected Poems*, ed. and trans. Peter Rickard (Edinburgh: Edinburgh University Press, 1971)

—— *Fernando Pessoa: Selected Poems*, trans Jonathan Griffin (Harmondsworth: Penguin, 1974)

—— *et al.*, *Orpheu: Edição facsimilada* (Lisbon: Contexto, 1989)

Sá-Carneiro, Mário de, *A Confissão de Lúcio* (Lisbon: Ática, 1945); *Lúcio's Confession*, trans. Margaret Jull Costa (Sawtry: Dedalus, 1993)

—— *Céu em fogo: novelas* (Lisbon: Ática, 1993)

—— *Poemas completos*, ed. Fernando Cabral Martins (Lisbon: Assírio & Alvim, 1996)

Further reading

Klobucka, Anna, and Mark Sabine (eds), *Embodying Pessoa: Corporeality, Gender, Sexuality* (Toronto: Toronto University Press, 2007)

Lisboa, Eugénio, and L. C. Taylor (eds), *A Centenary Pessoa* (Manchester: Carcanet, 1995)

McGuirk, Bernard (ed.), *Three Persons in One: A Centenary Tribute to Fernando Pessoa* (Nottingham: University of Nottingham, 1988)

Monteiro, George (ed.), *The Man Who Never Was* (Providence, RI: Gávea-Brown, 1982)

—— *The Presence of Pessoa: English, American, and Southern African Literary Responses* (Lexington: University Press of Kentucky, c.1998)

Sadlier, Darlene, *An Introduction to Fernando Pessoa: Modernism and the Paradoxes of Authorship* (Gainesville: University Press of Florida, 1998)

Santos, Maria Irene Ramalho Sousa, *Atlantic Poets: Fernando Pessoa's Turn in Anglo-American Modernism* (Hanover, NH: University Press of New England, 2003)

13

Narrative and Drama during the Dictatorship

PHILLIP ROTHWELL

The climate of fear the dictatorship of António de Oliveira Salazar fostered at various times during its long reign and its subtle and not-so-subtle censorship techniques had a profound impact on the cultural production of Portugal. Mediocre writers and playwrights were celebrated by the regime, through prizes and official approval. Yet, unlike under other authoritarian regimes, a significant amount of work that critiqued the premises and effects of Salazarism emerged within Portugal. The regime tended to use intimidation more than outright censorship, although some writers, such as José Cardoso Pires, did fall foul of the censor's blue pencil. However, Salazar preferred publishers and writers to police themselves, occasionally making examples of those who did not. This meant that much of the critique of and literary resistance to the regime was veiled, depending on metaphor and analogy.

The early years of Salazar's government saw the prominence of António Ferro (1895–1956) as the head of the state's propaganda machine. Ferro was himself a mediocre playwright and writer, who had been involved in the Modernist movement in Portugal. Through his friendship with the writer Mário de Sá-Carneiro (1890–1916), he had acquired, in 1915, the editorship of *Orpheu*, one of the movement's main publication venues. Ironically, given his future role in managing the Salazar regime's message through methods including censorship, his first play, *Mar Alto* (1923; *High Sea*), a rather dreary, one-dimensional depiction of an adulterous affair, was banned in 1923 when it was performed in Lisbon, on the grounds of public decency. The previous year, the play had been staged in Brazil as part of the aftermath of São Paulo's *Semana da Arte Moderna* (Modern Art Week).

Ferro rose to political prominence in Portugal writing positive narratives of dictatorships around Europe, including those of Mussolini and Mustapha Kemel. His *Viagem à Volta das Ditaduras* (1927; *Journey Around the Dictatorships*) was published the year after the coup that ended the First Republic, aligning him with an ideology that favoured culture's deployment in the cause of a national dictatorship. In 1932, he published a series of interviews with Salazar, and was soon thereafter put in charge of the National Propaganda

Secretariat. Under his stewardship, the secretariat (which would become the Office of Tourism, Popular Culture and National Information in 1944 once Goebels had given propaganda a bad name) promoted what became known as the *Política do Espírito* (Politics of the Spirit), a wholesale effort to bolster support for the Salazar regime with a series of banal films, popular art museums, theatre constructions, mobile libraries, invitations to foreign writers to visit Portugal, literary prizes and drama competitions. The policy lasted sixteen years, until Ferro fell out of favour with Salazar and was made an ambassador first to Switzerland and then to the Holy See to remove him from Lisbon. Its main intention was to foster a culture that entertained at a very superficial level, and avoided any hint of social critique or any space for thought-provoking political discussion that might threaten the regime. It gave resources to writers whose purpose was to be a joyful palliative to the austerity of the government.

Clearly, prior to the military coup that established the *Estado Novo*, writers existed under the Republic, some of the most notable of whom were sympathetic to its democratic ideals. Perhaps the most famous in the category, who continued to write under the *Estado Novo*, is Aquilino Ribeiro (1885–1963). His literary career spanned over five decades, beginning with fictional propaganda advocating the Republic. He produced an enormous quantity of novels under both the Republic and the *Estado Novo*. Born in the rural north of Portugal, his language often reflected the regional hues of his birthplace, and his favoured themes included the peasantry and countryside. His tone is, at times, gently ironic, while he consistently critiques abuses of power and exploitation, as well as rejecting political fanaticism. He founded the Portuguese Writers' Association in 1956 and initially presided over it. He was also, on several occasions, the target of the *Estado Novo*'s censor. The regime was never able to co-opt his liberal humanism into its service.

It was against the backdrop of the regime's *Política do Espírito* that neorealism emerged as an important force of literary resistance. Feeding into as well as taking its cue from similar movements in Europe, particularly in Italy, as well as in Brazil, neorealism was a politically committed form of literature, more concerned with following the prescribed ideological format of the class struggle than indulging in imaginative aestheticism or psychological introspection. By depicting in detail the exploitation of the masses, the movement hoped, like realism had done in the nineteenth century, to provoke change. An essential part of neorealism was to depict social circumstances in great detail, in the hope that the portrayal would foster unity among the exploited classes and thus trigger revolutionary change. *Gaibéus* (1939; *Field Hands*) by Alves Redol (1911–69) is generally considered to be one of the pioneering works of the Portuguese neorealist movement, alongside *Esteiros* (1941; *Creeks*) by Joaquim Soeiro Pereira Gomes (1909–49). The objective of both, like the movement to which they gave birth, was to lay bare the abject conditions suffered by the masses, in a society that remained, thanks to the policies followed by the Salazar regime, predominantly rural and uneducated, with an enormous differential between the richest and the poorest. Redol is said to have spent time in the rice-growing area of the Ribatejo, researching for the book prior to writing it. This type of connection with the masses would be a principal characteristic of the movement. The first edition of Pereira Gomes's work included drawings by Álvaro Cunhal, who would later go on to dominate the Portuguese Communist Party as its general secretary.

One of Portuguese neorealism's recurrent themes is the issue of land distribution and subsistence. Characters are forced to move away from the land of their ancestry because it no longer sustains them, or because they have no legal rights. Underpinning the movement's characterisations is, of course, the class struggle – invariably defined in binary terms roughly corresponding to the proletariat versus the capitalist, or the agent of the regime versus the oppressed. Often, the proletariat is portrayed as passive, waiting for the raising of consciousness necessary for the fulfilment of the movement's revolutionary ideals. Key figures in the movement included the Brazilian-born Carlos de Oliveira (1921–81) and Fernando Namora (1919–89). Oliveira was particularly adept at critiquing economic liberalism rather than explicitly the Salazar regime, underlining the neorealists' firm belief that the solution to Portugal's woes did not lie in following the liberal democratic model of Western Europe, but in something more akin to an idealised form of revolutionary socialism. The movement's close association with the Portuguese Communist Party (often considered to be the most sympathetic to Stalinism in Western Europe) was pivotal to its broad attacks on capitalist exploitation and its abhorrence at depictions of the psychological (bourgeois) angst provoked by living under a dictatorship.

Oliveira's novels became increasingly more complex, reaching an apex of literary sophistication in his enigmatic, post-revolutionary, *Finisterra* (1978), some forty-five years after the publication of his first novel, *Casa na Duna* (1943; *House on the Dune*). His tone was often melancholy, communicating a tragic sense of existence rather than an optimistic outlook for the future.

Namora's work also evolved considerably over his lifespan. Like most notable writers in Portugal at the time, he wrote poetry as well as prose. His first published work, *Relevos* (1937; *In Relief*), was influenced by the *Presença* movement, to which we will return shortly, and against which neorealism would also react. Early prose works like *A Noite e a Madrugada* (1950; *The Night and the Dawn*) and *O Trigo e o Joio* (1954; *The Wheat and the Tares*) shared the rural concerns of early neorealism, before Namora deployed more urban settings in *O Homem Disfarçado* (1957; *The Disguised Man*) and later works. Like Oliveira, Namora's concerns became more nuanced, and while he never abandoned social commitment in his work, he did adopt a line more influenced by the existentialism that was in vogue in France, with the need to delve more into the psychology of his characterisations that implied.

In some ways, psychological characterisation in Namora could also be traced back to his initial debt to the *Presença* movement.[1] *Presença* was a literary journal, first published in 1927. Initially edited by Branquinho da Fonseca (1905–74), *Presença* is generally considered to mark the second wave of Portuguese Modernism (the first wave having coalesced around the journal *Orpheu*). Fonseca was the son of another Portuguese writer, Tomás da Fonseca, who had been an ardent supporter of the First Republic, and was sidelined with the rise of the *Estado Novo*. Branquinho, a prolific writer himself, is remembered more for his role in *Presença*, and the importance the journal had in cementing the reputation of the Portuguese modernists, most notably Fernando Pessoa. The journal was fundamental to the introduction in Portugal to some of the key European writers of the first half of the twentieth century, such as Proust, Gide, and Pirandello. It also helped to establish the career of João Gaspar Simões (1903–87), one of the most influential Portuguese literary critics of the twentieth century, as well as to introduce to Portugal two of its greatest writers of the era, Miguel Torga (the pseudonym of Adolfo Correia da Rocha) (1907–95) and José Régio (the pseudonym of José Maria dos Reis Pereira) (1901–69).

Miguel Torga was born in the north-eastern region of Trás-os-Montes. In 1989, he was the first ever recipient of the highly prestigious Prémio Camões, the most important literary prize for work published in the Portuguese language. He adopted the name Torga for the first time with the publication of his *A Terceira Voz* (1934; *The Third Voice*) having already published poetry and prose under his legal name. The choice of name (it means heather, a shrub that grows extensively in the region of his birth) somehow corresponds to his literary production. He never forgot his rural roots, and as much in his choice of words as in his choice of themes, rural Portugal is ever present. Initially, he self-published, using his income as a medical doctor with a reputation for treating for free the patients who could not afford to pay. While his political posture was never as blatant in his work as in that of the neorealists, he did incur the displeasure of the Salazar regime, and was arrested several times as well as spending a short period in exile in France.

In 1941, he began to publish what would become a sixteen-volume journal (known in Portuguese as his *Diário*). It was a unique literary endeavour, and is full of poems, prose, political commentary and an array of studies on Portuguese customs and culture that is a profound form of witnessing to the period it covers. He also penned a number of plays, including *Mar* (1941; *The Sea*) – an ever-present trope in Portuguese literature from the time of

---

[1]   See also chapter 12, pp. 151–3.

Camões – and *Terra Firme* (1941; *Dry Land*), which portrays the fate of women left behind in rural regions by men to whom they are betrothed.

Torga had extraordinary ability as a writer of short stories. The various volumes of short stories that he published deal with the foibles of humanity, and constantly bring to the fore an agnostic anguish and doubt. Amongst his best known are *Contos da Montanha* (1941; translated as *Tales from the Mountain*) and *Novos Contos da Montanha* (1944; translated as *Tales and More Tales from the Mountain*).

The other literary titan to emerge from the *Presença* generation was José Régio. Régio's literary output mirrored almost exactly the duration of the *Estado Novo*, or at least, Salazar's grasp on the nation's government. Régio's first published literary work, *Poemas de Deus e do Diabo* (*Poems of God and the Devil*), dates from 1925, and at the time of his death from heart failure in December 1969, he was still actively writing. He is not an easily categorisable literary figure. An ambivalence in his political stance towards the *Estado Novo* led to severe criticism of him by those who more bluntly opposed the Salazar regime. However, a close reading of his work reveals a constant questioning of the mechanisms of power as they came to operate in Portugal, and particularly the way in which Salazar propagated a stifling patriarchal structure at every level of Portuguese society. In his work, Régio avoids the Manichean binaries of oppressor and oppressed, or victim and perpetrator, preferring instead to depict both complex psychological positions and the way in which society's imposed expectations came to strangle the individual.

Régio was born in Vila do Conde. During his life, he repeatedly courted controversy. He taught in a secondary school in Portalegre, and was considered by many who actively opposed the Salazar regime as almost an apologist for the dictator. Régio's designation of Salazar as one of Portugal's good visionary writers drew the ire of Jorge de Sena, among others, who could not believe that anyone of Régio's intelligence would credit the dictator with anything approaching critical thought. Another criticism often levelled against Régio was that he indulged in introspection. For left-leaning materialist critics of the *Estado Novo*, like those of the neorealist movement, there was no room for the psychological dramas that were repeatedly played out in Régio's texts. For them, a work of art must critique the system and assume an obvious stance that favours the proletariat. Régio famously became embroiled in a polemic with the leader of the Portuguese Communist Party, Álvaro Cunhal, in which Cunhal accused him of being overly self-obsessed and of 'worshipping his own navel'.

Régio's stance was misunderstood. He was not prepared to sign up to any dogma or sacrifice critical thought. He was aware that in so doing the world that would be created to replace the dictatorship, against which he had actively campaigned in the 1949 presidential campaign, would replicate the irrational lack of thought of the *Estado Novo* and its rhetorically strong leader. By delving into the psychological depths of the human character, Régio's project was not just an analysis of the conflicts between God and man, or between the individual and society, nor was he just riding a wave of fashionable psychoanalytic theory as literary critics often imply. Instead, Régio was offering the means to transform society by understanding what, within the individual, makes society behave the way that it does.

Régio understood and profoundly critiqued the patriarchal structures of Portugal. His book of short stories, *Histórias de Mulheres* (1946; *Women's Stories*), is a sensitive and sympathetic portrayal of the various forms of female abjection in a political climate that increasingly sought to curtail women's rights.

Régio's work is repeatedly dominated by issues of faith or loss of faith in the existence of the divine. He focuses on the conflicts inherent in the human condition. His plays draw on biblical references, like Jacob, or the Virgin Mary, to provide profound commentaries on existential crises that these very references are designed to obviate. *Benilde, ou a Virgem Mãe* (1947; *Benilde or the Virgin Mother*), for example, relates the story of a girl who appears to become pregnant through divine intervention, but who may be lying or simply deluded. In typical Régio fashion, every shade of opinion, from the most cynical to the most fervent believer, is represented on the stage, and no conclusive answer is given to the question of who is responsible for the pregnancy. Instead, in a dramatic conclusion, the girl herself dies.

Régio also used his plays to raise questions about the recurrent messianic theme that saturates Portuguese cultural discourse, particularly its Sebastianist strain.[2] In Régio's version of the myth – the play *El-Rei Sebastião* (1949; *King Sebastião*), which may be read as a thinly veiled critique of Salazar's appropriation of the myth – the eponymous antihero, the young king, reveals the extent to which he is willing to sacrifice the nation's well-being in order to secure a place in the roll-call of national heroes. In other words, Sebastião is presented not as a deluded king who dared to dream of greatness for his nation, as in Fernando Pessoa's description of the boy-king, but as a calculating man who knows the only way to avoid being written into history as the mediocrity that he is, is to put the very future of the nation in jeopardy, dying in the process.

While some in the neorealist movement remained vehemently critical of Régio and his failure to push a Marxist alternative to the *Estado Novo* in his literature, the more skilled writers in the movement gradually moved away from prescription and became more innovative in the way they communicated their critiques. Vergílio Ferreira (1916–96), for example, moved away from initial neorealism towards existentialism, with portrayals of the innate soli-

---

2   For Sebastianism, see chapter 1, pp. 11–12.

tude of man. A case in point is his novel *Manhã Submersa* (1954; *Submerged Dawn*).

One of the most popular writers, with an enormous body of plays, novels, essays and satires to his name, who moved away from neorealism, was José Cardoso Pires (1925–98). José Cardoso Pires was born in São João de Peso, in the north-eastern part of Portugal. He studied mathematics at the University of Lisbon, before holding various jobs including Lector of Portuguese and Brazilian Literature at King's College, London. Early on, he fell foul of Salazar's censors, following the publication of his *Histórias de Amor* (1952; *Love Stories*). He was arrested by Salazar's security police, and deprived of sleep during his detention, as a warning to the young writer to watch his words. Following his release, he was brought before the board of censors, who wanted the young writer to amend his book so that it could be published with the state's approval. The offensive words that were ravaged by the censor's blue pencil included adjectives such as 'naked', as Cardoso Pires remembered many years later in an autobiographical set of interviews entitled *Cardoso Pires por Cardoso Pires*. As Cardoso Pires realised, his youthful experience of the censors had nothing to do with any offence caused or content that threatened the security of the state. It was merely an exercise to let the young writer know that he was not master of his own words.

Cardoso Pires enjoyed considerable popularity in Portugal, a popularity that went alongside critical acclaim. The secret of his success has been variously attributed to his appropriation of the tropes of detective fiction, in that the reader is often enticed to continue reading by well-timed revelations, and also to his cinematographic technique, by which is usually meant his ability to capture the visual in words. Indeed, at least five of his works have been adapted to film, including one of his most famous novels, *O Delfim* (1968; *The Dauphin*). Cardoso Pires attributed its uncensored publication to what is known as the Caetano Spring.[3] He also attributed its unshackled publication, in typical humour, to the illiteracy of the censor board. The book is blatantly critical of the hegemonic structure – particularly its feudal aspects – that dominated Portugal at the time, portraying it as dying and decadent.

His novella, the parody *Dinossauro Excelentíssimo* (1972; *Most Excellent Dinosaur*), caused considerable political controversy when it was first published. It is a satirical take on a second-rate dictator whose discourse leads him to lose touch completely with the stagnant reality around him. The controversy that projected *Dinossauro Excelentíssimo* to prominence was an absurd own-goal on the part of supporters of the dictatorship. In a debate in the National Assembly, the Member of Parliament Miller Guerra suggested that there was no freedom in Portugal. One of the regime's most ardent and

[3] The period 1968–74, presided over by Salazar's successor, Marcello Caetano.

sycophantic supporters, Cazal Ribeiro, in a fit of anger, cited the case of *Dinossauro Excelentíssimo*, which had just gone on sale, as proof of the fact that there was no censorship in Portugal. The result was that the censor could not ban the book, as appeared to be their intention. Of course, the usual intimidating tactics of the *Estado Novo* soon kicked in, and while the book could not be seized, book stores were afraid to stock it. It was a continuation of the strategies of the Salazar era, in which self-censorship was the greatest weapon of the regime. As Cardoso Pires once put it, Salazar managed to get those he oppressed to perform the oppressive tasks of oppression.

The oppressive atmosphere Salazar fomented led many to seek exile during his regime. While the principal destination of economic exiles was Europe, several notable Portuguese writers ended up in the United States. The most famous of these was Jorge de Sena (1919–78), who after a stay in Brazil and then at the University of Wisconsin, eventually settled in California. Sena influenced a generation of American academics, raising the profile of Portuguese literary studies in the United States, and contributing an enormous body of scholarship on a wide range of writers, including Portugal's sixteenth-century epic poet, Camões. He wrote an array of prose, theatre and poetry in his life, which did not subscribe to any particular paradigm or ideology, but which did continually reference intertextually other works of literature. One of his concerns was the condition of belonging to a nation, while not living in its geographical space, a theme which comes to the fore in his poetry. Another of his concerns was the nature of erotic desire, most innovatively depicted in his novella *O Físico Prodigioso* (1966; translated as *The Wondrous Physician*). His partly autobiographical *Sinais de Fogo* (1978; translated as *Signs of Fire*) depicts the plight of two Spanish Republicans on the run during the Spanish Civil War who hide in Portugal, a country that officially supported Franco's Nationalists. It graphically narrates the Portugal of his youth.

Sena also wrote a play, *O Indesejado* (1951; *The Undesired One*), first read in public in 1945. It is an innovative reworking of Portugal's constant concern over its national identity. In it, Sena references the Sebastianic myth by absenting the sixteenth-century king who was often termed the *Desejado*, or desired one. As the title indicated, Sena is more interested in the Undesired, in this case, the unsuccessful claimant to the Portuguese throne on King Sebastião's demise, the Prior of Crato. The play deals with the condition of being exiled from one's own country, and has been read as a premonition of Sena's future state of exile.

Like Sena, Torga and Régio, many of Portugal's great writers in the twentieth century also wrote poetry and plays. As with Portuguese narrative, European trends exercised considerable influence over theatrical endeavours. Perhaps the two most notable playwrights of the era were Bernardo Santareno (1924–80) and Luís de Sttau Monteiro (1926–93). Both had plays banned, and both brought European innovations to traditional Portuguese themes.

Luiz Francisco Rebello (b. 1924), himself a playwright as well as a literary critic, comments in his *História do Teatro Português* (*History of Portuguese Theatre*) on the constant divorce during the *Estado Novo* between plays being written and plays being performed. The latter category was considerably smaller, not because of issues of quality but rather, once again, because of censorship.

Some of the most innovative theatre in Portugal during the dictatorship, characterised by experimentation, was based at the *Teatro-Estúdio do Salitre* (Salitre Studio Theatre), founded in 1946 by Gino Saviotti, the then director of the Institute of Italian Culture in Lisbon. It was allied to the Modernist movement, but, unlike the *Teatro Novo* theatre António Ferro had founded with José Pacheco in 1925, there was an overwhelming desire to critique the tenets of the *Estado Novo*, but in a way that also moved Portuguese theatre away from the influence of Naturalism. A generation of writers, including Alves Redol, Pedro Bom (b. 1914), David Mourão-Ferreira (1927–96) and Luiz Francisco Rebello, experimented with theatre at the Salitre.

The other great theatrical centre during the dictatorship was the Experimental Theatre in Oporto, founded in 1953, and directed by António Pedro (1909–66), a Cape Verdean who was an artist intimately linked to the Surrealist movement. The TEP, as it was known (an acronym for the *Teatro Experimental do Porto*) exercised an enormous influence over university drama groups, and produced Bernardo Santareno, the literary pseudonym of António Martinho do Rosário (1924–80) and the keystone of Portuguese Modernist theatre. His work shows a constant interest in the interplay between good and evil, flesh and the spirit, social injustice and Portuguese superstitions, as well as existential concerns around religious doubt that had been popularised in France. One of his first plays, *A Promessa* (1957; *The Promise*), was banned ten days after it was first performed and could only be produced again ten years later, in one of the periodic relaxations that characterised the *Estado Novo*'s censorship practice. In a form reminiscent of Brecht's epic theatre, Santareno's *O Judeu* (1966; *The Jew*) drew on the story of the Inquisition's execution of António José da Silva, an eighteenth-century playwright. His *Português, Escritor, 45 Anos de Idade* (1974; *Portuguese, Writer, Forty-five Years Old*) was the first new Portuguese play to be performed after the Carnation Revolution.

Sttau Monteiro spent several years of his childhood in London, where his father was Portugal's ambassador until Salazar recalled him. His *Felizmente Há Luar* (1961; *Fortunately, There Is Moonlight*) placed him on the *Estado Novo*'s blacklist because of its use of a historical setting to provide a damning portrayal of contemporary Portuguese society. It was quickly banned, and was only restaged in 1978, after the return of democracy to Portugal, when it was directed by Sttau Monteiro himself.

A rather amusing play that captured the nausea of the censorship with which Portuguese writers and playwrights had to interact during the *Estado Novo*, is Augusto Abelaira's *A Palavra É de Oiro* (1961; *Words Are Made of Gold*). Abelaira (1926–2003), one of the most committed neorealists, more known for his novels, depicts a state of affairs in which characters have to pay for their words, entering the stage with a word counter hung around their necks to ensure they pay for everything they say. In many ways, this dark parody captures perfectly the political attitudes of the *Estado Novo*, those summed up by Cardoso Pires when he pointed out that the dictatorship expected writers to partake in their own oppression. Yet the literary legacy of those barren years of dictatorship was the fertile ground of ideas and ideals of resistance that would be part of the process that led Portugal back to the path of democracy.

Texts and translations

Abelaira, Augusto, *A Palavra É de Oiro: Comédia em Dois Actos e um Prólogo* (Lisbon: Bertrand, 1961)
Ferreira, Vergílio, *Manhã Submersa* (Lisbon: Sociedade de Expansão Cultural, 1954)
Ferro, António, *Mar Alto* (Lisbon: Portugália, 1924)
—— *Viagem à volta das Ditaduras* (Lisbon: Diário de Notícias, 1927)
Gomes, Joaquim Soeiro Pereira, *Esteiros* (Lisbon: Sírios, 1941)
Miguéis, José Rodrigues, *A Man Smiles at Death with Half a Face*, tr. George Monteiro (Hanover and London: Brown University Press, 1991)
—— *Happy Easter*, tr. John Byrne (Manchester: Carcanet, 1995)
—— *Steerage and Ten Other Stories*, tr. George Matos and Carolina Matos (Providence, RI: Gávea Brown, 1983)
—— *The Polyhedric Mirror*, tr. David Brookshaw (Providence, RI: Gávea-Brown, 2006)
Monteiro, Luís de Sttau, *Felizmente Há Luar* (Lisbon: Jornal do Foro, 1961)
Namora, Fernando, *A Noite e a Madrugada* (Lisbon: Inquérito, 1950)
—— *O Trigo e o Joio* (Lisbon: Guimarães, 1954)
—— *O Homem Disfarçado* (Lisbon: Arcádia, 1957)
—— *Relevos* (Coimbra: Portugália, 1937)
Oliveira, Carlos de, *Casa na Duna* (Coimbra: Coimbra Editora, 1943)
—— *Finisterra: Paisagem e Povoamento* (Lisbon: Sá da Costa, 1978)
Pires, José Cardoso, *Cardoso Pires por Cardoso Pires: Entrevista de Artur Portela* (Lisbon: Dom Quixote 1991)
—— *Dinossauro Excelentíssimo* (Lisbon: Arcádia, 1972)
—— *Histórias de Amor* (Lisbon: Gleba, 1952)
—— *O Delfim* (Lisbon: Moraes, 1968)
Rebello, Luiz Francisco, *História do Teatro Português* (Lisbon: Europa–América, 1967)
Redol, Alves, *Gaibéus* (Lisbon: A. Redol, 1939)

Régio, José, *Benilde, ou a Virgem Mãe* (Porto: Portugália, 1947)
—— *El-Rei Sebastião* (Coimbra: Atlântida, 1949)
—— 'Four Poems', tr. Richard Zenith, in *Tabacaria*, 4, *Portuguese Poetry after Pessoa* (Lisbon: Contexto, 1997)
—— *Histórias de Mulheres* (Porto: Portugália, 1946)
—— [*O Meu Caso*] *My Problem*, tr. Gregory Rabassa, *Odyssey* Review 3.2 (1963), 130–43
—— *Poemas de Deus e do Diabo* (Coimbra: Lumen, 1925)
—— *The Flame-Coloured Dress and Other Stories*, tr. Margaret Jull Costa (Manchester: Carcanet (1999)
Santareno, Bernardo, *A Promessa: O Bailarino: A Excomungada: Teatro* (Lisbon: B. Santareno, 1957)
—— *O Judeu* (Lisbon: Ática, 1966)
Sena, Jorge de, *O Físico Prodigioso* (Lisbon: Edições 70, 1977); *The Wondrous Physician*, tr. Mary Fitton (London: Dent, 1986)
—— *O Indesejado* (Porto: Maranaus, 1951)
—— *Sinais de Fogo* (Lisbon: Edições 70, 1978); *Signs of Fire*, tr. John Byrne (Manchester: Carcanet, 1999)
Torga, Miguel, *A Terceira Voz* (Coimbra: Atlântida, 1934)
—— *Contos da Montanha* (Coimbra: Atlântida, 1941); *Tales from the Mountain* (Fort Bragg, CA: Q.E.D. Press, 1991)
—— *Diário*, 16 vols (Coimbra: Atlântida, 1934)
—— *Novos Contos da Montanha* (Coimbra: Coimbra Editora, 1944); *New Tales from the Mountain*, tr. Ivana Rangel-Carlsen (Manchester: Carcanet, 1991); *Tales and More Tales from the Mountain*, tr. Ivana Rangel-Carlsen (Manchester: Carcanet, 1995)
—— *Teatro: Terra Firme: Mar* (Coimbra: Atlântida, 1941)

Further reading

Kelley, Charles (ed.), *Fiction in the Portuguese-Speaking World* (Cardiff: University of Wales Press, 2000)
Rothwell, Phillip, *A Canon of Empty Fathers* (Lewisburg PA: Bucknell University Press, 2007)
Sapega, Ellen, *Consensus and Debate in Salazar's Portugal: Visual and Literary Negotiations of the National Text, 1933–1948* (University Park, PA: Pennsylvania State University Press, 2008)

14

Women Writers up to 1974

HILARY OWEN and CLÁUDIA PAZOS ALONSO

In 1858, with his usual sharp wit, Camilo Castelo Branco remarked that 'Over the course of the last fifty years ladies had not been reading novels, the reason for which took me many a sleepless night to figure out: they did not know how to read.'[1] With this statement, he was succinctly expressing his dismay at the negative effect of women's lack of educational opportunities, but equally how puzzling he found this situation at a time when change was already, slowly but surely, under way.

Indeed, the visible rise of, not only the woman reader, but also the 'woman of letters' in Portugal, from the 1860s onwards, was heralded by women such as Guiomar Torresão (1844–98), Maria Amália Vaz de Carvalho (1848–1921), and Caiel (Alice Pestana) (1860–1929), who left their imprint on a male-dominated cultural landscape, through various permutations of the following: political writing, journalism, moral treatises and work on education, as well as fictional, dramatic and/or poetic output. The most significant writer in the late nineteenth century, however, was arguably Ana Plácido (1831–95), author of the autobiographical work *Luz Coada por Ferros* (1863; *Light Filtered Through Bars*) and her masterpiece, the novel *Herança de Lágrimas* (1871; *A Legacy of Tears*).

Regrettably, to this day, literary history continues to privilege her role as a muse (she was the lover, and later the wife, of Camilo Castelo Branco) and neglect her as a gifted writer in her own right. Accordingly, there was (and still is) a missing link, which means that, unlike their British or French counterparts, Portuguese women writers at the dawn of the twentieth century did not have an established literary female legacy to look back to. This state of affairs is all the more ironic given that *Herança de Lágrimas* seeks precisely to voice a female-centred perspective on life. The first part of the novel records, through letters, the increasing attraction of Diana, a married woman, to a

---

[1] 'Há cinquenta anos que as senhoras não liam romances, por uma razão cujo desco-brimento me custou longas vigílias: – não sabiam ler.' Quoted by Teresa Leitão de Barros, *Escritoras de Portugal*, 2 vols (Lisbon: the author, 1924), vol. 2, p. 171.

dashing prospective lover, Nuno. At the last minute, Diana rejects the path of adultery, prompted by the reading of a manuscript which forms the second part of the novel and recounts the story of her mother's tragic abandonment and death after giving in to illicit love. Plácido thus somewhat modifies the generic convention of the nineteenth-century novel, in which the maintenance of the social status quo is more often than not negotiated over the body of the sacrificed woman (a model reproduced, for instance, in Eça's *O Primo Basílio*), by staging Branca's bid from beyond the grave to avoid a legacy of tears.[2] Admittedly, this cautionary tale is handed over to Diana by her husband/guardian/father figure, Álvaro, and, as such, may on one level reinforce sexual conformism within marriage. On another level, however, the novel displays an ongoing questioning of male privilege, while drawing attention to female solidarity as potentially empowering.

By the early twentieth century, as educated women become increasingly endowed with political consciousness and active in women's organisations and Republicanism, the transformation of the 'woman of letters' into an identifiable feminist entity is apparent. Ana de Castro Osório's feminist manifesto, *Às Mulheres Portuguesas* (*To Portuguese Women*), in 1905, and her co-founding with Adelaide Cabete (1867–1935) in 1909 of the *Liga das Mulheres Republicanas* (Republican Women's League) are landmark moments. While the League divided in 1912 over the rejection of educationally restricted women's suffrage by the new Republican government, the Republic did bring other major improvements in women's status, notably divorce laws.

If, politically speaking, the stage was therefore set for women to take a more prominent role in the public sphere, in literary terms what is striking is that women remain all but excluded from the Modernist movement. Tellingly, the *Orpheu* generation opted to invent a couple of token minor women contributors. The hunchback woman created by Pessoa was symptomatically handicapped from birth, could only write in confessional prose (i.e. a letter) and spent her days longingly looking at the man she loved from a window, without ever stepping out into the wider world. By contrast, her potential suitor, a locksmith, remains quite simply unaware of her existence. In Sá-Carneiro's masterpiece *A Confissão de Lúcio* (1914; translated as *Lúcio's Confession*), the character of Marta turns out to be likewise a male creation, a means to an end, and more specifically a bridge between two men.

In a context where women were still ventriloquially spoken by male-authored artistic creations, what could a modern educated woman do? One answer may arguably be provided by Teresa Leitão de Barros, who in 1924 published the first volume of her monumental *Escritoras de Portugal* (*Portu-*

---

[2] See Elisabeth Bronfen, *Over Her Dead Body* (Manchester: Manchester University Press, 1992).

guese Women Writers), subtitled *Génio Feminino Revelado na Literatura Portuguesa* (*Feminine Genius Revealed in Portuguese Literature*). Submitted as an undergraduate thesis to the University of Lisbon, this overview is a pioneering, if not entirely sucessful, attempt to recover Portuguese women's writing from centuries of near oblivion. Another more pragmatic answer is the way in which women writers en masse become more visible as 'poetesses': riding on the wave of modernity and progress, they successfully court the limelight through newspapers and magazines, erupting onto the literary stage of the 1920s. Alongside writers who included Fernanda de Castro (who was married to Salazar's propaganda minister António Ferro) and the popular Virgínia Vitorino, the two most outstanding poets of the period unquestionably turn out to be, retrospectively at least, Florbela Espanca (1894–1930) and Judith Teixeira (1880–1959).

Espanca was *persona non grata* on account of her scandalous life and final suicide, but was posthumously re-evaluated for her three sonnet collections, which give her a foundational role in twentieth-century women's letters in Portugal. Teixeira was equally reviled during her lifetime: her first collection was seized in 1923 by the *Governo Civil* of Lisbon, at the same time as a volume of homoerotic poetry by António Botto and the pamphlet *Sodoma Divinizada* (*Divinised Sodom*) authored by Raul Leal. Unlike Espanca, she remained almost completely forgotten until the 1990s, when her poetry, out of print for many decades, was finally republished.

Espanca's textual engagements with the overwhelmingly male Portuguese literary canon are certainly unprecedented in scope. Her first collection, *Livro de Mágoas* (1919; *Book of Sorrows*), teeming with intertextual references to the two most celebrated poets of the nineteenth century, António Nobre and Antero de Quental, as well as to Camões, articulates her yearning for artistic recognition and social acceptance. She laments at length the inability of her readers and society at large to acknowledge her as a woman writer in the making, vividly showing how her dream of becoming 'a Poetisa eleita' (the chosen Poetess) is consequently bound to fail. In her second collection, *Livro de Soror Saudade* (1923; *Book of Sister Longing*) however, she confidently starts to adopt parody to turn the tables on man-made assumptions about female literary genius (or lack thereof), through a revision of centuries-old stereotypical images. By seemingly accepting what she is expected to be, but subsequently subversively portraying herself as something other, she rejects the role of the muse. Initially enshrined as virginal nun and/or princess, fixed as an object of desire by her male literary contemporaries, she increasingly rebels and seeks to carve out for herself a discursive space which would allow for 'A glória! ... A fama! ... O orgulho de criar! ...' ('Glory! ... Fame! ... The pride of creating! ...'). Her third and most famous work, *Charneca em Flor* (1931; *Heath in Flower*), published posthumously, confirms her as thematically groundbreaking, for the way in which she textualises the taboo topic of female desire. Although she sticks to the use of a conventional form, the sonnet, she displays many thematic affinities with modernist impulses to break free from the shackles of a monolithic self, not least through her dazzling 'performance' as a multifaceted persona. Her prose writings *As Máscaras do Destino* (1931; *The Masks of Destiny*) and *O Dominó Preto* (1982; *The Black Domino*), and the diary *Diário do Último Ano* (1981), likewise question the boundaries of identity and reality. Unsurprisingly, since her death, her colourful life story has been subjected to various interpretations and stage adaptations, including several authored by successive generations of women writers.

Rather less well-known, but equally groundbreaking, is the modernist poetry of Judith Teixeira: *Decadência* (1923; *Decadence*), *Castelo de Sombras* (1923; *Castle of Shadows*), and the strikingly titled *Nua* (1926; *Naked Woman*). In 1925, she was the director of the short lived but significant modernist magazine *Europa*. Teixeira was pigeonholed and dismissed as a decadent poet, yet on closer inspection she shows thematic points of contact with Pessoa's most famous heteronym, Álvaro de Campos, and like him displays a predilection for free verse. Only in recent times has Teixeira enjoyed a revival: one may posit that for many decades the increasingly daring lesbian subtext of her work – for instance her first collection of poetry featured a poem entitled 'A minha amante' ('My Female Lover') – had to be expurgated from literary history and collective memory in the name of morality. Her two short novellas from *Satânia* (1927) continued to challenge assumptions of sexual orthodoxy through plot: *Insaciada* (*Unsatisfied*), the second novella from that collection, culminates in the suicide of a male protagonist, potentially allowing room for the continuation of a close friendship between the two main female characters.

Satânia was published a year before Salazar first rose to prominence. Within the next five years, the consolidation of Europe's longest dictatorship would become a *fait accompli*. By 1933, the new Political Constitution, and its (in)famous Article 5, explicitly excluded women from equal citizenship in terms of their 'specific nature' and the 'well-being of the family'.[3] It is unquestionable that Salazar's views on women, alongside his well documented politics of censorship, restricted women's literary activity: the authoritarian family-oriented ethos of the dictatorship was undoubtedly detrimental to their visibility as creators (rather than procreators). But needless to say, women continued to publish, though the extent to which they were excluded for their differences at the point of reception is telling: only a handful of women made it into anthologies and literary histories, which have such a prominent

---

[3]   See Ana Paula Ferreira, 'Homebound: The Construct of Femininity in the Estado Novo', *Portuguese Studies* 12 (1996), 133–44.

part to play in the shaping of the literary canon.[4] This problem was further compounded, as the case of the modernist generation had amply demonstrated, by the fact that women's writing, in the 1940s and beyond, often remained tangential to predominant canonical movements such as neorealism.

The most versatile and talented writer of the 1930s and 1940s is Irene Lisboa (1892–1958). Her works, like those of Maria Archer (1905–82) and many others, negotiate her marginal position and encode criticism of society under the Salazar regime. She was accordingly persecuted by the dictatorship, being forced to take early retirement from her job as a teacher and teaching inspector. Lisboa's most significant works include two collections of poetry, *Um Dia e Outro Dia ...* (1936; *One Day and Another*) subtitled 'diário de uma mulher' ('diary of a woman'), and *Outono Havias de Vir* (1937; *Autumn You Had to Come*), both of which make predominant use of *vers libre*, and her diary *Solidão* (1939; *Solitude*). All three were published under the male pseudonym João Falco.

Her literary projects question fixed categories and existing mental positions disseminated by the primarily male literary establishment at the start of the dictatorship. Despite ongoing pressure from some of her influential male contemporaries such as José Régio and João Gaspar Simões, Lisboa steadfastly refused to produce a novel. Her unwillingness to fit into existing literary moulds is a rhetorical strategy through which she seeks to question essentialist assumptions which effectively disempower women writers at all stages of literary production. In that connection her short story 'Um Dito' ('A Remark'), included in the self-published collection *Esta Cidade!* (1942; *This City!*), is a masterpiece of irony, subtly exposing the mechanisms which prevent women's access to publication and subsequent literary dissemination on an equal footing with their male counterparts.

As an illegitimate daughter, a condition she shared with Espanca, Lisboa chose to revisit her precarious condition and social exclusion on a personal level, in two autobiographical novellas, one situated at the beginning of her literary career *Começa uma Vida* (1940; *A Life Begins*) and the other towards the end *Voltar Atrás Para Quê?* (1954; *Why Go Back in Time?*). Her dramatic foregrounding of the plight of the illegitimate daughter can be read on a broader collective level, as emblematic of women being deprived of the right to function as equals within the household and, by extension, society at large. In so doing, her work undoes the rhetoric of Salazar's central tenets of 'Deus, Pátria, Família' ('God, Fatherland, Family'), pointing to social and intellectual exclusion, while providing an exemplary case-study of the strategies, such as self-publishing, that a gifted woman writer could generate to bypass silencing.

---

[4]   See Chatarina Edfeldt, *Uma história na História. Representações da autoria feminina na História da Literatura Portuguesa do século XX* (Montijo: Câmara Municipal do Montijo, 2006).

In the 1940s and 1950s resistance centred primarily on the novel, echoing the predominance of neorealism in Portuguese fiction. Given that women by and large did not fit into the ideological and stylistic formats beloved of the neorealists, it comes as no surprise that Agustina Bessa Luís, one of the most important women writers of this period, rose to prominence initially by demarcating her differences from neorealism. Maria Agustina Ferreira Teixeira Bessa Luís was born in 1922 in Vila Meã, near Amarante in the northern Douro region of Portugal, a region that acquires mythical dimensions in many of her novels. Her long career spans the pre- and post-revolution periods. She began writing in the 1940s and her published work to the present day includes more than forty novels, as well as literary criticism, short stories, novellas, biographies, plays and film scripts, many of her works winning literary prizes.

Her representations of women draw attention to their inner lives, their intimate conflicts, their attachment to mysticism and the sublime, and their sense of alienation in relation to the roles scripted for them by dominant masculine culture. Her writings before the revolution particularly tend to focus on the limits, frustrations and constraints of women's existence in a world where sex roles are rigidly defined, and women's revolt consists of ironising their own passivity whilst compelled to internalise their oppression. Her penchant for historical novels, revisions of Portuguese romanticism, and film collaborations with the director Manoel de Oliveira, best characterise her post-1974 reputation.

Bessa Luís made her name in the mid-1950s with her novel *A Sibila* (1954; *The Sibyl*). The novel was heralded by the essayist Eduardo Lourenço as a major turning point of neo-romanticism that would regenerate national literature, acting as a counterpoint to the male-authored Marxist neorealist protest genres of the era.[5] Most traditional literary histories of Portugal treat Bessa Luís's work, particularly *A Sibila*, as a watershed for twentieth-century women's writing in Portugal.

Adopting a Proustian aesthetic of memory and a circular temporal structure, the novel follows an urban bourgeois woman remembering her rural ancestral past. Set in the northern region of the Minho, *A Sibila* details three generations of a rural family, the Teixeiras, through the lives of three women. The central figure Joaquina Augusta or Quina is marked out from infancy by a birthmark like a burn. She survives a harsh childhood as the family's unfavoured younger sister, and subsequently becomes gifted with apparently mystical, sibylline powers following a serious childhood illness. Emerging into adulthood as a powerful local figure, she becomes astute at acquiring land and managing the family properties, using her unmarried status and her

---

[5] See Eduardo Lourenço, 'Agustina Bessa Luís ou o neo-Romantismo', *Colóquio/Letras* 6 (1963), 49–52.

business acumen to create a strong image of independence that fascinates her unmarried niece Germa, on her visits to the old family homestead, the *Vessada*. Nonetheless, Quina's wisdom and authority are undermined when she adopts an abandoned backward boy, Custódio, who exploits her emotional vulnerabilities and attempts to inherit the family property and disinherit Germa. Resisting Custódio's entreaties, and leaving her farm to Germa, the city niece who will not continue her rural legacy, Quina dies a lonely death. She is compared throughout the novel to a Prometheus figure punished for usurping the fire of the gods, in her encroachment on male domains of power. It is left to Germa to inscribe her aunt's memory in writing, and to ponder her own future in the light of the sacrificial example set by Quina's pursuit of masculine influence, aspirations and ambitions at the expense of a female, reproductive destiny. Lauded by the critics at the time of publication and for decades later, *A Sibila* was, for many years, a secondary-school syllabus text in Portugal, further underlining Bessa Luís's canonical status.

   In addition to novels, Bessa Luís also wrote collections of short stories such as *A Brusca* (1971; *The Brusque Woman*), drawing on the rural folklore of the north to spin her own powerful allegories of gender roles. 'A Mãe de um Rio' ('The Mother of a River'), published in 1971 but written much earlier (between 1958 and 1967) was a particularly well known story in which a young village woman Fisalina goes to seek the mythical 'mother of a river', an ancient goddess recalling Ceres or Demeter, who is in charge of wisdom and water. She has golden fingertips and is feared and revered by the villagers who depend on her. As the goddess grows weary of her role, she loses touch with the peasants, and their lives become morbid, hunger-stricken, dark and barren. When Fisalina goes to visit her in her quest to find the secret of being individual and different, she is tricked into receiving the same golden finger-tips, and is driven away from her community, forced to take on the Mother of the River's isolated destiny as the symbol of life and continuity, the guardian of truth. The story can be read, on one level, as an ironic statement on the castration and disembodiment that society metes out to the desiring ego of the female creator.

   Politically speaking, restrictions placed on women culminated publicly after the Second World War, when the National Council of Portuguese Women (created during the First Republic by Adelaide Cabete) was dissolved in 1947 and its leader, Maria Lamas, was exiled to Paris in 1948. But this did not deter growing numbers of women from continuing to voice their cultural resistance to *Estado Novo* politics. Amongst the most influential, not least by virtue of their longevity, were Sophia de Mello Breyner Andresen (1919–2004) and Natália Correia (1923–93).

   Mello Breyner is the author of more than a dozen collections of poetry, spanning nearly half a century, and several volumes of short stories and children's fiction. Her inaugural collection *Poesia* (1944; *Poetry*) immediately showcases the emergence of a distinctive poetic voice. From the 1950s onwards, her poetry becomes increasingly concerned with political issues: *Mar Novo* (1958; *New Sea*) includes a magnificent reworking of Rimbaud's 'Le dormeur du val'; in *Livro Sexto* (1962; *Sixth Book*), the third and final section is clearly political, as implied in the title 'As Grades' ('Prison Bars'). The allusions to a context of dissidence and colonial war become ever more explicit in the last section of *Dual* (1972) entitled 'Em Memória' ('In Memory'), featuring titles which would have been self-explanatory for a Portuguese audience, such as 'Caxias 68' (referring to a notorious jail for political prisoners) or 'A Paz sem Vencedor e sem Vencidos' ('Peace Without Winners or Losers'), where the reiterated noun 'peace' draws attention to the necessary censoring of its missing opposite, 'war'. It is worth noting, especially since Mello Breyner has often been praised for the way in which her poetry deals with universal and timeless themes, that the closing poems of *Dual*, including 'Retrato de uma Princesa Desconhecida' ('Portrait of an Unknown Princess') and 'Catarina Eufémia' (a pregnant peasant woman killed during a political uprising), poignantly evoke the plight of women as victims of social and political oppression, throughout the centuries and in a more localised context, that of Portugal in the 1950s.

In her poetry and prose works, Mello Breyner is scathing about the hypocrisy of those, men and women alike, through whom the status quo is perpetuated. Accordingly 'Retrato de Mónica' ('Portrait of Monica'), one particularly witty short story belonging to the celebrated collection of short stories *Contos Exemplares* (1962; *Exemplary Tales*), traces how an upper-class woman named Mónica has secured an influential place in society, by colluding with existing patriarchal structures of power. As the story draws to a close, the platonic relationship between the two caricatural characters, Mónica and 'o Príncipe deste Mundo' ('The Prince of This World'), a character who may be a veiled reference to Salazar himself or, by extension, to any man in a position of authority, allows them to co-authorise each other, exclusively for their own self-centred mutual benefit, in the pursuit of what is damningly described as 'uma vontade sem amor' (a loveless will), the will to power. In so doing, as readers are told, Mónica has renounced poetry, in marked contrast to Mello Breyner, who of course remained a committed poet until her death.

Natália Correia was a significant voice of literary resistance during the same period as Sophia de Mello Breyner Andresen, and she was also the exact contemporary of Agustina Bessa Luís. Her approach to women and writing was, in contrast to Bessa Luís's, centred on the exuberant affirmation of maternal mythical culture as the source of women's creativity. However, the writings of Natália Correia also embody the tensions and contradictions that beset women who sought to develop their own literary and political voices as part of an active cultural resistance to the *Estado Novo*.

A native of the Azores, Correia arrived in Lisbon to study in 1934, and became involved in anti-fascist opposition as a young adult in the 1940s, joining the communist-linked MUD (Movimento de Unidade Democrática) in 1944/5. She began to publish in earnest in the 1950s and was particularly influential in the propagation of Portuguese surrealism during that period, producing the collection *A Dimensão Encontrada* (1957; *The Found Dimension*), which includes her famous 'Queixa das Almas Jovens Censuradas' ('Lament of the Young Souls that are Censored') calling vigorously for the freedom of poetic voice and creativity. She also went on to edit the important anthology *O Surrealismo na Poesia Portuguesa* (*Surrealism in Portuguese Poetry*) in 1973.

In addition to pursuing her own literary resistance to the Salazar/Caetano regime, Correia supported leading oppositional male writers such as David Mourão-Ferreira and Urbano Tavares Rodrigues. In the early 1970s Correia became a co-owner of the Botequim Bar in Lisbon, a significant political and artistic meeting place over which she regularly presided, both during and after the 1974 Revolution. Correia was elected to Parliament in 1979 as an independent on the PPD (*Partido Popular Democrático*, Popular Democratic Party) lists, and re-elected in 1987, again as an independent. She maintained a high public profile in politics, national culture and the media in the 1980s, offering public support for campaigns to decriminalise abortion, and broadcasting her own television programme on feminine images in national culture, *Mátria*, for RTP (the national television channel).

Among her enormous opus, three particular aspects are worth noting here in respect of her contribution to the history of women's writing: first, her mystical poetry, appealing for national regeneration and emphasising her ties to the Azorean island motherland or 'ilha mãe' and to maternal culture; second, her focus on the Mátria or Mother Goddess figure from classical and other mythologies (in the manner of Mother Right theorists in Social Anthropology such as Robert Briffault), which underpinned the claim in many of her works, particularly the novel *A Madona* (1968; *The Madonna*), and the poetry collection *Mátria* (1968; *Motherland*), that patriarchy's historical defeat of matriarchal socio-cultural systems must be urgently reversed in order to save man from his own self-destructive rationalism; third, her fascination with Nietzschean masking and performance, Brechtian epic theatre and Theatre of Cruelty, which inspired her many plays on themes of national interest, most notably *O Encoberto* (1969; *The Hidden One*).[6] Originally written in 1969, at the height of the Colonial Wars in Africa, *O Encoberto* was censored by the

---

6   On the sources of Correia's matriarchy theories, see Luís Adriano Carlos, 'A Mátria e o Mal', *Natália Correia. 10 anos depois ...*, org. Secção de Estudos Franceses do DEPER (Porto: Faculdade de Letras da Universidade do Porto, 2003).

regime and only staged in 1977. The play deals with a reluctant fake King Sebastião forced to act out the role of a saviour, in a scathing, farcical revision of Portugal's historical propensity to passivity and inactivity in the face of oncoming crisis, such as the ongoing colonial debacle.

Correia's literary work suffered *Estado Novo* censorship on more than one occasion, the most famous being the furore caused by the *Antologia de Poesia Portuguesa Erótica e Satírica* (*Anthology of Erotic and Satirical Portuguese Poetry*) that she edited in 1966 and for which she was tried and sentenced in 1970 to a three-year suspended prison sentence. Given this highly repressive climate, it is not surprising that some of her most important dramatic work was not published or performed until after the 25 April Revolution, most notably *A Pécora* (1983; *The Hooker*), her satire on Marian cults such as Fátima, written in 1967 but not staged until 1989. In this play the 'role' of the Virgin Mary appearing at the shrine is played by a prostitute called Melânia, generating the business that sustains the town, only to be murdered when she seeks to reveal her true identity, and then duly canonised again when she is safely dead.

There can be no doubt that Natália Correia provided an important inspiration for many women writers whose work she supported, particularly during the 1960s and 1970s. As new generations of literary and political dissenters emerged and Anglo-American and French feminist ideas from abroad also began to circulate in translation, albeit tentatively and often clandestinely, Portuguese women became involved in active resistance to the *Estado Novo* regime, and to the Colonial Wars in Africa (1961–74), through their membership in protest movements, student activism and their literary and journalistic defiance of censorship.

By the 1960s and 1970s, a substantial number of women were publishing novels and poetry. To select only a few, in the prose genre, Maria Judite Carvalho (b. 1921) stands out for the novel *Os Armários Vazios* (1966; *Empty Wardrobes*), in which she details the isolation, instability and repression experienced by a widowed woman trying to live in New State society without the support of a husband. In contrast to this, the limits of women's freedom and identity were challenged by the works of Maria Ondina Braga (b. 1932), whose extensive journeying as a Portuguese teacher in Goa, Angola, China and Macau in the 1960s led to her producing autobiographical works, fiction, chronicles and travel accounts, such as *Eu Vim Para Ver a Terra* (1965; *I Came to See the Land*), *A China Fica ao Lado* (1968; *China is Next Door*) and *Estátua de Sal* (1969; *Pillar of Salt*). These afforded a specifically female perspective on the closing years of Portuguese empire in Africa and the Far East. The use of poetry as a protest medium grew in significance in the 1960s and early 1970s, thereby also increasing the possibility for artistic dialogue between women writers. The *Poesia 61* movement, which arose partly in response to neorealism, included three important women poets, Maria Teresa

Horta (b. 1937), Luiza Neto Jorge (1939–89) and Fiama Hasse Pais Brandão (1938–2007).

In this climate, the high-profile artistic resistance undertaken by Natália Correia, for instance, extended well beyond her own publications. In her position as cultural editor for the publishers Estúdio Cor, Correia supported the publication of *Novas Cartas Portuguesas* (translated as *New Portuguese Letters*) in 1972. Co-authored by Maria Isabel Barreno (b. 1939), Maria Teresa Horta and Maria Velho da Costa (b. 1938), later known as the Three Marias, *Novas Cartas Portuguesas* was to become the most emblematic and scandalous feminist work of twentieth-century Portugal.

The three co-authors of this text all began writing in the 1960s. Maria Velho da Costa, who went on to become one of the most significant writers of the post-revolution period, produced an experimental novel, *Maina Mendes* (1969), which famously charts a woman overcoming muteness as she becomes aware of how women's cultural ancestry has been silenced. The poet and journalist Maria Teresa Horta wrote a volume of erotic poetry, *Minha Senhora de Mim* (1971; *Milady of Myself*), which was suppressed by the regime. Horta also published her first novel *Ambas as Mãos sobre o Corpo* (*Both Hands on the Body*), in 1970, describing a woman's self-discovery through the appropriation of language. Maria Isabel Barreno's novel *Os Outros Legítimos Superiores* (*Our Elders and Betters*), also from 1970, describes young women's rejection of Church and fascist State conditioning. Here, Barreno plays ironically on the prevalence of the Catholic name Maria, moulding women's individuality to the image of the Virgin in Portuguese society.

An amalgamated fabricated quotation from these three titles provides the epigraph to *Novas Cartas Portuguesas*, the text that the three women decided to write together, in 1971, as a means of consciously challenging the *Estado Novo* censors through collective literary action. *Novas Cartas Portuguesas* thus carries, as a forewarning banner of solidarity, the epigraph 'ou de como Maina Mendes pôs ambas as mãos sobre o corpo e deu um pontapé no cu dos outros legítimos superiores' ('Or how Maina Mendes put both hands on her body and gave her elders and betters a kick up the arse').

Like *A Sibila*, *Novas Cartas Portuguesas* is often taken as a twentieth-century turning point for women's literature in Portugal. Its basic literary premise is a reworking of *Lettres Portugaises*, the set of anonymous letters penned in French, supposedly translated from the Portuguese, and published in 1669. The original letters are written from the perspective of Mariana Alcoforado, a lovelorn, abandoned Portuguese nun in a convent in Beja in the Alentejo. Early twentieth-century scholarship has shown them to be, in all likelihood, the work of the French male writer Gabriel-Joseph Lavergne de Guilleragues, who had pretended to 'discover' and translate the letters, but had in fact written them himself, mimicking the feminine narrative voice of sentimental, epistolary discourse.[7] While long academic debates, and issues of national pride, have marked the discussion on *Lettres Portugaises*, Barreno, Horta and Velho da Costa set out simply to produce their own modern version, meeting twice a week to exchange and discuss their own unsigned fragments, essays, letters, word games and poems on the theme, effectively creating an ahistorical web of cross-references, and establishing a cast of new fictitious relations, descendants, and friends for the original Mariana Alcoforado, moving from the seventeenth century up to the present, the *Estado Novo* and the Colonial War in Africa.

One effect of this structure was to expose the unchanging oppression of women throughout the ages, and to narrate women's survival and self-expression against the odds. Taking a daring stand on sexual taboo with passages about incestuous rape, domestic violence, women's desire, female masturbation, and abortion, the book certainly set out to challenge Catholic convention. It met a somewhat more draconian response that it expected in the Caetano Spring of the early 1970s, being prosecuted for offending public decency. Its veiled references to the Colonial War in Africa, its coded call for the military men to return to their women folk, and its critique of the conventional sexual roles required by the defence of empire, were clearly also factors in its suppression. It became the subject of a long and much-publicised trial of its three co-authors and its publisher, giving rise to support from anti-fascist resistance in Portugal and from international feminist groups abroad. The Marias were able to use the anonymity of each individual text to avoid naming the specific authors of the passages on which the prosecution rested. They were officially pardoned shortly after the Caetano regime fell.

Although the Three Marias occupy a very important place in the histories of both the Portuguese revolution and 1970s feminism, their choice of a fictional source of inspiration, *Lettres Portugaises*, with no ultimate scholarly consensus regarding its authorship, marks a strong poststructuralist turn away from the grand narratives of literary history and canons, pointing in a multitude of different directions for women of future generations. As an iconoclastic statement about women's fraught relationship to canons and literary histories, *Novas Cartas* defines a consciously new beginning, distancing itself from possible foremothers such as Florbela Espanca and Agustina Bessa Luís. Undoing the structures of dynastic lineage, and taking an antihistoricist view, the text emphasises instead the lateral bonds of sisterhood

---

[7] On *New Portuguese Letters* and its relationship to the French original, *Lettres Portugaises*, see Anna Klobucka, *The Portuguese Nun: Formation of a National Myth* (Lewisburg, PA: Bucknell University Press, 2000); Hilary Owen, *Portuguese Women's Writing, 1972 to 1986. Reincarnations of a Revolution* (Lewiston: Edwin Mellen, 2000); and Linda S. Kauffman, *Discourses of Desire: Gender, Genre and Epistolary Fictions* (Ithaca, NY: Cornell University Press, 1986).

between the three co-authors, undermining the *Estado Novo* authoritarianism associated with both maternal and paternal genealogies.

At the same time, *Novas Cartas* reinforces its own political point about women's exclusion or marginality in relation to hegemonic national and literary History. Through their ironic reading of Mariana Alcoforado, the Three Marias point clearly to the gaps, exclusions and silences of women's literary history in Portugal. By establishing new paradigms of feminist critical reading for the Portuguese context, *Novas Cartas* also effectively foresees the potential offered by French poststructuralism for theories and practices of feminist textual rebellion within and against the masculine symbolic, ideas that would later be more fully and famously expounded by French Feminist philosophers Luce Irigaray, Hélène Cixous and Julia Kristeva.

The retrieval of lost, suppressed and forgotten women's writing in Portugal, particularly pre-1950s and earlier, remains an urgent work in progress for feminist scholars, following the initiatives taken by Ferreira and Edfeldt in relation to the first half of the twentieth century. If our emphasis on key canonical women writers of the twentieth century up to 1974 has traced a very selective history of women's writing up until the Revolution, the need for women's full integration into Portugal's national literary tradition *per se*, constitutes an ongoing and unavoidable imperative that continues to structure the political field of women's writing in Portugal.

Texts and translations

Andresen, Sophia de Mello Breyner, *Contos Exemplares* (Lisbon: Portugália, n.d.)
—— *Log Book: Selected Poems*, tr. Richard Zenith (Manchester: Carcanet, 1997)
—— *Obra Poética*, vols 1–3 (Lisbon: Caminho, 1995–6)
Barreno, Maria Isabel, *Os Outros Legítimos Superiores. Folhetim de Ficção Filosófica*, 2nd edn (Lisbon: Caminho, 1993)
Barreno, Maria Isabel, Maria Teresa Horta and Maria Velho da Costa, *Novas Cartas Portuguesas*, 7th edn (Lisbon: Dom Quixote, 1998); *New Portuguese Letters*, tr. and pref. Helen R. Lane (London: Readers International, 1994)
Braga, Maria Ondina, *A China Fica ao Lado* (Lisbon: Editores Associados, n.d.)
—— *Estátua de Sal* (n.p.: Sociedade de Expansão Cultural, n.d.)
—— *Eu Vim para Ver a Terra* (Lisbon: Agência-Geral do Ultramar, 1965)
Cartas Portuguesas, atribuídas a Mariana Alcoforado, edição bilingue, Prefácio e tradução. Eugénio de Andrade (Lisbon: Assírio & Alvim, 1993); Gabriel-Joseph de Lavergne (Vicomte de Guilleragues), *The Love Letters of a Portuguese Nun*, trans. Guido Waldman (London: Harvill Press, 1996))
Carvalho, Maria Judite de, *Os Armários Vazios* (Mem-Martins: Publicações Europa-America, 1993)
Correia, Natália, *A Madona*, 4th edn (Lisbon: Editorial Notícias, 2000)

—— *A Pécora*, 2nd edn (Lisbon: O Jornal, 1990)
—— *Antologia Poética*, org. Fernando Pinto do Amaral (Lisbon: Dom Quixote, 2002)
—— *O Encoberto* (Alfragide: Galeria Panorama, 1969)
—— (ed.), *Antologia de Poesia Portuguesa Erótica e Satírica (dos Cancioneiros Medievais à Actualidade)* (n.p.: Fernando Ribeiro de Mello. Edições Afrodite, n.d.)
—— (ed.), *O Surrealismo na Poesia Portuguesa* (Mem Martins: Publicações Europa-América, 1973)
Costa, Maria Velho da, *Maina Mendes*, 2nd edn (Lisbon: Morães Editores, 1977)
Espanca, Florbela, *Obras Completas* (Lisbon: Dom Quixote, 1985–86), vols 1–6
Horta, Maria Teresa, *Ambas as Mãos sobre o Corpo* (Lisbon: Publicações Europa–América, 1970)
—— *Minha Senhora de Mim* (Lisbon: Editorial Futura, 1974)
Lisboa, Irene, *Obras Completas* (Lisbon, Editorial Presença, 1991), vols 1–5
Luís, Agustina Bessa, 'A mãe de um rio', in *A Brusca* (Lisbon: Verbo, 1971)
—— *A Sibila*, 12th edn (Lisbon: Guimarães, n.d.)
Plácido, Ana, *Luz Coada por Ferros, Herança de Lágrimas*, ed. fac-simile (Vila Nova de Famalicão: Lello & Irmão – Câmara Municipal de Vila Nova de Famalicão, 1995)
Teixeira, Judith, *Poemas* (Lisbon: &etc, 1996)
—— *Satânia* (Lisbon: Livraria Rodrigues, 1927)
Garay, René Pedro, *Judith Teixeira: o modernismo sáfico português* (Lisbon: Universitária Editora, 2002) [includes an anthology of Teixeira's poems, with English and Spanish translations]

Further reading

Bronfen, Elizabeth, *Over Her Dead Body* (Manchester: Manchester University Press, 1992)
Edfeldt, Chatarina, *Uma história na História. Representações da autoria feminina na História da Literatura Portuguesa do século XX* (Montijo: Câmara Municipal do Montijo, 2006)
Ferreira, Ana Paula, *A Urgência de Contar* (Lisbon: Caminho, 2000)
Kauffman, Linda S., *Discourses of Desire. Gender, Genre and Epistolary Fictions* (Ithaca, NY: Cornell University Press, 1986)
Klobucka, Anna, *The Portuguese Nun. Formation of a National Myth* (Lewisburg, PA: Bucknell University Press, 2000)
Owen, Hilary, *Portuguese Women's Writing, 1972 to 1986. Reincarnations of a Revolution* (Lewiston, NY: Mellen, 2000)
Pazos Alonso, Cláudia (ed.), *Women, Literature and Culture in the Portuguese-Speaking World* (Lewiston, NY: Mellen, 1996)
Sapega, Ellen, *Consensus and Debate in Salazar's Portugal: Visual and Literary Negotiations of the National Text, 1933–1948* (University Park, PA: Pennsylvania State University Press, 2008)

15

Writing after the Dictatorship

MARK SABINE and CLAIRE WILLIAMS

Esta é a madrugada que eu esperava	This is the dawn I waited for
O dia inicial e limpo	The new day clean and whole
Onde emergimos da noite e do silêncio	When we emerge from night and silence
E livres habitamos a substância do tempo	To freely inhabit the substance of time

Sophia de Mello Breyner Andresen, '25 de Abril' (1974),
translated by Richard Zenith[1]

No matter how often Sophia de Mello Breyner Andresen's salutation to 25 April 1974 is quoted, it avoids the status of cliché through its succinct encapsulation of so much of the ethos of the 'Carnation Revolution'. Into four lines are concentrated not simply the euphoria and optimism inspired by the almost bloodless fall of the *Estado Novo*, and the belief in a fresh beginning, but also, and more significantly, the liberty to partake of a new and more dynamic relationship with time and history. After having their eyes, ears and mouths confounded by the night and silence of tyranny, and having being trapped in the socio-economic and cultural time-warp forged by Salazarism's reactionary cult of tradition, the Portuguese were now free not only to engage with a fast-changing outside world, but equally to reflect upon and debate established accounts of their history and heritage, and even to question notions of their collective cultural identity. It is no coincidence that so much of the literary production in Portugal of the thirty-five years since the Carnation Revolution discusses the social and political functions of art, reinvestigates the national and imperial past, and explores newly accessible cultural models and means of adaptation to the country's post-dictatorship and post-imperial situation.

The Carnation Revolution is often cited as the forerunner and model for the wave of mostly peaceful transitions to parliamentary democracy in

---

[1]   *Log Book*, tr. Richard Zenith (Manchester: Carcanet, 1997), p. 78.

southern, central and eastern Europe from 1975 to the early 1990s. What has been examined less is the worldwide influence of the impassioned discussion, at many levels in mid-1970s Portuguese society, of the means by which writing and culture might be deployed to consolidate democratic and libertarian principles, to articulate and address popular concerns, and to undo or at least to mitigate Salazarism's legacy of illiteracy and ignorance. Literary production and consumption had become ever more politicised in the last decade of dictatorship, but the demise of censorship in 1974 brought both political theorisation and polemic out into the open, rendering the newspaper *crónica*, the essay, and even the lyric an open field of ideological confrontation. Writers positioned across the spectrum of resistance to the Salazarist regime achieved new profiles, both as political and educational activists within the newly-formed writers' unions, and as spokespersons, and often electoral candidates, for the newly-legalised parties. The distinguished political careers of, for example, Natália Correia (MP from 1980 to 1991) or Manuel Alegre (b. 1936; Independent Socialist presidential candidate in 2006), together with the highly publicised interventions in public affairs of the Portuguese PEN Club and of internationalist writer-activists such as José Saramago, have shown that this new affirmation of political intervention as the prerogative of (canonised) writers was no flash-in-the-pan. Helder Macedo cites as evidence of this the case of the 1986 presidential election, where an open letter signed by two hundred prominent intellectuals was a factor in the victory of Socialist Party candidate Mário Soares.[2]

   The freer environment and a hunger for the works of formerly prohibited or restricted authors fostered a proliferation of periodicals and small independent publishing houses, of which some 1,337 were operating by 1975.[3] While the country's traditions of patronage and deference remained formidable, and while many new publishing enterprises concentrated on servicing the newly-liberalised markets for left-wing political theory and for soft pornography, it became easier for non-established or marginal authors to get their works into at least limited circulation. Essayistic writing, and particularly the traditionally prominent format of the newspaper *crónica*, was strongly invigorated by these developments.

---

[2]   As Macedo claims, this 'apparently quixotic gesture [...] which in other countries would have attracted little more than a patronizing comment in the press (or might even have been regarded as the kiss of death) [...] was widely noted and commented on, and, in the finely balanced state of relative support for the three nonconservative candidates, probably tipped the balance'. Helder Macedo, 'Portuguese Culture Today', in Kenneth Maxwell and Michael H. Haltzel (eds), *Portugal: Ancient Country, Young Democracy* (Washington, DC: Wilson Center Press, 1990), pp. 101–6, at pp. 103–4.

[3]   Eduarda Dionísio, *Títulos, Acções, Obrigações: Sobre a Cultura em Portugal 1974–1994* (Lisbon: Salamandra, 1993), p. 481.

The decade following April 1974 brought into print the unfettered expression of such eloquent cultural and social commentators as Vergílio Ferreira (1916–96), Jorge de Sena (1919–78), António José Saraiva (1917–93), and above all the unique figure of Eduardo Lourenço (b. 1923), whose writing, balancing a surpassing lucidity with dazzlingly wrought prose, articulated a whole tradition of leftist thinking in modern Portugal. Lourenço's ingenious exploration of the Portuguese lyric tradition, and, particularly, of Fernando Pessoa's irruption within it, spurred the advance of a more meticulous, combative and rigorously theorised literary criticism. He is however most renowned for his proposition, first fully realised in *O Labirinto da Saudade* (1978; *The Labyrinth of Nostalgia*), of mapping the national psyche through a tracing of the origins and impact of treasured cultural tropes and myths of origin. Lourenço's later essay collection, *Nós e a Europa* (1988; *Europe and Us*), developed his notion of a Portuguese 'hyperidentity' based on a narcissistic fixation on the lost 'solar moment' of maritime expansion as a national myth that is at once sustaining and demotivating. As a thesis of the nation's apprehension of its post-colonial role as historically privileged intermediary between Europe and the wider world, Lourenço's 'hyperidentity' paradigm has been extolled, adapted or decried in innumerable discussions of contemporary Portuguese cultural identity, but provides only one instance of the beguiling mix of erudition and intuition that makes his prose a joy to read.

While the winding-down of censorship breathed new life into publication across all literary genres, still more vital was the impact of the new freedoms on theatrical culture. Art theatre in Portugal had been driven into seemingly terminal decline by the recession of the early 1970s and the prohibition of the defining works of a whole dramatic generation: foreign authors partly or wholly forbidden included Brecht, Sartre, Weiss, Ionesco, O'Casey, Arrabal, Gatti and Anouilh, and in 1972 only one premiere of a Portuguese play featured among the paltry forty-six theatre performances staged nationwide.[4] After April 1974, the student theatre groups and other (often semi-amateur) outfits that had thus sustained contemporary theatre were joined by new ventures such as Fiama Hasse Pais Brandão's *Teatro Hoje* (Theatre Today) group, leading the way to the first stagings of hugely influential plays by Natália Correia, Luís de Sttau Monteiro and Bernardo Santareno. These productions fostered a boom in Brechtian productions attuned to a post-revolutionary concern to expose the relationship between power and representation, and to exploit theatre as a forum for popular education and debate. The untimely

---

4   José Oliveira Barata, 'The Historical Parable in Contemporary Portuguese Drama', in Helena Kaufman and Anna Klobucka (eds), *After the Revolution: Twenty Years of Portuguese Literature* (Lewisburg, PA: Bucknell University Press, 1997), pp. 108–26, at p. 116.

death of Santareno in 1980 robbed Portuguese theatre of a distinctive voice who, in late works such as the quartet of one-act plays *Os Marginais e a Revolução* (1979; *The Outsiders and the Revolution*), had tackled taboos undisturbed by the new left cultural ascendency (e.g. homosexuality, gender norms, and sexual recreation) even as he sustained his attack on those forces (the Church, patriarchal laws, private capital) that perpetuated the values and structures of Salazarism. Nevertheless, an ambitious and increasingly mature Portuguese theatre scene steadily established itself through the 1980s. An early high-water mark was the 400th anniversary of the death of Camões in 1980, when fresh attempts to wrest the great bard from his reductive and reactionary framing by the *Estado Novo* included José Saramago's *Que Farei com Este Livro?* (1980; *What am I to do with this Book?*), Natália Correia's *Erros Meus, Má Fortuna, Amor Ardente* (1980; *Errors of Mine, Misfortune, Fires of Love*), and Luiza Maria Martins's *O Homem que se Julgava Camões* (1980; *The Man who Thought he was Camões*).

Dramatic writing was perhaps the one genre to confirm the widely-held presumption that democratisation would release into the public sphere a wealth of masterpieces formerly lying hidden and unpublishable in an author's drawer. However, before the decade reached its close it was widely recognised that the majority of oppositional writers had been astute in adapting their output to elude the censor's strictures, rather than writing for an imagined posterity that, as it had transpired, would swiftly be obliged to elaborate a radically different cultural agenda. Many well-established writers sought new narrative strategies in order to perpetuate the political and social agenda of mid-twentieth-century 'neo-realism', while adapting both to the receptive practices of a freer, more knowing readership, and to new critiques of old-school Marxism's allegiance to a 'realist' aesthetic.

Amongst the most acclaimed experiments in narrative technique was Almeida Faria's (b. 1943) plurivocal (and partly epistolary) Lusitanian Tetralogy – *A Paixão* (1965; *Passion*), *Cortes* (1978; *Parliament*), *Lusitânia* (1980; *Lusitania*), and *Cavaleiro Andante* (1983; *Knight Errant*) – embedding subjective accounts of the Revolution's consequences into a study of the disintegration of rural tradition. Olga Gonçalves (1929–2004) published what she called 'I was there' writing; pseudo-sociological texts that relayed the voices of the marginalised or alienated, such as migrants (to France, and returning from Germany), teenagers, prostitutes, and the uneducated. Her perspective on society immediately after the Revolution, in *A Floresta em Bremerhaven* (1975; *The Forest at Bremerhaven*), *Mandei-lhe uma Boca* (1977; *Tongue in Cheek*), *Este Verão o Emigrante là-bas* (1978; *This Summer the Migrant Worker là-bas*) and *Ora Esguardae* (1982; *Come and Behold*), punctures the residual euphoria by tracing the not always wholly positive concatenations of change in family and social structures. José Cardoso Pires now turned to pastiche of the popular detective novel to explore the iniquities of dictatorship in *Balada da Praia dos Cães* (1982; translated as *Ballad of Dogs' Beach*).

The pursuit of more apposite formats for socially engaged writing itself is the basis for fiction in José Saramago's (b. 1922) first mature novel, *Manual de Pintura e Caligrafia* (1977; translated as *Manual of Painting and Calligraphy*), in which a society portrait painter recounts the experience of political and artistic radicalisation and 'rebirth'. In the short story collection *Objecto Quase* (1978; *Quasi-Object*) and the epic saga of working-class struggle in the rural Alentejo, *Levantado do Chão* (1980; *Risen from the Ground*), Saramago developed a playfully mercurial narrative voice that, by interrupting its own account of historical events, encourages the reader to reflect both on the limitations of representation and on the ideological ramifications of all choices of narrative and linguistic strategy, including the author's own ingenious rehabilitation of late neo-realism's censor-evading use of allegory and symbolic encryption. The exploitation of multiple or mutating narrators, their identities blurred or elided through unconventional punctuation and obfuscated factual detail, and their unstable position relative to the diegesis they recounted, was crucial also to the early works of António Lobo Antunes (b. 1942) and Lídia Jorge (b. 1946), and taken to unsettling but remarkable extremes by Maria Gabriela Llansol (1931–2008) and Rui Nunes (b. 1947).

In the realm of poetry, the excitation prompted by the Revolution confronted the weight of a tradition whose vigour and diversity had suffered less under dictatorship. A lively debate arose regarding the viability of modernist aesthetics in a post-censorship era concerned with culture's potential as a democratising force. This discussion dominated the reception of the mature and uncensored work of authors associated with the influential *Poesia 61* publication, notably Luiza Neto Jorge (1939–1989) and Gastão Cruz (b. 1941). Viewed variously as reinvigorating the lyric with its pursuit of verbal plasticity and expressive concentration, and as reductive and depoliticised hermeticism, such poets' output was both an inspiration and a provocation to a younger cohort that included Nuno Júdice (b. 1949), João Miguel Fernandes Jorge (b. 1943), Joaquim Manuel de Magalhães (b. 1945), Vasco Graça Moura (b. 1942), and a number of (mostly male) figures returning from exile. Certainly, the extensive and complex intertextual allusion that juxtaposes diverse literary quotation with popular cultural reference in, for example, the work of António Franco Alexandre (b. 1944) or Manuel António Pina (b. 1943) repudiates the *Poesia 61* pursuit of the poem's formal and enunciatory unity. Claims of the typically postmodernist sensibility characterising the poetry of the so-called '1970s generation' also derive from recognition of the self-consciously cosmopolitan focus that abets these texts' challenges to the traditional laws of a national canon that they cannot help but evoke. Younger poets of the post-revolutionary era evinced an unprecedented interest in anglophone and central European literary models, though engagement with contemporary innovations in Brazilian poetry (for example the conceptual 'concrete poetry' of Haroldo de Campos, and the 'pop anthropophagism' of Tropicália) was notably limited.

For aesthetic reasons as much as historical ones, one of the most significant cultural developments of the post-revolutionary era was the explosion of literary publishing by women authors. After 1974, women were granted much more freedom by law, and the 1976 Constitution accorded equal rights to men and women and made discrimination illegal. Just as women steadily became more visible in more high-status jobs and in politics, so too did they begin to win prominence and respect in the literary world. Some established women authors, like Agustina Bessa Luís (b. 1922), Luísa Dacosta (b. 1927) and Fernanda Botelho (b. 1926), continued to publish as they had done under the regime, without significant changes to form or content. Others returned from abroad, or finally felt more confident to publish their fiction and/or poetry, which was often experimental, sometimes erotic, frequently not merely pushing the boundaries of social convention but also critiquing the presumptions of a new, 'democratic' political ascendency from expressly female perspectives. The Three Marias, acquitted of the charge of offending public morals, continued to publish along the diverging lines of their particular interests: Maria Velho da Costa (b. 1938) penning a series of award-winning dense novels and short stories, Maria Isabel Barreno (b. 1939) authoring science fiction novels and essays on education and Europe, and Maria Teresa Horta (b. 1937) making a unique contribution to post-revolutionary poetry's foregrounding of the life of the body.

While the work of her *Poesia 61* fellows Gastão Cruz and Luiza Neto Jorge and that of Joaquim Manuel de Magalhães also explored the experience of erotic desire and of gendered sexuality with unprecedented depth and nuance, age-old taboos were defied most candidly in Horta's vociferously feminist, but never simplistic, celebration of female corporeality, and in Al Berto's (1948–97) LSD- and sex-fuelled existential ruminations, drawing inspiration from the likes of William Burroughs, Jean Genet and the lyricists of punk and new wave. While these writers' texts were a far cry from the limpid classicism of those supreme figures of the older generation, Eugénio de Andrade (1923–2005) and Sophia de Mello Breyner Andresen (1919–2004), rarely in the poetry of the 1970s and 1980s can one fail to find traces of Andrade's evocation of erotic sensuality or of Andresen's consciousness of material actuality.

By the early 1980s, as the ink dried on a sequence of documents committing Portugal to the EEC and a free market economy, a realisation was abroad that the discursive innovations and didactic initiatives of the revolutionary period had effected only a limited democratisation or radicalisation of culture. While literature maintained its significance as a means of political intervention, there was a growing emphasis on the identification of long-term tropes and tendencies in Portuguese society and culture, and with it an implication that artists might assist social regeneration as much through the analysis of such past continuities as through a focus on current turbulence. It is perhaps unsurprising, given that the *Estado Novo* had reduced historical discourse to jingoistic pageantry in order to claim continuity with the aims and values of a past national golden age, that historiographical fiction should have become the most vital literary genre of the period. Already in 1980, Al Berto's poem 'O mito da sereia em plástico português' ('The Myth of the Portuguese Plastic Mermaid') had strikingly evoked both the latter-day fabrication of identity out of ideologically-loaded myths of seafaring, and the attempts to confect a new imagined community out of the debris of a collapsed totalitarianism. Over the 1980s the 'new historicism' of Georges Duby and Hayden White and the historiographical fiction booming in the formerly-colonised world informed Portuguese novelists' innovation of formats that reassessed the mythologised past events prominent in debates about national identity, priorities and ethics, without losing sight of the inherent problematics of narrative as a vehicle for historical representation. The resulting exploration of the 'silenced years of the Salazar regime and the so-called remote past [...]; the African experience and colonial war; the "provincial condition" characterising a majority of Portugal's population; and the concept of national identity' ushered in perhaps the Portuguese novel's most remarkable epoch to date.[5] Established figures were joined by mostly younger authors such as João de Melo (b. 1949), Hélia Correia (b. 1949), Mário Cláudio (b. 1941), Helena Marques (b. 1935), Maria Gabriela Llansol, Teolinda Gersão (b. 1940), Mário de Carvalho (b. 1944), and the three Portuguese novelists who have established considerable international profiles: José Saramago, António Lobo Antunes and Lídia Jorge.

José Saramago had enjoyed a modest reputation as a poet and essayist since the mid-1960s, but the appearance of *Memorial do Convento* (translated as *Baltasar and Blimunda*) in 1982 confirmed his maturation into a novelist possessed of outstanding originality and imagination. An instant commercial and critical hit, *Memorial* has become Portugal's best-selling modern novel, and established its author's international profile, being translated into more than forty languages. Conjuring the reign of Portugal's 'Sun King', João V (1706–50), in terms alternately rhapsodic, Rabelaisian, elegiac and macabre, the novel displaces the official account with the histories of working people and religious dissenters struggling for justice and enlightenment amid the

5   Helena Kaufman and Anna Klobucka, 'Politics and Culture in Postrevolutionary Portugal', in *After the Revolution*, pp. 13–36, at p. 19.

squalor of a decadent state and in the shadow of the Portuguese Inquisition. Saramago elaborates these histories through his trademark device of
the re-creation of history based on a fantastical proposition. While railing
against both the crushing of human initiative and dignity by a purportedly
Christian state, and the effacement of state crimes and popular heroism from
the historical record, *Memorial* speculates on how altered historical circumstances could call forth a more equitable, loving and productive social order.
If *Memorial*'s excavation of suppressed histories also suggests the Portuguese establishment's recurrent tendency towards reactionary authoritarianism, this foreshadows and informs Saramago's dissection, in subsequent
novels, of incipient practices of institutional totalitarianism and of the cant
and doublespeak of officialdom.

   This comes to the fore in *O Ano da Morte de Ricardo Reis* (1984; translated as *The Year of the Death of Ricardo Reis*), where the brutal authoritarianism of the 1930s *Estado Novo*, and reports of the bloody rise of fascism
worldwide, set the scene for a lyrical yet bleak meditation on the problematics of textuality and on the politics of writing and reading. *História do
Cerco de Lisboa* (1989; translated as *The History of the Siege of Lisbon*)
relates two apocryphal histories: that of a proof-reader who deliberately
falsifies a text recounting the foundation of the Portuguese kingdom in
the twelfth century, and the alternative account of the same events that his
boss challenges him to write, building on the spurious revisions that he
made to the historical record. This playfully semi-autobiographical tale is
Saramago's most direct analysis of how fiction contributes to the writing
and rewriting of history, and his boldest attempt to move historiographical
discourse beyond narrative formats that lend plausibility to false teleologies
of human development. Juxtaposing Portugal's founding myth of 'Christians versus Moors' with present-day life in multicultural Lisbon, *História*
was also Saramago's contribution to the historiographic novel's belated
treatment of the nation's long cultural, economic and political relationship
with Africa, and, particularly, of the dirty colonial wars of 1961–74.

   Challenging though they were in both form and content, works like Lídia
Jorge's *A Costa dos Murmúrios* (1988; translated as *The Murmuring Coast*),
Manuel Alegre's *Jornada de África* (1989, *Africa Campaign*), Helder
Macedo's *Partes de África* (1991; *Some Parts of Africa*) and Domingos
Lobo's (b. 1946) *Os Navios Negreiros não Sobem o Cuando* (1993; *Slave
Ships do not Go up the Kwando*) contributed significantly to a slow process
of coming-to-terms with the trauma, guilt and recrimination engendered by
the *Estado Novo*'s military campaigns. Previously, an on-going 'conspiracy
of silence' about the horrors of the conflict had been challenged only by a
few voices; notably Wanda Ramos (1948–98) in *Percursos: Do Luachino
ao Luena* (1981; *From Luachino to Luena*), João de Melo in *Autopsia de
um Mar de Ruínas* (1984; *Post-Mortem on a Sea of Ruins*), and the writer

widely deemed to have mapped the trouble-spots in the nation's post-imperial psyche with most devastating accuracy, António Lobo Antunes.[6]

Lobo Antunes's extraordinary blend of dense and phantasmagoric prose poetry with vivid character narration emerges at its rawest in his debut *Os Cus de Judas* (translated as *South of Nowhere*) and its close successor *Fado Alexandrino* (translated as *Fado Alexandrino*), both published in 1979. In *Os Cus de Judas*, a veteran of gruesome counter-insurgency operations in Angola obsessively recounts his experiences to a woman he has picked up in a Lisbon bar. In a manner inevitably reminiscent of the work of Joseph Conrad, the narrator's recollections of complicity in colonialist violence dominate and pervert his interaction with present surroundings and company. The hallucinogenic quality of Lobo Antunes's famously 'neo-baroque' narrative (the novelist has spoken of his deep admiration for the work of the seventeenth-century Spanish poet Francisco de Quevedo) does not correspond to a simple scorn for verisimilitude in the fictionalisation of history.[7] Rather, the fantastic, the non-sequitous and the absurd deturpation of stock cultural references serve to express, and simultaneously deconstruct, the viewpoint of historical subjects trapped between imaginary ideals that have lost their plausibility, and material realities that are too alienating or traumatising to be recognised or believed in. An outstanding example is the later *As Naus* (1988; translated as *The Return of the Caravels*), a carnivalesque anti-epic depicting the heroes of the Discoveries washed up in post-revolutionary Lisbon as *retornados* from the colonies. Concluding with Vasco da Gama and his deluded comrades escaping the confines of a psychiatric ward to await the rumoured return of King Sebastião at the beach resort of Ericeira, *As Naus* suggests that only when the Portuguese affirm an alternative national narrative to that of imperialist primacy will they be able to transcend an ultimately psychotic misrecognition of their post-colonial circumstances.

The increasing symbolic and conceptual density of Lobo Antunes's later work – presenting a Herculean challenge to his translators – has gone hand in hand with the use of ever more fragmentary and labyrinthine narrative frameworks. The experience of fragmentation – of the nation, of the family, and most tragically, of the self and of the memories and value-systems upon which an individual sense of self and of purpose depend – is arguably Lobo Antunes's primary concern, and informs his unremittingly bleak, yet rarely dispassionate, judgement on the human condition. Knowledge, and especially self-knowledge, are seen only to undo the subject's ontological security; and memory, unreliable, traumatic and remote from external reality though it

---

6   Rui de Azevedo Teixeira, *A Guerra Colonial e o Romance Português* (Lisbon: Notícias, 1998), 98.

7   See, for example, Lobo Antunes's interview with Alexandra Lucas Coelho and Enric Vives-Rubio in *Público*, 29 October 2006, 44–54, at p. 47.

may be, offers the only reference point or refuge from a sense of rootlessness and cosmic insignificance.

A critique of the false consolations of both mythographic and positivist histories combines with a rather less solitary psychological focus in the works of Lídia Jorge, who has become the Portuguese woman writer best known internationally, having been widely translated and been awarded a number of national and international prizes. Her native Algarve provides the setting for her first two novels, the highly innovative *O Dia dos Prodígios* (1980; *The Day of Wonders*) and *O Cais das Merendas* (1982; *The Picnicking Harbour*). Both use the experience of the 1974 revolution and the social and ideological transformations that it precipitated to address not just the manipulative power of notions of collective history and identity, but also more universal dilemmas. *O Dia dos Prodígios*'s depiction of the impact of the 25 April coup in a remote Algarve village explores the significance of cultural marginalisation, as the villagers struggle to conceptualise the new 'people's democracy' proclaimed from Lisbon in their name, yet remain bound by age-old patriarchal laws and definitions imposed by the heads of their community. Jorge explores the seemingly inevitable violence inherent in self/Other relations in *A Costa dos Murmúrios* using an army wife's account of her short, ill-fated marriage in war-time Mozambique to allegorise both the fallacy of 'brandos costumes' ('gentle ways') informing Portuguese colonialism and the culture of denial that abetted state suppression of the grisly truth about the wars. Twenty years on, Jorge has amassed a large body of work, including the particularly acclaimed novels *O Vale da Paixão* (1998; translated as *The Migrant Painter of Birds*) and *O Vento Assobiando nas Gruas* (2002; *The Wind Whistling in the Cranes*). The latter focuses directly on pressing social problems in modern Portugal, including racism, subtly presenting shocking events through unconventional figures coping with unexpected upheavals, and scratching the surface of a seemingly more prosperous, fully-functioning and civilised society.

The new confidence in Portuguese fiction in the 1980s and early 1990s and the remarkable sales figures achieved by such highbrow figures as Saramago and Cardoso Pires did not end the preeminent status of lyric poetry in Portuguese culture. While the poets who made their debuts in the 1970s and 1980s were supported by a host of mostly small-scale publishing houses and journals, the major presses considered it a mark of prestige to produce increasingly high-quality anthologies and collected works of senior figures like António Ramos Rosa (b. 1924), Miguel Torga (1907–95), Alexandre O'Neill (1924–86), Ruy Belo (1933–78) and Herberto Helder (b. 1930). Pessoa's centenary in 1988 occasioned unprecedented commodification of his work as cultural heritage, but also genuine recognition of its scope and originality, and of the diverse responses it provoked from later writers.

Sophia de Mello Breyner Andresen, picking up on Pessoa's own reformulation of national and classical myth in *Mensagem*, lovingly evokes Pessoa as a poetic Ulysses, while Al Berto's *Luminoso Afogado* (1995), a lyrical mono- logue addressed to the corpse of the eponymous 'luminous drowned man', pays tribute by reworking the premises of Pessoa's 'static drama' *O Marin- heiro (The Mariner)*. Meanwhile, in the scabrous satire *O Virgem Negra* (1989; *The Male Black Virgin*), the pioneer of Portuguese surrealism Mário Cesariny (1923–2006) debunked the Pessoan myth of the sublimely immate- rial 'man who never was'.[8] A different kind of riposte to Pessoa is implicit in the writing of Herberto Helder, probably Portugal's most revered poet of the late twentieth century. Where Pessoa stresses the loss of the author's exterior identity in the mass of textuality opened up in the poem, Helder has reaffirmed the poet's vocation of demiurgic sublimation in verse that recalls 'visionary writing as practiced by Lautréamont, Rimbaud, Milton or Blake'.[9] An outstanding new voice in the 1980s was that of Luís Miguel Nava (1957– 95), whose verse and prose-poetry is distinguished by a concentrated prosody and startling originality of metaphor, often alluding to intense, frequently homoerotic, corporeal experiences.

The questions of language's translation of spiritual insight, corporeality and desire exercised prose writers as well, some of whom had had enough of fiction infused with political comment and turned their attentions to renewed formal and hermeneutic experimentation, to the subjective, and to interper- sonal relationships. Indeed, Luísa Costa Gomes's often cited epigraph to *O Pequeno Mundo* (1988; *Small World*) triumphantly declares: 'Reader! This book does not speak about the 25 April. It does not refer to the 11 March and it is not bothered about the 25 November. Worse, nowhere does it mention the war in Africa. It does not reflect upon our cultural identity as a people, our future as a nation, our place in the European community.' Regarding this last, however, Gomes was swimming against the tide, as Portugal became firmly involved in European initiatives: the Lisbon Expo of 1998 being crowned by the award of the Nobel Prize for Literature to Saramago that autumn, the euro being successfully adopted in 1999, and Oporto following Lisbon's success as European City of Culture in 2001. In 2007, the Portuguese presidency of the EU oversaw the signing of the Lisbon treaty, relating to the historic but controversial project of a European constitution. This swift process of internationalisation was reflected, at the close of the twentieth century, by a recognition of the growth of capitalism and consumerism in a more urban, materialistic and cynical Portugal. The 'total urban realism' of Rui Zink

8   Fernando Cabral Martins, 'Appearances of the Author', in Anna Klobucka and Mark Sabine (eds), *Embodying Pessoa: Corporeality, Gender, Sexuality* (Toronto: University of Toronto Press, 2007), pp. 245–57, at pp. 250–2.
9   António Ladeira, ' "The Poet is not a Faker": Herberto Helder and the Myth of Poetry', *Portuguese Literary and Cultural Studies* 7 (2001 [2008]), 43–62, at p. 56.

(b. 1961), Jacinto Lucas Pires (b. 1974) and Inês Pedrosa (b. 1962) echoes the pessimism and social disorientation characteristic of Portuguese literature at the end of the nineteenth century.[10]

Against this backdrop, there were exceptions, of course. As well as the tongue-in-cheek celebration of a postmodern Portugal in *Requiem* (1991), by the lusophile Italian Antonio Tabucchi (b. 1943), there were the now bankable writers like Saramago, Lobo Antunes and Jorge, and the experimentalists, who rejected traditional form and content. The most prolific and idiosyncratic of these was Maria Gabriela Llansol, who characterised her own work as a deliberate move away from narrativity towards textuality, having found the conventions of traditional literature too restrictive. She was not concerned about describing reality but rather believed that language is an organic, living process: writing, for her, was reality. Already in 1985, in her diary *Um Falcão no Punho* (*A Falcon on my Fist*), she wrote 'literature doesn't exist. When you are writing, the only thing you need to know is which reality you are entering and whether or not there is a suitable technique that can open up the way to others.' Peopling her works with maverick figures and historical heretics from central Europe, as well as versions of Fernando Pessoa, Bach and King Sebastião, she created a philosophy of community and cooperation between humans, animals, plants and minerals, eschewing hierarchy of any kind. Key works include *O Livro das Comunidades* (1977; *The Book of Community*), the first of her truly innovative works, and *Amigo e Amiga* (2006; *Lover and Beloved*), an elegy to her deceased husband. Another highly individual and hermetic prosodist to have won belated acclaim is Rui Nunes. Nunes has memorably described works such as *O Grito* (1997; *The Cry*) and *Rostos* (2001; *Faces*) as 'texts that are beyond redemption [...] that suffer from a nostalgia for the regard of God, while knowing that regard to be non-existent, and believing that words only prolong further the lack that they aim to make good'.[11]

Teolinda Gersão's career has gone from strength to strength since her debut novel *O Silêncio* (1981; *Silence*). Family and love relationships form the core of works like *Paisagem com Mulher e Mar ao Fundo* (1982; *Landscape with Woman and Sea in the Distance*), *O Cavalo de Sol* (1989; *The Sun Horse*) and *A Árvore das Palavras* (1997; *The Tree of Words*), often set in the day-to-day reality of the protagonists. Hélia Correia's adult fairy and folk tales, like the gloriously irreverent *Montedemo* (1981; *Devil Mountain*), question taboos and restrictions and invert classical myths. Correia and Gersão, together with

---

[10] Miguel Real, *Geração de 90: Romance e Sociedade no Portugal Contemporâneo* (Oporto: Campo das Letras, 2001), 21–2.

[11] Nunes, quoted in Maria João Cantinho, 'Rui Nunes: A Experiência da Desconstrução da Linguagem', *Espéculo* 31 <http://www.ucm.es/info/especulo/numero31/ruinunes.html>, accessed 21 February 2007.

the talented and prolific Mário Cláudio, have also built on the achievements of the 1980s novel, adapting tried and tested formulae for combining historical data with myth, fantasy or literary parody and *mise-en-abîme*. Correia's novel *Lilias Fraser* (2001) is a fine example: set against the backdrop of the Lisbon earthquake in 1755, it unites the beleaguered Scottish émigrée of its title with the clairvoyant Blimunda from Saramago's *Memorial do Convento*. Cláudio's *As Batalhas do Caia* (1995; *The Battles of Caia*) reworks tropes from 'A Catastrofe' ('The Disaster'), Eça de Queirós's tale of finisecular Portugal's annexation by Spain, in order to query the wisdom of ever-deeper integration into the European Union.

Other writers of fiction who came to prominence in the 1990s include Helder Macedo (b. 1935), whose novels are intricate narrative puzzles that shrewdly examine Portugal's engagement with its recent past (the colonial war, abuses under the dictatorship) and its situation as a country on the periphery of Europe. *Pedro e Paula* (1998; *Pedro and Paula*) weaves intertextual references to Eça de Queirós and Wagner into the story of the complicated relationship between the eponymous twin protagonists and how they come to terms with their family's (and Portugal's) past. Mário de Carvalho provides a more light-hearted treatment of the historical novel. Carvalho's primary concern with satirising contemporary political practices and social mores, rather than with interrogating the epistemology of history, is clearest in his 2003 novel *Fantasia para Dois Coronéis e uma Piscina* (*Fantasia for Two Colonels and a Swimming Pool*).

Since the mid-1990s Saramago has transferred his trademark imagining of the possibility of the impossible from Iberian cultural contexts to more universally accessible scenarios for allegories of foundational questions of Western philosophy. The apocalyptic *Ensaio sobre a Cegueira* (1995; translated as *Blindness*) imagines notions of humanity and civilisation tested to breaking point by an incurable epidemic of blindness. While arguably lacking much of his earlier works' intricate wordplay and ingenious manipulation of intertextual reference, *A Caverna* (2000; translated as *The Cave*) – where a replica of Plato's cave is unearthed beneath a gigantic shopping centre – and *O Homem Duplicado* (2002; translated as *The Double*) – whose protagonist encounters and confronts a man who is his precise physical double – are remarkable meditations on the continuing pertinence of Platonic discussions of representation, perception, identity and self–Other relations in the age of capitalist globalisation, simulacra and cyber-communication.

Even in periods of straitened financial circumstances, theatrical culture has continued to deepen its roots and diversify, with a bright younger generation of dramatists including Carlos J. Pessoa (b. 1966), Jacinto Lucas Pires (b. 1974), Pedro Eiras (b. 1975) and José Maria Vieira Mendes (b. 1976). Longer-established writers particularly applauded for their dramatic writing include Jaime Rocha (b. 1949) and Luísa Costa Gomes (b. 1954), whose international profile was raised through an acclaimed operatic collaboration with the American minimalist composer Philip Glass.

The vitality of the Portuguese lyric tradition has also prevailed through the 1990s and beyond, despite the shocking murder of rising star Luís Miguel Nava in 1995 and the equally untimely loss two years later of Al Berto, who confronted his imminent mortality – and his consequent transfiguration into literary myth – with his most intense and distinguished work in *Horto de Incêndio* (1997; *Burning Garden*). Nava's near contemporaries Ana Luísa Amaral (b. 1956) and Fernando Pinto do Amaral (b. 1960) have both produced numerous collections of distinction, the former's idiosyncratic and expressly female-voiced take on the literary canon evident in her debut *Minha Senhora de Quê* (1990; *Milady of What?*), a play on the title of Maria Teresa Horta's 1970 collection *Minha Senhora de Mim* (*Milady of Myself*). A uniquely controversial voice is the self-styled 'pop poetess' and literary 'housekeeper' Adília Lopes (b. 1960). Lopes's prolific output, most of it first published independently, has become particularly familiar through her much-commented-upon appearances on daytime TV and reality shows. Lopes's literary pranks, the candour with which she alludes to details of her personal life, and her frequent recourse to slang, obscenity, and children's verse, have provoked some consternation, but also, increasingly, admiration.

Contemporary Portuguese literary criticism and academe have not ignored international discussions concerning pluralism and identity politics, though institutional endorsement of such causes is often lukewarm or limited. Women's Studies departments and university courses focusing on women's writing, for example, are few and far between in Portugal. The reception of literary treatments of lesbian, gay, bisexual and queer identities and/or homoerotic experience has followed a similar pattern. The early twenty-first century has seen exponential growth in the formerly unacknowledged discipline of LGBQT (Lesbian, Gay, Bisexual, Queer and Transexual) studies, with queer readings of Al Berto, Luís Miguel Nava, Isabel de Sá (b. 1951), Mário Cesariny, Eugénio de Andrade, Pessoa and others, and debate regarding notions of a queer literary canon.[12] Novels by such writers as Guilherme de Melo (b. 1931) and Marta Tasmânia (b. 1975), and Frederico Lourenço's (b. 1963) trilogy *Pode um Desejo Imenso* (2002–03; *Boundless Desire*) are often referred to as 'gay', or 'lesbian', fiction, a label not always welcomed by their authors.[13]

While between five and ten per cent of Portugal's population can claim to have African roots or to have lived in Africa, and while the country –

---

[12] See Eduardo Pitta, *Fractura. A Condição Homossexual na Literatura Portuguesa Contemporânea* (Coimbra: Angelus Novus, 2003), and Fernando Cascais (ed.), *Indisciplinar a Teoria – Estudos Gays, Lésbicos e Queer* (Lisbon: Fenda, 2004).

[13] The title of Lourenço's novel is an allusion to the opening of a famous poem by Camões.

and Lisbon in particular – has an increasingly large and visible population of immigrants from Brazil, Africa, and central and eastern Europe, it is notable that there have been few attempts (at least on the part of publishers, retailers, critics and scholars) to identify 'immigrant', 'diasporic', or 'black Portuguese' writers or writing in the manner now commonplace in the UK or Germany. The content of much published fiction, meanwhile, declines to acknowledge the growing multicultural and increasingly diverse nature of Portuguese society, focusing on middle-class white heterosexual characters rather than disturbing entrenched taboos. Recent novels to address contemporary racism and interracial relationships are Maria Velho da Costa's *Irene ou o Contrato Social* (2000; *Irene, or The Social Contract*) and Lídia Jorge's *O Vento Assobiando nas Gruas* (2002).

The turn of the millennium has also been the era in which Portugal's literary scene has embraced the post-colonial project of 'lusofonia' – the linguistic link between all Portuguese-speaking countries. The relationship between Portugal and Brazil, like that between all nations previously connected through colonisation, has often been a delicate one and the exchange of cultural products eyed with suspicion, condescension or resentment.[14] Literature from lusophone Africa, meanwhile, remained for most Portuguese readers inextricably linked with revolutionary politics and the struggle against colonialism, long after the Portuguese Writers' Association controversially awarded a prize to the Angolan novelist and pro-independence activist José Luandino Vieira in 1965. Nevertheless, modern Portugal has significantly curtailed inherited tendencies towards cultural chauvinism and isolationism.

There is considerable discussion in all Portuguese-speaking countries about the precise usefulness of the concept of 'lusofonia' as a political category, but the debate is also evident in the fields of literature and culture. An intriguing reality-check for notions of a happy band of brother lusophone nations is provided by the international success of ocean-hopping cosmopolitanist José Eduardo Agualusa (b. 1960), born in Angola, but resident for some time in Brazil and also in Europe. While the majority in Portuguese academe and criticism remain insistent on categorising writing according to national schools, Agualusa's output raises questions about the nomadic identity of texts within the lusophone context; questions that are further compounded by their enthusiastic reception when published in translation. Agualusa's biggest international hit, *O Vendedor de Passados* (2004; translated as *The Book of Chameleons*), satirises the link between corporate corruption and historical revisionism in post-conflict Angola. He has also ruffled Brazilian

---

[14] Fernando Arenas, 'Introduction', in *Utopias of Otherness: Nationhood and Subjectivity in Portugal and Brazil* (Minneapolis: University of Minnesota Press, 2003).

and Portuguese feathers respectively with *O Ano em que Zumbi Tomou o Rio* (2002; *The Year Zumbi Took Rio*), a speculative novel about an uprising in Rio's shantytowns, and with *Nação Crioula* (1997; translated as *Creole*), an epistolary romance dealing with the illicit but thriving slave trade in late nineteenth-century Luanda.

In twenty-first-century Portugal, trends in publishing have followed the popularity of formats that have found success around the world, such as 'chick lit', and the huge success of historical novels set in the not-so-distant past (though many of these avoid historiographical reflection or debate). Miguel Sousa Tavares's best-seller *Equador* (2003; translated as *Equator*) describes the political, diplomatic and amorous challenges befalling the newly appointed governor of the islands of São Tomé and Príncipe, between 1905 and 1908, when the rest of the world was concerned that the Portuguese were using slave labour on their coffee and cacao plantations. Another best-seller, *A Filha do Capitão* (2004; *The Captain's Daughter*), by José Rodrigues dos Santos (b. 1964), depicts Portuguese soldiers fighting in Flanders in the First World War, while the plot of the same author's *O Códex 632* (2005; *Codex 632*) revolves around documents which might prove that Christopher Columbus was, in fact, Portuguese. A big hit of 2006 was Domingos Amaral's (b. 1967) astute Second World War espionage thriller *Enquanto Salazar Dormia* (*While Salazar Slept*).

Júlio Magalhães's (b. 1963) *Os Retornados* (2008; *Returning Settlers*) is one of what has grown to a stream of works tackling the still-painful subject of the colonial wars; a number of these are historical accounts and memoirs or testimonials of veterans. Another audacious, if perhaps lurid, popular fictional treatment of the African conflicts is António Brito's thriller *Olhos de Caçador* (2007; *Hunter's Eyes*). As the trauma, mistrust and disaffection born of wars and a shambolic decolonisation have faded, Portuguese readers have developed an appetite for both scholarly and more creative treatments of the history of 'their' Africa. Journalist Pedro Rosa Mendes (b. 1968) has published two volumes of postmodern travel literature that analyse the effects of war and corruption in Portugal's former colonies: *Baía dos Tigres* (1999; translated as *Bay of Tigers*), a fictionalised journey from Angola to Mozambique, and *Lenin Oil* (2006), set like *Equador* in the tiny equatorial island of São Tomé, whose fortune may lie in offshore oil reserves.

It has become a commonplace to observe that Portugal, in the thirty-five years since its April Revolution, has changed almost beyond recognition. In those years of preponderantly positive but challenging and often turbulent flux, literature (in particular poetry and the novel) has defied gloomy predictions of the death of the book, articulating renewed hopes and demands for the future and revised interpretations of the past, and offering reassuring intimations of a distinctive cultural identity as the nation finds itself ever more beholden to globalised markets and to its new European partners. It would be rash to pronounce upon which of Portugal's living writers will be most acclaimed by posterity, or to attempt any more precise delineation of the contemporary canon than this chapter's panoramic sketch. It is, however, rather safer to surmise that the writing of the last few decades will continue to be regarded as compelling confirmation of the vivacity and distinctive qualities of Portuguese literature.

Texts and translations[15]

Agualusa, José Eduardo, *Nação Crioula* (1997); *Creole*, tr. Daniel Hahn (London: Arcadia, 2002)

—— *O Ano em que Zumbi Tomou o Rio* (2002)

—— *O Vendedor de Passados* (2004); *The Book of Chameleons*, tr. Daniel Hahn (London: Arcadia, 2006)

Alegre, Manuel, *Jornada de África* (1989)

Amaral, Ana Luísa, *Minha Senhora de Quê* (1990)

Amaral, Domingos, *Enquanto Salazar Dormia* (2006)

Andrade, Eugénio de, *Forbidden Words: Selected Poetry*, tr. Alexis Levitin (New York: Norton, 2005)

Andresen, Sophia de Mello Breyner, *Log Book: Selected Poems*, tr. Richard Zenith (Manchester: Carcanet, 1997)

Antunes, António Lobo, *Os Cus de Judas* (1979); *South of Nowhere*, tr. Elizabeth Lowe (London: Chatto & Windus, 1983)

—— *Fado Alexandrino* (1979); *Fado Alexandrino*, tr. Gregory Rabassa (New York: Grove, 1990)

—— *Explicação dos Pássaros* (1981); *An Explanation of the Birds*, tr. Richard Zenith (London: Secker & Warburg, 1992)

—— *Auto dos Danados* (1985); *Act of the Damned*, tr. Richard Zenith (London: Secker & Warburg, 1993)

—— *As Naus* (1988); *The Return of the Caravels*, tr. Gregory Rabassa (New York: Grove, 2002)

—— *A Ordem Natural das Coisas* (1992); *The Natural Order of Things*, tr. Richard Zenith (New York: Grove, 2000)

—— *O Manual dos Inquisidores* (1996); *The Inquisitors' Manual*, tr. Richard Zenith (New York: Grove, 2003)

Berto, Al, *Luminoso Afogado* (1995)

—— *Horto de Incêndio* (1997)

Brito, António, *Olhos de Caçador* (2007)

Carvalho, Mário de, *Um Deus Passeando pela Brisa da Tarde* (1994); *A God Strolling in the Cool of the Evening: A Novel*, tr. Gregory Rabassa (London: Weidenfeld & Nicolson, 1997)

—— *Fantasia para Dois Coronéis e uma Piscina* (2003)

Cesariny, Mário, *O Virgem Negra* (1989)

---

15 The works of individual authors are presented in chronological order.

Cláudio, Mário, *As Batalhas do Caia* (1995)
Correia, Hélia, *Montedemo* (1981)
—— *Lilias Fraser* (2001)
Correia, Natália, *O Encoberto* (1969)
—— *Erros Meus, Má Fortuna, Amor Ardente* (1980)
Costa, Maria Velho da, *Irene, ou o Contrato Social* (2000)
—— *Myra* (2008)
Faria, Almeida, *A Paixão* (1965)
—— *Cortes* (1978)
—— *Lusitânia* (1980)
—— *Cavaleiro Andante* (1983)
Gersão, Teolinda, *O Silêncio* (1981)
—— *Paisagem com Mulher e Mar ao Fundo* (1982)
——*O Cavalo de Sol* (1989)
—— *A Árvore das Palavras* (1997)
Gomes, Luísa Costa, *O Pequeno Mundo* (1988)
Gonçalves, Olga, *A Floresta em Bremerhaven* (1976)
—— *Mandei-lhe uma Boca* (1977)
—— *Este Verão o Emigrante là-bas* (1978)
—— *Ora Esguardae* (1982)
Jorge, Lídia, *O Dia dos Prodígios* (1980)
—— *O Cais das Merendas* (1982)
—— *A Costa dos Murmúrios* (1988); *The Murmuring Coast*, tr. Natália Costa
    and Ronald W. Sousa (Minneapolis: University of Minnesota Press, 1995)
—— *O Vale da Paixão* (1998); *The Migrant Painter of Birds*, tr. Margaret Jull
    Costa (London: Harvill, 2001)
—— *O Vento Assobiando nas Gruas* (2002)
Llansol, Maria Gabriela, *O Livro das Comunidades* (1977)
—— *Um Falcão no Punho* (1985)
—— *Amigo e Amiga* (2006)
Lobo, Domingos, *Os Navios Negreiros não Sobem o Cuando* (1993)
Lourenço, Eduardo, *O Labirinto da Saudade* (1978)
—— *Nós e a Europa* (1988)
—— *Chaos and Splendor: Selected Essays of Eduardo Lourenço*, ed. Carlos
    Veloso (Dartmouth, MA: Center for Portuguese Studies and Culture, 2003;
    Adamastor Series, 1)
—— *This Little Lusitanian House: Essays on Portuguese Culture*, ed. Ronald W.
    Sousa (Providence, RI: Gávea-Brown, 2003).
Lourenço, Frederico, *Pode um Desejo Imenso*, 3 vols (2002–03); single vol.
    (2006)
Macedo, Helder, *Partes de África* (1991)
—— *Pedro e Paula* (1998)
Magalhães, Júlio, *Os Retornados* (2008)
Martins, Luiza Maria, *O Homem que se Julgava Camões* (1980)
Melo, João de, *Autopsia de um Mar de Ruínas* (1984)

Mendes, Pedro Rosa, *Baía dos Tigres* (1999); *Bay of Tigers: A Journey Through War-Torn Angola*, tr. Clifford Landers (London: Granta, 2004)
—— *Lenin Oil* (2006)
Monteiro, Luís de Sttau, *Felizmente há Luar!* (1961)
Nunes, Rui, *O Grito* (1997)
—— *Rostos* (2001)
Pedrosa, Inês, *Nas Tuas Mãos* (1997)
Pires, José Cardoso, *O Delfim* (1968)
—— *Balada da Praia dos Cães* (1982); *Ballad of Dogs' Beach*, tr. Mary Fitton (London: Dent, 1986)
Ramos, Wanda, *Percursos: Do Luachino ao Luena* (1981)
Santareno, Bernardo, *O Judeu* (1966)
—— *Os Marginais e a Revolução* (1979)
Santos, José Rodrigues dos, *A Filha do Capitão* (2004)
—— *O Códex 632* (2005)
Saramago, José, *Manual de Pintura e Caligrafia* (1977); *Manual of Painting and Calligraphy: A Novel*, tr. Giovanni Pontiero (Manchester: Carcanet, 1994)
—— *Que Farei com Este Livro?* (1980)
—— *Levantado do Chão* (1980)
—— *Viagem a Portugal* (1981); *Journey to Portugal*, tr. Amanda Hopkinson and Nick Castor (London: Harvill, 2000)
—— *Memorial do Convento* (1982); *Baltasar and Blimunda*, tr. Giovanni Pontiero (London: Harvill, 1994)
—— *O Ano da Morte de Ricardo Reis* (1984); *The Year of the Death of Ricardo Reis*, tr. Giovanni Pontiero (London: Harvill, 1992)
—— *A Jangada de Pedra* (1986); *The Stone Raft*, tr. Giovanni Pontiero (London: Harvill, 1994)
—— *História do Cerco de Lisboa* (1989); *The History of the Siege of Lisbon*, tr. Giovanni Pontiero (London: Harvill, 1996)
—— *O Evangelho segundo Jesus Cristo* (1991); *The Gospel According to Jesus Christ*, tr. Giovanni Pontiero (London: Harvill, 1993)
—— *Ensaio sobre a Cegueira* (1995); *Blindness: A Novel*, tr. Giovanni Pontiero (London: Harvill)
—— *O Conto da Ilha Desconhecida* (1997); *The Tale of the Unknown Island*, tr. Margaret Jull Costa (New York: Harcourt Brace, 1999)
——*Todos os Nomes* (1997); *All the Names*, tr. Margaret Jull Costa (London: Harvill, 2000)
——*A Caverna* (2000); *The Cave*, tr. Margaret Jull Costa (London: Harvill, 2002)
—— *O Homem Duplicado* (2002); *The Double*, tr. Margaret Jull Costa (London: Harvill, 2004)
—— *Ensaio sobre a Lucidez* (2004); *Seeing*, tr. Margaret Jull Costa (London: Vintage, 2007)
—— *As Intermitências da Morte* (2005); *Death at Intervals*, tr. Margaret Jull Costa (London: Harvill Secker, 2008)
Sena, Jorge de, *Os Grão-Capitães* (1976)
—— *By the Rivers of Babylon*, tr. Daphne Patai (London: Polygon, 1989)

—— *O Físico Prodigioso* (1977); *The Wondrous Physician*, tr. Mary Fitton (London: Dent, 1986)

—— *Sinais de Fogo* (1979); *Signs of Fire*, tr. John Byrne (Manchester: Carcanet, 1999)

Tabucchi, Antonio, *Requiem* (1991)

Tavares, Miguel Sousa, *Equador* (2003); *Equator*, tr. Peter Bush (London: Bloomsbury, 2008)

Anthologies

Clemente, Alice, org. *Sweet Marmalade, Sour Oranges: Contemporary Portuguese Women's Fiction* (Providence, RI: Gávea-Brown, 1994)

From the Edge/Onde a Terra Acaba – Portuguese Short Stories (Lisbon: 101 Noites, University of Lisbon Centre for English Studies, n.d.)

Passport to Portugal: A Passport Anthology (London: Serpent's Tail, 1994)

Further reading

Arenas, Fernando, *Utopias of Otherness: Nationhood and Subjectivity in Portugal and Brazil* (Minneapolis: University of Minnesota Press, 2003)

Frier, David, *The Novels of José Saramago: Echoes from the Past, Pathways into the Future* (Cardiff: University of Wales Press, 2007)

Kaufman, Helena, and Anna Klobucka (eds) *After the Revolution: Twenty Years of Portuguese Literature* (Lewisburg, PA: Bucknell University Press, 1997)

Owen, Hilary (ed.), *Gender, Ethnicity and Class in Modern Portuguese-Speaking Culture* (Lewiston, NY: Edwin Mellen, 1996)

—— *Portuguese Women's Writing 1972–1986: Reincarnations of a Revolution* (Lewiston, NY: Edwin Mellen, 2000)

Pazos Alonso, Cláudia (ed.), *Women, Literature and Culture in the Portuguese-Speaking World* (Lewiston, NY: Edwin Mellen, 1996)

Perkins, Juliet, *The Feminine in the Poetry of Herberto Helder* (Lampeter: Mellen, 1991)

Portuguese Literary and Cultural Studies 2 (1999): 'Lídia Jorge in Other Words'

Portuguese Literary and Cultural Studies 6 (2001): 'On Saramago'

Portuguese Literary and Cultural Studies 7 (2001 [2008]): 'Contemporary Portuguese Poetry'

Portuguese Literary and Cultural Studies 15/16 (2008): 'Facts and Fictions of António Lobo Antunes'

Sadlier, Darlene, *The Question of How: Women Writers and New Portuguese Literature* (New York: Greenwood, 1989).

16

Portuguese Literature in English Translation

PATRICIA ODBER DE BAUBETA

Relatively few histories of Portuguese literature have been written in English, perhaps because the subject is unlikely to attract sufficient readers to justify such an undertaking and there is a general assumption that anyone with an interest in this subject will have, at the very least, a reading knowledge of Portuguese. This rationale inevitably excludes readers with an interest in comparative literature who do not possess the required linguistic knowledge. Histories of the translation of Portuguese literature into English are even scarcer: the potential readership is extremely small, and the information required to produce such a history is difficult to locate. And yet, works of Portuguese literature have been translated into English – from Portuguese, Latin and Spanish – for more than six centuries and for the most varied reasons. It is not easy to arrive at a complete overview of this intercultural activity: the timespan in question is simply too long, the translated works do not belong to one specific genre and could never have been aimed at a single, homogeneous readership. Works have been translated because their content is deemed to have some intrinsic value or aesthetic quality, because of their social, cultural or political significance, or on account of some particular relevance for potential readers. In any event, translations do not happen by accident: for every translation that makes it into print, other potential translations have been left by the wayside.

Information about Portuguese literature translated into English may at first seem sparse but a reasonable amount can be tracked down and pieced together from surveys beginning with Thomas in the first half of the twentieth century.[1]

---

[1]   Henry Thomas, *English Translations of Portuguese before 1640* (Coimbra: Universidade, 1930); Félix Walter, *La Littérature Portugaise en Angleterre à l'Époque Romantique* (Paris: Champion, 1927); Fran Paxeco, *The Intellectual Relations between Portugal and Great Britain* (Lisbon: Editorial Império, 1937); Anthony Francis Allison, *English Translations from the Spanish and Portuguese to the year 1700: An Annotated Catalogue of the Extant Printed Versions (excluding Dramatic Adaptations)* (London: Dawson, 1974); George Monteiro,

Some works have been translated and published in English within just a few years of their first appearance in print. *The legacye or embassate of the great emperour of Inde prester Iohn, vnto Emanuell kyng of Portyngale, in the yere of our lorde M.v.C.xiii*, was printed in 1533, the year after the publication of Damião de Gois's Latin original.[2]

What readers may find surprising, however, is the length of time that can elapse between the date of composition or publication of a text or corpus of texts, and its first appearance in English. This is very much the case of the medieval Galician-Portuguese lyrics, composed between the twelfth and fourteenth centuries, but not translated until the late nineteenth or early twentieth. The gap of some 800 years can be explained by the fact that the source texts were simply not accessible: the manuscripts were lying dormant in different European libraries waiting to be rediscovered and edited. Furthermore, the poems were viewed as either 'antiquarian' or 'primitive', written in an obscure dialect, as well as being incomplete or illegible. It was only when scholars began to produce editions or anthologies of the lyrics that translations could be made and published, Henry Roseman Lang's article in 1905 marking the beginning of this process.[3] Since then, approximately 370 of the 1,680 profane *cantigas* have been translated into English by 55 different translators, some of them just once, others in as many as twenty-one distinct versions, namely King Dinis's 'Ai flores, ai flores do verde pĩo' and Nuno Fernandez Torneol's 'Levad', amigo, que dormides as manhãas frias'. Individual lyrics from the religious *Cantigas de Santa Maria* have appeared in anthologies, and the complete collection was published by Kathleen Kulp-Hill in 2000.[4]

Following the chronology of Portuguese literature rather than that of the translators, the next substantial body of works to have been translated into English are the plays of Gil Vicente. As with the Galician-Portuguese lyrics, there is a hiatus between the period when the plays were first composed and

---

'Checklist of Modern Portuguese Literature in English Translation – Books', *Gávea-Brown* 17–18 (1996–97), 49–57; P. A. Odber de Baubeta, 'The Sir Henry Thomas Project: Towards a History of Portuguese Literature in English Translation', *Revista de Estudos Anglo-Portugueses* 10 (2001), 43–65; Helen Kelsh, 'Towards a History of Portuguese Literature in English Translation: Volume II: From the Nineteenth Century to the Present Day', *Revista de Estudos Anglo-Portugueses* 10 (2001), 67–8.

[2] Thomas, p. 2.

[3] Henry Roseman Lang, 'Old Portuguese Songs', *Baustgeine zur Romanischen Philologie: Festgabe für Adolfo Mussafia* (Halle, 1905), pp. 27–45; Jean R. Longland, 'Preliminary Bibliography of Medieval Galician-Portuguese Poetry in English Translation', *Studies in Honour of Lloyd A. Kasten* (Madison, WI: Hispanic Seminary of Medieval Studies, 1975), pp. 135–53.

[4] Kathleen Kulp-Hill, *Songs of Holy Mary of Alfonso X, the Wise: A Translation of the Cantigas de Santa Maria* (Tempe, AZ: Arizona Center for Medieval and Renaissance Studies, 2000).

performed, the sixteenth century, and their subsequent recovery and dissemination in the nineteenth. Once the plays come to the attention of scholars,
they are referred to by the literary historians Bouterwek and Sismondi, themselves translated into English in 1823.[5] Gil Vicente is also mentioned in the
Foreign Quarterly Review of 1832. His plays were more readily accessed
than the Galician-Portuguese lyric because the (supposedly) complete works
had been printed in 1562 and 1586. However, it should be noted that Gil
Vicente's literary production is known to the English-speaking world principally through translations of the lyrics as opposed to the complete plays,
and especially because, for historico-cultural reasons, Vicente composed his
verse in Castilian as well as Portuguese. Interest in Vicente's works is further
due to his standing as the 'Father of Portuguese theatre' (he was also desig-
nated 'the Portuguese Plautus') and he undoubtedly appealed to successive
generations of Romantics. Translations of Gil Vicente begin to appear in the
nineteenth century, produced by gentleman-scholars and academics on both
sides of the Atlantic, among them Bowring, Ticknor, Longfellow, William
Cullen Bryant, followed by Edgar Prestage, Aubrey Fitz Gerald Bell and Sir
George Young in the early decades of the twentieth.[6]

At least fifty-five scholars, poets or professional translators have translated complete Vicentine plays, selected extracts or 'stand-alone' poems,
either for play collections, academic journals, histories of literature or poetry
anthologies. Of these, at least sixteen have also translated Galician-Portuguese lyrics. More recently, Vicente's work has attracted attention because
of its relevance for students of the Discoveries or those who wish to discuss
feminist issues (especially the *Auto da Sibila Cassandra*).[7] Complete plays
have been adapted for performance on stage while others have been translated as part of a doctoral thesis.[8] By far the most popular – or most trans-

---

5   Frederick Bouterwek, *History of Spanish and Portuguese Literature*, tr. Thomasina
Ross, Volume II: *Portuguese Literature* (London: Boosey and Sons, 1823); J.-C.-L. Simonde de
Sismondi, *Historical View of the Literature of the South of Europe*, tr. Thomas Roscoe, Volume
4 (London: Henry Colburn and Co., 1823).

6   John Bowring, *The Ancient Poetry and Romances of Spain* (London: Taylor & Hessey,
1824); Henry Wadsworth Longfellow (ed.), *The Poets and Poetry of Europe* (London: Sampson
Low, Son and Co., 1855); George Ticknor, *The History of Spanish Literature*, 3 vols (London:
John Murray, 1849); William Cullen Bryant, *Library of World Poetry, being the Choice Selec-
tions from the Best Poets* (New York: Avenel Books, 1870); Sir George Young, *Portugal: An
Anthology* (Oxford: Clarendon Press, 1916).

7   Anthony Lappin (ed.), *Gil Vicente. Three Discovery Plays: Auto da Barca do Inferno,
Exortação da Guerra, Auto da Índia* (Warminster: Aris & Phillips, 1997); Aubrey F. G. Bell,
The Ship of Hell (Watford: Voss & Michael, 1929).

8   *The Boat Plays: The Boat to Hell, The Boat to Purgatory, The Boat to Heaven*,
translated and adapted by David Johnston (London: Oberon Books, 1997); Cheryl Folkins
McGinnis, *The Sibyl Cassandra. A Christmas Play with the Insanity and Sanctity of Five
Centuries Past* (Lanham, NY: Oxford University Press, 2000); Ann Adele Arney, *The Play*

lated – plays are the *Auto da Sibila Cassandra*, four complete versions and one abridged; *Auto da Barca do Inferno*, three complete versions and one abridged; *Quem tem farelos?*, three versions. The most translated lyrics all derive from Castilian source texts. Thus, from the *Auto da Sibila Cassandra*, 'Muy graciosa es la doncella', twenty-eight English versions; 'Dicen que me case yo', sixteen; 'A la guerra', ten; 'Sañosa está la niña', ten; 'En la huerta nasce la rosa', this time taken from the *Auto dos Quatro Tempos*, again with ten different English translations, then, with nine different translations, 'Si dormis, doncella', from *Quem tem farelos?*, widely known in English as 'Art thou sleeping maiden?' because it has been set to music. The Portuguese plays or lyrics have received less attention, though Aubrey Bell was certainly undeterred by the difficulty of the language.[9]

Poems by Francisco de Sá de Miranda have not yet been translated to any significant extent, while the prologue to Bernardim Ribeiro's *História da Menina e Moça* or *Saudades* appeared in 1985.[10] Complete plays by António Ferreira, on the other hand, have been translated into English, primarily his tragedy *Castro*, of which numerous versions and adaptations exist.[11] A very small number of his poems have been translated and anthologised, while the comedy *Bristo* was translated by John Martyn.[12]

The works of Portugal's iconic (epic and lyric) poet Luís de Camões, on the other hand, may be found in multiple English versions and have been the subject of numerous studies.[13] The epic poem *Os Lusíadas* is first translated

---

of the Sibyl Cassandra, unpublished dissertation, Department of English, University of South Carolina, 1969; *Quem tem farelos?* translated as *Who Has Bran?* in Mariana Leanna Smolen, *Bilingualism as Semiotic Code in the Theatrical Code Systems of the Theater of Gil Vicente*, PhD dissertation, Arizona State University, 1990, pp. 144–66; *Inês Pereira* and *Quem tem farelos?*, rendered as *Hay for the Horses*, in Ann MacLaren, *Page and Stage: Translation and Transformation for Gil Vicente's New Audience*, PhD, University of Glasgow, 1999.

[9] P. Odber de Baubeta, 'Gil Vicente in English Translation', *Gil Vicente 500 Depois. Actas do Congresso Internacional realizado pelo Centro de Estudos de Teatro da Faculdade de Letras da Universidade de Lisboa*. 2 vols (Lisbon: Imprensa Nacional–Casa da Moeda, 2003), vol. II, pp. 291–306; Aubrey F. G. Bell, *Four Plays of Gil Vicente* (Cambridge: Cambridge University Press, 1920; reprinted New York: Kraus, 1969); Aubrey F. G. Bell, *Lyrics of Gil Vicente* (Oxford: Blackwell [1914; second edition 1921, different in some respects from the previous edition; third edition 1925, reprint of the second]).

[10] Suzette Macedo, 'Translation of the Prologue of *Menina e Moça ou Saudades*, "The Young Girl's Story or the Book of Longing"', *Portuguese Studies* 1 (1985), 58–67.

[11] Maria Leonor Machado de Sousa, *D. Inês e D. Sebastião na Literatura Inglesa* (Lisbon: Vega, 1980), and *Inês de Castro: Um Tema Português na Europa* (Lisbon: Ediçoes 70, 1987).

[12] *The Comedy of Bristo, or, The Pimp*, tr. John R. C. Martyn (Ottawa: Dovehouse, 1990)

[13] George West, 'The Work of W. J. Mickle, the First Anglo-Portuguese Scholar', *Review of English Studies* 10 (1934); Fernando de Mello Moser, *Discurso Inacabado. Ensaios de Cultura Portuguesa* (Lisbon: Fundação Calouste Gulbenkian, 1994); George Monteiro, *The Presence of Camões: Influences on the Literature of England, America, and Southern Africa* (Lexington, KY: University Press of Kentucky, 1996), and 'Articles about Poems by, References to, and

by Sir Richard Fanshawe in 1655, while the lyrics first appear in English in 1803. Each century throws up its own readings of Camões, who has never really been absent from the translator's landscape but continues to be translated in the twenty-first century.[14] It is worth noting that certain lyrics have acquired the status of what Riding and Graves dismissed as 'anthology pieces'.[15]

The prose of the Portuguese Middle Ages and Renaissance has also attracted translators' attention, for instance in Beazley and Prestage's translation of Zurara, and selections from Fernão Lopes's chronicles published under the title *The English in Portugal*.[16]

The literature of the Discoveries, exploration and shipwrecks, and travel writing in general has consistently aroused interest in the English-speaking world, because of competing imperial aspirations, a desire to learn about Europe's African or Asian 'other' or quite simply, a taste for 'ripping yarns' with episodes of horror and tragedy thrown in for good measure. The first volume of Fernão Lopes de Castanheda's *História do Descobrimento e Conquista da Índia pelos Portugueses* was published in London in 1582, shortly after his death in 1559. The translator probably used the Spanish version (Antwerp, 1554). British historians such as Charles Boxer have translated excerpts from a range of Portuguese texts in order to illustrate their expositions, as has A. R. Barter for his anthology *Portugal through her Literature*.[17] The Hakluyt Society has also been instrumental in disseminating works of Portuguese history. Individual scholars have singled out particular works for translation and analysis. Afonso de Albuquerque's *Commentaries*

Mentions of Luiz de Camões in US Periodicals [1791–2002]', *Revista de Estudos Anglo-Portugueses* 16 (2006), 25–153.

14 Luís de Camões, *Selected Sonnets*, translated by William Baer (Chicago and London: University of Chicago Press, 2005); *The Collected Lyric Poems of Luís de Camões*, tr. Landeg White, Lockert Library of Poetry in Translation (Princeton University Press, 2008).

15 Laura Riding and Robert Graves, *A Pamphlet against Anthologies* (London: Cape, 1927). See, for instance, Collard J. Stock's *Translations in Verse from the French, Spanish, Portuguese, Italian, Swedish, German and Dutch* (London: Elliot Stock, 1891), Julian Cooper's *Versions* (London: St George's Gallery, 1959), Harold B. Segel, *The Baroque Poem* (New York: Dutton, 1974), and Samuel Dennis Proctor Clough, *An Iberian Anthology: Versions of Spanish and Portuguese Literature* (Author's edition, 1991), *Further Poems and Translations* (Oxford: Author's edition, 1992).

16 *The Chronicle of the Discovery and Conquest of Guinea* by Gomes Eannes de Azurara, by Charles Raymond Beazley and Edgar Prestage (Hakluyt Society, 2 Volumes, First Series, 95 and 100, 1896 and 1899 respectively); *The English in Portugal*, tr. Derek Lomax and Robert J. Oakley (Warminster: Aris & Phillips, 1988).

17 Arthur Reginald Barter, *Portugal through her Literature: an anthology of prose and verse with introduction, notes on authors, and parallel translations* (Glastonbury: Walton Press, 1972); Charles Boxer, *The Tragic History of the Sea* (Cambridge: Hakluyt Society, 1959), and *Further Selections from The Tragic History of the Sea 1559–1565* (Cambridge: Hakluyt Society, 1968).

were translated for the Hakluyt Society in four volumes from 1875 to 1884, and texts by Albuquerque and his son were published by Earle and Villiers in 1990.[18] Rebecca Catz reviewed previous versions of Fernão Mendes Pinto's *Peregrinação*, before producing one of her own in 1989. Michael Lowery published an abridged translation in 1992.[19]

Historical interest also accounts for Ford's translation of correspondence from the Court of João III.[20]

Key works of the Portuguese Baroque period include the *Carta de Guia de Casados*, translated by Captain John Stevens as *The Government of a wife; or wholsom and pleasant Advice For Married Men. In a Letter to a Friend, written in Portuguese* and presented to Catherine of Braganza in 1697. Edgar Prestage also published extracts from this work in 1905 and 1922.[21] Regrettably, Dom Francisco's *O Fidalgo Aprendiz* has yet to be translated.

The Labyrinth of Crete by the ill-fated playwright António José da Silva has been studied in depth and translated by Juliet Perkins (2004).[22] The poetry of Soror Violante do Céu and her sisters-in-Christ may be found in anthologies, but not in single-author volumes. The *Lettres Portugaises*, attributed to a Portuguese nun, Soror Mariana Alcoforado, have been translated almost a dozen times in the last 300 years, by at least ten named translators.[23] Selected sonnets by Bocage were published in English by Flávio Pinto Leite in 1899, others appear in various anthologies. Ironically, his literary patroness, the Marquise de Alorna, has been less fortunate; herself a noted translator, she remains virtually unknown outside the Portuguese-speaking world.

The nineteenth century sees an upsurge in Portuguese literary production, clearly an affirmation of national identity in the wake of the Peninsular War and a response to different waves of Romanticism. Portugal is well served in this respect by Almeida Garrett and Alexandre Herculano, yet despite their

[18] T. F. Earle and John Villiers, *Albuquerque, Caesar of the East: Selected Texts by Afonso de Albuquerque and his Son* (Warminster: Aris & Phillips, 1990).

[19] Rebecca Catz, 'A Note on Previous Translations of the *Peregrinação*', *Portuguese Studies* 4 (1988), 70–81; Fernão Mendes Pinto, *The Travels of Mendes Pinto*, translated by Rebecca D. Catz (Chicago and London: University of Chicago Press, 1989); *The Peregrination of Fernao Mendes Pinto*, abridged and tr. Michael Lowery, introd. Luís de Sousa Rebelo (Manchester: Carcanet, 1992).

[20] *Letters of John III King of Portugal, 1521–1557* (1931), followed by the companion volume, *Letters of the Court of John III, King of Portugal* (1933).

[21] Edgar Prestage, *Dom Francisco Manoel de Mello. His Life and Writings* with *Extracts from the 'Letter of Guidance to Married Men'* (Manchester: Sherrat & Hughes, 1905).

[22] Juliet Perkins, *A Critical Study and Translation of António José da Silva's 'Cretan Labyrinth': A Puppet Opera* (Lampeter: Mellen, 2004).

[23] P. A. Odber de Baubeta, 'Travels (and Travails) of a Portuguese Nun', in *Estudos Anglo-Portugueses. Livro de Homenagem a Maria Leonor Machado de Sousa*, Organização de Carlos Ceia, Isabel Lousada & Maria João da Rocha Afonso (Lisbon: Colibri/Faculdade de Ciências Sociais e Humanas, Universidade Nova de Lisboa, 2003), 33–57.

political exile in the United Kingdom, little of their work was translated until the following century. English translators like Sir John Bowring (1792–1872) seem to be more concerned with the Peninsular ballad tradition. Garrett comes to the attention of the gentleman-scholar John Adamson (1787–1855) whose *Lusitania Illustrata* is essentially an early translation anthology.[24] The play *Frei Luís de Sousa* was translated by Edgar Prestage.[25] *Viagens na Minha Terra* (*Travels in My Homeland*) appeared in 1987, translated by John Parker. A new translation of *Frei Luís de Sousa, The Pilgrim*, made by Nicholas Round in the 1990s, for stage as much as page, is scheduled for publication in 2009. For Herculano we have John Branner's 1926 *History of the Origin and Establishment of the Inquisition in Portugal* (*História da Origem e Estabelecimento da Inquisição em Portugal*) and a recent, as yet unpublished translation of *Eurico o Presbítero* (*Euric the Presbyter*) done by Jorge Salgueiro.

Despite his prolific output and canonical status, only two novels by Camilo Castelo Branco have been translated into English, *The Fall of an Angel* (*A Queda dum Anjo*) by Samuel Dennis Proctor Clough, and *Amor de Perdição*, translated as *Doomed Love (a family memoir)* by Alice Clemente in 2000.

Another important nineteenth-century prose fiction author, Júlio Dinis, has only two works in translation, *Os Fidalgos da Casa Mourisca* and *Tia Philomela*.[26]

Members of the Generation of 1870 are reasonably well represented in English. Poems by Antero de Quental were translated by Prestage in 1894 and by S. Griswold Morley in 1922, while the American poet and translator Richard Zenith published *The Feeling of Immortality* in 1998.[27]

Oliveira Martins, the historian of the *Geração de '70*, also had a work translated into English, in 1896, by C. J. Willdey, *The England of Today (As Others See Us)*. The work was obviously selected because of its intrinsic

---

[24] John Adamson, *Lusitania Illustrata. Literary Department. Part II. Minstrelsy* (Newcastle: M. A. Richardson, 1846), and *Ballads from the Portugueuze*, translated & versified by J.A. and R.C.C. (Newcastle: M. A. Richardson, 1846).

[25] '*Brother Luiz De Sousa*', *Dublin Review* 118:17 (January 1896); *The 'Brother Luiz de Sousa' of Viscount de Almeida Garret* (1909).

[26] *The Fidalgos of Casa Mourisca* by the North American Roxanna Dabney in 1891, and *Tia Philomela* by Luiz Marques in 1943.

[27] By Prestage in 1894 under the title *Anthero de Quental: Sixty-four Sonnets* (1894); by S. Griswold Morley as *Sonnets and Poems* (1922; reprinted 1973); Richard Zenith, *The Feeling of Immortality* (1998). Individual poems have been anthologised by Aubrey Fitz Gerald Bell, *Poems from the Portuguese* (Oxford: Blackwell, 1913); Young, *Portugal: An Anthology*; Morland in Neville Braybrooke and Elizabeth King (eds), *Translation*, Second Series (London: Phoenix Press, 1947); and Roy Campbell, *Portugal* (London: Max Reinhardt, 1957), *Collected Works: Volume II: Poetry Translations*, ed. Peter Alexander, Michael Chapman and Marica Leveson (Craighall, AD: Donker, 1985).

interest (or novelty value) for an English readership – England seen through the eyes of her oldest ally.

Translations of works by Eça de Queirós have proved no less controversial than the novels themselves when they first appeared in print, mainly because of serious concerns about accuracy, fidelity and general translation quality. For instance, on the strength of the title at least, Portuguese readers would be hard pressed to identify the American translator Mary Serrano's *Dragon's Teeth* with its source text, *O Primo Basílio*,[28] and several scholars have commented scathingly on Roy Campbell's 1953 rendering of this work and other novels by Eça.[29]

Edgar Prestage translated Eça's *A Relíquia* as *The Sweet Miracle*, and was also responsible for a translation of *O Defunto, Our Lady of the Pillar*.[30]

Not unexpectedly, given his self-imposed mission of setting Portuguese literature before the English, Aubrey Bell also translated Eça, with *The Relic* (1915), as did Luiz Marques, *José Mathias and A Man of Talent* in 1947. Campbell continued to mistranslate Eça (*The City and the Mountains*, 1954). Nan Flanagan did *The Sin of Father Amaro* in 1962. Richard Franko Goldman translated *The Mandarin and Other Stories* in 1965, and Patricia McGowan Pinheiro and Ann Stevens produced their version of *The Maias* in the same year. Ann Stevens translated *The Illustrious House of Ramires* and gave us Eça's *Letters from England*, later updated by Alison Aiken for Carcanet in 2000.[31] *Alves & Co* was translated by Robert Fedorcheck.[32] *The Yellow Sofa and Three Portraits* was translated by Goldman, Marques and John Vetch, who did *To the Capital* for Carcanet in 1995.[33] However, the 1990s marked

---

[28] *Dragon's Teeth*, trans. Mary Serrano (Boston: Ticknor, 1889).

[29] Roy Campbell, *Cousin Bazil* (London: Max Reinhardt, 1953); Alison Aiken, 'Eça in English Translation: Some Treasures and Some Travesties', *Portuguese Studies* 14 (1998), 92–103; Helen Kelsh, 'O Primo Basílio no Mundo Anglo-Saxónico', *Actas do Congresso de Estudos Queirosianos. IV Encontro Internacional de Queirosianos*, 2 vols (Coimbra: Almedina/ Instituto de Língua, 2002).

[30] *The Sweet Miracle* (London: Nutt, 1902). He was also responsible for a translation of *O Defunto, Our Lady of the Pillar* (London: Archibald Constable, 1906).

[31] *José Mathias and A Man of Talent*, tr. Luiz Marques (London: Harrap, 1947); *The City and the Mountains*, tr. Roy Campbell (London: Max Reinhardt, 1954); *The Sin of Father Amaro*, tr. Nan Flanagan (London: Reinhardt, 1962); *The Mandarin and Other Stories*, tr. Richard Franko Goldman (London: Bodley Head, 1965); *The Maias*, tr. Patricia McGowan Pinheiro and Ann Stevens (London: Bodley Head, 1965); *The Illustrious House of Ramires*, tr. Ann Stevens (London: Bodley Head, 1968). *Letters from England*, tr. Ann Stevens (London: Bodley Head, 1970).

[32] *Alves & Co*, tr. Robert M. Fedorcheck (New York and London: University Press of America, 1988).

[33] *The Yellow Sofa and Three Portraits*, tr. John Vetch, Richard Franko Goldman and Luís Marques (Manchester: Carcanet, 1993); *To the Capital*, tr. John Vetch (Manchester: Carcanet, 1995).

a new departure in Eça translation: instead of merely reprinting old translations (the publishing strategy adopted by Carcanet and Quartet), Dedalus inaugurated a new era with Margaret Jull Costa's high-quality translations of *The Mandarin* (1993), *The Relic* (1994), *The Tragedy of the Street of Flowers* (2000), *The Crime of Father Amaro* (2002), *Cousin Bazilio* (2003), *The Maias* (2007) and *The City and the Mountains* (2008).

Relatively few English-speaking readers are familiar with poems of João de Deus or Cesário Verde.[34] Others may be familiar with Mário de Sá-Carneiro through the translations of Macedo and Jull Costa, but anyone with a genuine interest in Portuguese Modernism or the Western Canon will have had ample opportunity to read the iconic Fernando Pessoa and his heteronyms. Multiple translations of Pessoa exist in print and on line, made by scholars, academics and distinguished poets such as Jonathan Griffin, Richard Zenith and John Betjeman. Pessoa's 'Mar português' from *Mensagem* easily competes with King Dinis's 'Ai flores, ai flores do verde pĩo' or Camões's 'Alma minha gentil' (at least 18 versions, from the eighteenth century onwards) for the title of most translated, and, according to that criterion, most canonical Portuguese poem. The translations are too numerous to list, but abundant information and commentary has been published by George Monteiro.[35]

The writers of Portugal's Second Modernism, embodied principally in the *Presença* generation, can also be accessed by English-speaking readers. Unusually, José Régio had the privilege of being translated within his lifetime. The poem 'Fado-Canção', translated by Roy Campbell, appeared in 1966 in *The Penguin Book of Modern Verse Translation*. More interesting, however, is the fact that Régio's 1957 play *My Problem* (*O Meu Caso*) was published in the *Odyssey Review*.[36] The *Review* was published by the Latin American and European Literary Society between 1961 and 1963, and numbered among its sponsors W. H. Auden, Jorge Luis Borges, Robert Graves and Stephen Spender. More recently, poems by Régio have been translated by Richard Zenith while Margaret Jull Costa has published some of his short stories.[37]

[34] Keith Bosley, 'On Being a Westerner: A Translation of "O Sentimento dum Ocidental" by Cesário Verde', *Portuguese Studies* 2 (1986), 120–4, for a partial translation.

[35] George Monteiro, *The Presence of Pessoa: English, American and Southern African Literary Responses* (Lexington, KY: University Press of Kentucky, 1997), *Fernando Pessoa and Nineteenth-Century Anglo-American Literature* (Lexington, KY: University Press of Kentucky, 2000); 'Fernando Pessoa's reception in the United States: an annotated checklist of items in journals, periodicals, and newspapapers', *Revista de Estudos Anglo-Portugueses* 15 (2005), 211–43.

[36] José Régio, *My Problem*, tr. Gregory Rabassa, *Odyssey Review* 3.2 (1963), 130–43.

[37] José Régio, Four Poems translated by Richard Zenith, in *Tabacaria*, 4, *Portuguese Poetry after Pessoa* (Lisbon: Contexto, 1997); José Régio, *The Flame-Coloured Dress and Other Stories*, tr. Margaret Jull Costa (Manchester: Carcanet, 1999).

Régio's contemporary, Miguel Torga, has also been translated into English, first by Denis Brass and then by Ivana Rangel-Carlsen.[38]

Other major figures of the twentieth century who attracted the attention of critics and translators are the writers-in-exile José Rodrigues Miguéis and Jorge de Sena. Miguéis's 'Gente da Terceira Classe' was transformed into 'Steerage' (1983) and other short stories have appeared in anthologies.[39] Sena's prose and poetry have also been published in English, in the United Kingdom or the United States.[40] Various other twentieth-century Portuguese short stories, novels and plays have been translated into English because of a publisher, scholar or translator's personal commitment to disseminating Portuguese literature. A perusal of on-line catalogues for major libraries or booksellers will throw up translations of Aquilino Ribeiro, Ferreira de Castro, Vitorino Nemésio, Pedro Homem de Mello, Branquinho da Fonseca, Alves Redol, Manuel da Fonseca, Fernando Namora, Eugénio de Andrade, Bernardo Santareno, José Cardoso Pires, Luís de Sttau Monteiro, David Mourão-Ferreira, Alberto Lacerda, Herberto Helder, Mário de Carvalho, Nuno Júdice, and Miguel Sousa Tavares, among others.

Now, in the twenty-first century, those Portuguese writers with whom English-speaking readers are most familiar are José Saramago, winner of the 1998 Nobel Prize for Literature, and António Lobo Antunes, who many believe is equally deserving.[41] Other authors may appear in anthologies or literary magazines, and translations of chapters or short stories by contemporary authors are commissioned annually by the Instituto Nacional do Livro e das Bibliotecas for their publication *Sights from the South*, for example Pedro Tamen, Helder Macedo, Manuel Alegre, Rui Zink, Rodrigo Guedes Carvalho, Gonçalo M. Tavares, valter hugo mãe, and Jacinto Lucas Pires.

Portuguese women writers have not always fared well in translation. The Marquise de Alorna, mentioned above, is a case in point. The nuns of the Baroque have not got any further than the occasional anthology, unlike the pseudo-religious Mariana Alcoforado, who took on an afterlife of her own. Women writers and intellectuals from the earliest decades of the twentieth century are scarcely known in Portugal, let alone overseas. Agustina Bessa Luís, unquestionably the most distinguished living Portuguese female author, has only a few short stories in translation, likewise Irene Lisboa, Maria

---

[38] Miguel Torga, *Farrusco the Blackbird and Other Stories from the Portuguese*, tr. Denis Brass (London: Allen & Unwin, 1950); *New Tales from the Mountain*, tr. Ivana Rangel-Carlsen (Manchester: Carcanet, 1991); *The Creation of the World*, tr. Ivana Rangel-Carlsen with Patricia Odber de Baubeta (Manchester: Carcanet, 2000).

[39] José Rodrigues Miguéis, *Steerage and Ten Other Stories*, tr. George Matos and Carolina Matos (Providence, RI: Gávea-Brown, 1983).

[40] Jorge de Sena, *The Wondrous Physician*, tr. Mary Fitton (London: Dent, 1986).

[41] For translations of works by these authors, see chapter 15.

Judite de Carvalho, Maria Ondina Braga, Fiama Hasse Pais Brandão, Maria Gabriela Llansol, and Helena Marques. *New Portuguese Letters* (1975) by the Three Marias was, however, published in English within three years of its publicatiõn in Portugal, because it raised crucial questions about gender, freedom of expression and censorship. The poet Sophia de Mello Breyner Andresen was translated into English, by the distinguished American poet Ruth Fainlight, and by Alexis Levitin and Richard Zenith. Lídia Jorge has achieved international recognition through the translation of *A Costa dos Murmúrios*,[42] short fiction by Hélia Correia appears in literary magazines and translation anthologies, as do stories by Teolinda Gersão.[43] Translations of Luiza Neto Jorge, Teresa Veiga (b. 1945) and Ana Teresa Pereira (b. 1958) have been commissioned by the Instituto Português do Livro e das Bibliotecas, and several plays by Luísa Costa Gomes (b. 1954) have been translated into English. This rather scant list may denote an imbalance in gender, but it is probably an accurate reflection of the realities of Portuguese publishing.

Far from any pretence of exhaustiveness, a survey like this can only hope to offer a brief glimpse of Portuguese literary works available to an English readership. The question of why some works are able to cross the linguistic and cultural divide while others do not, may never be fully answered. In some cases, a poem, a play or a novel may enshrine particular aesthetic values or present such manifest social or political interest that it would be an act of unpardonable neglect to leave it untranslated. Certain works are deliberately selected because they are bound to sell enough copies to justify the translation costs and make a healthy profit for the publishing house. And some authors are fortunate enough to have a champion who will transform them into a *cause célèbre* among the international community. Notwithstanding the gaps, just about all the main periods and movements of Portuguese literature are represented, as well as the main literary genres. Portuguese literature is neither invisible nor absent from the international landscape. We just need to look for it more attentively.

---

42 Lídia Jorge, *The Murmuring Coast*, tr. N. Costa and R. W. Sousa (Minneapolis: University of Minnesota Press, 1995).

43 Teresa F. A. Alves and Teresa Cid (eds), *Onde a Terra Acaba: Colectânea de Contos Portugueses / Views from the Edge* (Lisbon: Centro de Estudos Anglísticos da Universidade de Lisboa / 101 Noites, 2006).

Anthologies of translations

Gerrard, Mike and Thomas McCarthy, *Passport to Portugal* (Wistow, Huntington: Passport; London: Serpent's Tail, 1994)

Lisboa, Eugénio, and Helder Macedo (eds), *The Dedalus Book of Portuguese Fantasy* (Sawtry: Dedalus, 1995)

Lisboa, Eugénio (ed.), *The Anarchist Banker and Other Portuguese Stories* (Manchester: Carcanet, 1997)

Macedo, Helder and E. M. de Melo e Castro (eds), *Contemporary Portuguese Poetry. An Anthology in English* (Manchester: Carcanet, 1978)

Williams, Frederick G., *Poets of Portugal: A Bilingual Selection of Poems from the Thirteenth through Twentieth Centuries*. Introduction and notes by Frederick G. Williams; with a foreword by Maria de Lourdes Belchior (New York: Luso-Brazilian Books, 2007)

Zenith, Richard (ed.), *Translation, The Journal of Literary Translation* 25 (1991)

Zenith, Richard (ed.), *Fictions from the Portuguese, The Literary Review* 38.4 (1995)

Further reading

France, Peter (ed.), *The Oxford Guide to Literature in English Translation* (Oxford: Oxford University Press, 2000), pp. 441–3

Keenoy, Ray, David Treece and Paul Hyland, *Babel Guide to the Fiction of Portugal, Brazil and Africa in English Translation* (London: Boulevard, 1995)

McGuirk, Bernard, and Else R. P. Vieira, 'Portuguese Literature', in *Encyclopedia of Literary Translation into English*, Volume 2, ed. Olive Classe (London and Chicago: Fitzroy Dearborn, 2000), pp. 1105–7

Odber de Baubeta, Patricia, *The Anthology in Portugal: A New Approach to the History of Portuguese Literature in the Twentieth Century* (Oxford: Peter Lang, 2007)

INDEX

Portuguese authors and historical personages are indexed under the final element of their surname, patronymic or nickname.

CPSIA information can be obtained at www.ICGtesting.com
Printed in the USA
LVOW10s1814211113

362258LV00003B/9/P